America's Great Loop Cruise

www.greatloop.com

Other books by Ron Stob

Back Roads of the Central Coast
More Back Roads of the Central Coast
Exploring San Luis Obispo County and nearby coastal areas

"Honey, Let's Get a Boat..."

A Cruising Adventure
of
America's Great Loop

Ron Stob and Eva I. Stob

Raven Cove Publishing
Greenback, Tennessee

Published by: Raven Cove Publishing
                  P. O. Box 168
                  Greenback, TN 37742-0168 U.S.A.
                  Telephone: (865) 856-7888
                  Fax: (865) 856-7889
                  E-mail: REStob@aol.com

Printed in the United States of America

Cover Design by Kristin Williams, Glenmary Graphics
Cover Photograph by Ron Stob.
Photographs by Ron Stob and Eva I. Stob
Illustrated maps by Ken Hannel and Danny Garrison, Digital Color, Inc.

Cataloging-in-Publication Data
Stob, Ron.
        "Honey, let's get a boat...": a cruising adventure of America's great loop / Ron Stob and Eva I. Stob.— 1st ed.
            p.   cm.
        ISBN 0-9669140-0-7
        1. Voyages and travel.
        2. Boats and boating.
        3. Atlantic Intracoastal Waterway—Description and travel.
        4. Atlantic Coast (U.S.)—Description and travel.
        5. Great Lakes Region—Description and travel.
        6. Canals (Canada)—Description and travel.
        7. Rivers—United States—Description and travel.
        8. Gulf Coast (U.S.)—Description and travel.
            I. Stob, Eva I.   II. Title
G550.S86   1999
910.45—dc21
Library of Congress Catalog Card Number: 98-96957

To our kids,
who thought we were nuts for doing this
but who enthusiastically joined us along the way

DISCLAIMER

This book is designed to provide information in regard to cruising America's Great Loop. It is an account of the authors' experience and is not intended to be a comprehensive guidebook. It is not the purpose of the book to reprint all the information that is available, but to complement and supplement those resources. You are urged to read all the available material and learn as much as possible before venturing on your cruise. For more information, see the Resources section in the Appendix.

Every effort has been made to make this book as accurate as possible. However, there may be mistakes both typographical and in content. Therefore, this text should be used only as a general guide and not as the ultimate source of information on cruising America's Great Loop. Waterways, rivers, marine businesses, etc. change from year to year so it is vital to acquire and have on board the latest charts and guidebooks.

The purpose of this book is to inform and entertain. The authors and publisher shall have neither liability nor responsibility to any person or entity with respect to any loss or damage caused, or alleged to be caused, directly or indirectly by the information contained in this book.

If you do not wish to be bound by the above, you may return this book to the publisher for a full refund.

Contents

ACKNOWLEDGMENTS

When you begin an endeavor like this—buying and outfitting a boat, learning to pilot it, understanding the ways of the sea and inland waters, and preparing for a year on a boat in accommodations the size of a camper—you know you're going to need some help. Besides learning about the boat and boating, there were considerations of leaving our home and livelihood. We needed all the friends we could get. To them we are deeply indebted.

Eva's sister, Lelia Guilbert, was single-handedly the person who sowed the seed for this trip. If there was a number one cheerleader, it was Lelia. To encourage us to write our newsletter, the Stobette, she sent us a page of stamps, a check and cheers. Lelia, you're full of fun and one of the unforgettable characters who has made a significant contribution to our lives.

Kudos to the folks in Costa de Oro Power Squadron, a unit of the United States Power Squadrons on California's Central Coast who proved to be both friends and tutors.

...to Dave and Marci Hutson, who revived Costa de Oro Power Squadron from near-death and made it useful in the community to novices like us who needed to be nurtured, encouraged, rewarded and educated. Through their example we became better disciples of nautical education and good will to others.

...to Bill Schultz, Squadron Education Officer, who lined up courses and taught us until our brains were bursting while we awaited that fateful time when we would drop the lines and embark on the unknown. Those Power Squadron manuals accompanied us throughout the trip and were frequently consulted, as practical experience became overlays on conceptual knowledge.

...to Warner Taylor, world-wide sailor, who knew our ignorance and fear and gave us good advice and constant encouragement. He realized that any ill wind could knock us over and that prolonged considerations for finances and personal safety could derail the voyage. He understood that our trip, like his trans-oceanic voyages to Tahiti, would be life-changing.

And ...to "Skip" Louis Lippitt, meteorologist and teacher, who tutored us in his home and then, with his infectious smile, shoved us out the door as we headed to Florida for the beginning of a new life on the water. Skip was a fine and generous man, and a patient teacher. Skip has recently gone on an eternally long cruise and won't ever be back. Here's to you, Skip.

We are grateful to the community of boaters along the waterways who befriended us and gave a helping hand. To Julie and Bob on *Plastikos*, Bob and Jane on *Brass Ring*, Harry and Margaret on *Phoebe*, Barney and Madelyn on *Pilothouse*, Roger and Lea on *Knight-N-Gail*, Jack and Teasley on *Watermark* and Lou and Sara on *Dunflyn,* to name a few. Thanks to those who gave or loaned us charts and guidebooks with no assurance they would ever be returned.

Bill and Lynne Houston moved in and took over our house for the first several months while we were gone, tending to our properties and forwarding mail. It was wonderful to know someone was watching over the garden, the house and all the things that needed management.

When we left our California home for our year-long cruise, Ben and Barbara Horner were there to kiss us good-bye. Later when we needed someone to manage on the home front, they volunteered; and when we returned to resume our land-based lives, they were the ones who got our car ready, filled the house with breakfast muffins and set up the coffee pot for that first morning back home. Every couple probably has a sweetheart other-couple who they can hardly live without. For us, it has been the Horners. Thank you, Ben and Barbara.

Eva's co-workers at the Arroyo Grande Hospital Laboratory were green with envy as we planned this trip. These folks sent us away with gifts and the kind of brotherly and sisterly concern that made us realize that no matter how worried and forgotten we felt, there was a warm family back home cheering for us and awaiting our return. They read our monthly newsletter, wrote us along the way and reminded us from where we came. As soon as we flew home, they were there with seasonal cheer and a party and we were again surrounded by people whose friendship we always felt along the way.

Cousin Jane Lewenthal told us that one night during a snow storm she sat in her car by the mailbox at the side of the road and read the latest issue of the Stobette. Because Jane was interested enough to stop in her tracks to read our news, we knew that our effort to record our pilgrimage had an audience. We're indebted to all the forty-plus readers who got our monthly Stobette and indicated they were waiting for the next edition.

Thanks to Katie Bryant, dear friend and astute proofreader. Katie sat with her cat on her lap and groomed the manuscript until all the bugs were out. And she did it for the fun of it.

...to Don McGuire who bought one of the California books, then returned it a month later with the errata underlined. Don got a new book, of course, and an assignment to become our proofreader for future publications. We always knew Don was more than just a great organist.

...to our faithful followers and friends at the Arroyo Grande Methodist Church who prayed for our safe journey, made copies of the newsletters, passed them around, and sent us a bannerful of good wishes.

And a tribute to our seven children, who often doubted and acted parental. They didn't have to, but they knew if we killed ourselves, they'd have to somehow cut a forty-foot trawler into seven bits. Of course, they became crew members and play mates throughout the trip. Part of our dream was to share this adventure with them and most of them made it into the pages of our book.

And last but certainly not least, we each give special appreciation to the other. Without Eva's dreaming and scheming the trip wouldn't have become a reality; but without Ron's willingness to go along and be her Cap'n Ron, the *Dream O'Genie* would never have left the dock.

Fort Lauderdale, Florida
to
Norfolk, Virginia

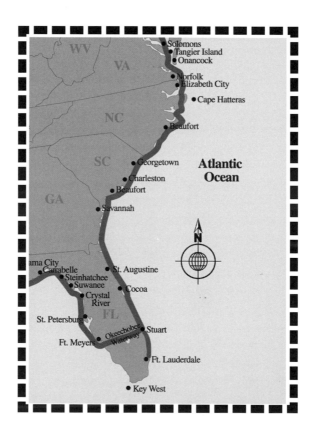

CHAPTER 1

IN THE BEGINNING

Lying in bed we heard crackling, like the unfolding of cellophane. Sea creatures clawing the boat's hull gave us a chilling intimacy with life in the water. Outside the wind howled, adding to our anxiety. We rocked uneasily in our amniotic sac, playing in our minds the events of the past weeks and the moment of our departure.

For days the coast had been whipped by high winds and rain, making the inland waters choppy and visibility poor. The weather was supposed to improve by morning, but it was an uncertain beginning to a trip that we had dreamed and planned for two years.

The previous day we had signed the papers making *Dream O' Genie* ours. We ended our stay in Fort Lauderdale at the Wish You Were Here Inn, turned in our rental car and moved aboard. We had ten days to go 400 miles to get out of Florida or we'd have to pay sales tax on the boat.

We had practically no boating experience and only a cursory acquaintance with the eleven year-old forty-foot powerboat that would be our home for a year. Standing at the helm and looking across that broad beam and forward deck brought on a weak-in-the-knees feeling. This was a lot of boat. It might as well have been the *Queen Mary*. If we could get through the first day of our trip without incident, we would add day 2, then 3 and 4.

We had just spent over two weeks making the boat into a cozy home and we were exhausted. Then there was the matter of the machinery—three diesel engines, refrigeration, water pumps, bilge pumps...it was all new to us, too much to learn, and some of it was in questionable condition despite the marine survey.

Bravery is one thing; foolhardiness is another. How did landlubbers with no boating experience get seduced into abandoning all sense of responsibility and set off in a trawler? I knew. The seducer lay next to me.

Her love affair with boating began innocently enough. I went along with the first idea: charter a boat in Canada with another couple, bump around for a week, have a good time, go back home and savor the memories. That was a few years earlier. I remember as if it were yesterday...

We chartered a 30-foot cruising tug on the Trent-Severn Waterway in Ontario, with Eva's sister, Lelia, and her husband. None of us had been on boats before. I was the old salt, having owned canoes and spent a childhood around rowboats on Minnesota lakes, but the other three were stone-cold. The women were from land-locked South Dakota, and my brother-in-law was a Los Angeles attorney with little interest in the water.

The boat's name was appropriate, *Audacity*, a one-of-a-kind little powerboat. Was our ignorance greater than our enthusiasm? That was the question. One skill we boasted: we knew how to cook.

With our priorities in order, we arrived at Port Severn on the eastern edge of Lake Huron's Georgian Bay and the western terminus of the Trent-Severn Waterway.

Dennis and Cynthia, the owners of the boat, were on board with cleaning pails and brushes. "Bring your things down from the car," Dennis called, "and we'll get you folks situated."

We trundled on board enough suitcases, camera gear, sleeping bags, pillows, and groceries to make us look like a relief team to a third-world country. Lelia even brought a bolt of raw silk to give to her Canadian craft friends, but thank goodness, we were not hauling her tuba and Guilbert's overstuffed golf bag which they had dragged along on a previous trip.

The boat was small. "Where are we going to put this stuff?" we asked each other. We soon discovered where. Back in the rental car. What stayed on the boat was stowed in obscure corners, hidden drawers, and teensie-weensie lockers.

Did we think about taking field glasses, hand-held compasses, or good rain gear and rubber boots? Get serious. We thought about recipes, sporty clothes and a guidebook to points of interest.

Like a father showing his kids how to drive the family car, Dennis oriented us to the boat, confident in the combination of the boat's unsinkability and our ability to learn the tasks. Our understanding of boat stuff was like a child's comprehension of metaphysics, but we leaned into the instruction with intensity until our minds were filled with the clutter of port and starboard, bilge and water pumps, charts and compasses, buoys and daymarks. Fortunately, Dennis stayed with us for the initiation.

Lelia, who drives her Mercury Marquis like Andretti drives a race car, got first crack at the wheel. She watched Dennis start the engine and he talked her through the procedure of getting us underway. I got myself into a fine sexist snit and muttered, "I'm the guy who should be driving this thing." Before long we each got a turn at the helm.

About an hour into the instruction we approached the Big Chute Marine Railway. Dennis guided Lelia into a slow approach toward the blue line. The boat kept going even after she took it out of gear and she looked surprised that bringing the boat to a stop was not as simple as she imagined. In the slippery medium of water floating things maintain their momentum. Eva, Guilbert and I stood on the deck with lines and poles, waiting for the boat to stop. Dennis called out orders, Lelia responded, and they got the boat close enough so we jumped off and tied her to the cleats.

Soon it was our turn for a carnival ride on the Big Chute Marine Railway. A monster platform with standing ribs rolled over the hill on rails, descended into the water, and let loose its cargo of runabouts suspended in nylon slings. Then we were coached into place with other boats.

With everyone secured, the monster rode the rails out of the water, leaving us high and dry; up one side and down the other, then we were in the water again. It was catch and release on a grand scale.

With nary a backward glance, Dennis left us. His wife, Cynthia, had driven our rental car to this point and Dennis joined her for the two-hour ride to their home in Toronto.

We came to the conventional lift lock at Swift Rapids and prepared for our first lock passage without a mentor. Lelia and Guilbert guided *Audacity* like a stealth bomber along the blue line under a barrage of directives from Eva and me (notice the lack of order or chain of command). We soon learned that the deck hands could make the person at the helm look like an ace or an oaf.

It was nearly 5 p.m. on that first day and the thought struck us that we hadn't devoted one brain cell to the task of figuring out where we were going to spend the night. We were between locks that were now closed, so we decided to stop in a shallow bay off Sparrow Lake.

We discovered we didn't know diddly-squat about anchoring, had never heard of rode and couldn't identify a windlass if we stepped on one. But common sense and group consensus came up with a technique: pitch the anchor out as far as possible, let it sink, reel in the excess rope, tie it to something, then have a drink and get ready for dinner.

Fortunately the wind did not come up, there were no tidal changes, and the locks were closed for the night so there was no movement in this quiet lagoon where loons call and the sound of cottage doors shutting on a late summer night is heard for miles. The bay was motionless and *Audacity* reflected off the water like a ship floating in mercury. A loon called. We all stood silently in reverie and respect, our heartbeats the only intrusion on nature's sepulchral void.

Then Guilbert pulled out his Eddie Bauer duck call and pierced the sacred silence with a series of obtrusive **gwalk, gwalk, gwalks**. The loon disappeared and we never saw or heard it again.

Like babes in the womb, we floated gently until the morning when we rose to see the lake steaming in the cool morning air.

Our little ship had four captains, all equal, all capable, and all full of authority. But soon enough, and just in time, division of labor arose among us, so while one couple was navigating and piloting, the other couple was preparing meals and doing chores.

In the historic canal town of Bobcaygeon, we shared space along the city wall with a retired navy officer and his wife who were on a forty-foot motor yacht, the *Sea Gill* from Norfolk, Virginia. Eva talked with them and learned that they began their trip on the east coast and had come up the Mississippi River.

Wide-eyed, she said, "How did you get here from the Mississippi?" The captain indicated that the Mississippi River connects to Lake Michigan by way of the Illinois and Chicago Rivers making the eastern half of

Eva amd Lelia lug bags of provisions to the Audacity at Bobcaygeon, Ontario.

the USA an island. They were going to return along the Atlantic Ocean. In the boating community, this circumnavigation trip is called The Great Loop Cruise. Even though Eva knew a trip like theirs was out of the realm of possibility for us, she looked longingly at that boat and murmured to me, "Honey, let's get a boat..."

She sent a postcard to her co-workers back in California, "I don't miss work at all. We've decided to buy a boat and cruise the world. Don't I wish!" The seed was planted.

Our brief encounter with the little tug *Audacity,* was enough to teach us to distinguish nuns from cans and "red right returning", but our only navigational tool was a compass. There were no electronics aboard; we had never heard of GPS, didn't know about Loran, or how to use radar or VHF radio if we had one. We had no experience reading charts as we groped our way through granite rocks the size of Buicks. We didn't know nuthin'.

Traveling along the Trent-Severn was like slot-boat touring. There were no tides or currents. The waterways were protected from strong winds and waves, except on Lake Simcoe, and line-of-sight navigation was always possible. We had no education on water safety, no knowledge of how boats were built, and only a rudimentary understanding of some of the mechanics of a boat.

Months later, after we were home from our Canadian odyssey, someone mentioned the protected Atlantic Intracoastal Waterway to us. You could hear the neural connections being made in Eva's brain like the slapping valves of an old pipe organ. You did not have to make long, open ocean runs. The image of a great white cruiser cutting through scenic waterways was taking shape.

This was where I could have put my foot down. She was hell bent on seeing this thing through, and I was becoming ever more apprehensive. Our income would be greatly reduced and our expenses would be a gamble. The cost of a used boat that met our needs would be anywhere from $50,000 to $150,000, and as far as I could see, that kind of money was not hanging from our trees.

I'm usually reckless and unaccountable with money and Eva is frugal. Accounting for every penny is her finest picayune quality. We had switched roles. I let go my tight-fistedness, trusting that if she calculated the real costs of this escapade, she would be overwhelmed with the enormity of the project and abandon ship before we owned one, so I let her go. Besides, she's a modern, independent, working woman and she can live any fantasy she likes, so long as it doesn't cost me anything.

She went to the library and looked up *Waterways, Atlantic Intracoastal,* then *Boats,* and compiled a reading list. She checked out books and ordered more. Books on boats cluttered the house. There was no way to avoid her obsession. We read Farley Mowat's book, *The Boat Who Wouldn't Float*, without realizing its prophetic nature.

A plan began to take shape. She wanted us to spend the next year or two learning all we could about boats and boating, then take off for a year and cruise the Great Loop aboard our own boat. I felt like I was being dragged...or was it seduced?

In a moment of weakness she asked, "Is this a pipe dream? Do you think we will be able to do it?"

I was skeptical, too. "Honey, do you realize how much money this is going to cost? And look at our experience—one week on a little 30-foot boat and my limited experience with canoes and rowboats. That's it."

Everyone who knew us thought it was my idea. I was the reckless fool who followed the rule: "Jump in and find out what it's like." Eva was cautious and level-headed. When we told people of our plan to take a year off and buy a boat, they were surprised she was the initiator. Daughter Amy's first words were, "Where are your wills and insurance papers?"

When we told sons, Phil and Jeff, they responded with long stares. People at church said, "You know nothing about boating and you're going to live on a boat for a year?" This was said with the tone of incredulity. Others said sarcastically, almost with a sneer, "Good luck," followed by a wicked chuckle.

But when Eva makes up her mind to do something, I may as well give in. She'll dig in and argue her point, she'll persist and insist, she'll research and talk; she'll cite a hundred reasons why we should do it.

I must admit, the idea of a great escape was fascinating to me too, and I promised to be an active and willing partner.

Both Eva and I were at turning points in our lives. Youngest son, Alan, was about to graduate from the University of California, so a financial burden would end. Eva was a hospital laboratory technologist with almost 30 years of experience, a high performance, never-make-a-mistake-because-you-are-dealing-with-peoples'-lives-kind of job, and she was worn out. Reducing the cost of medical care comes off the back of the hospital staff. In her 50's, with a house, a camper, and a devoted husband, what more could she want? Out of her job would be good, even if temporarily.

I taught for 23 years before buying and operating a residential care business and establishing a writing career with a local newspaper. I sold the business a few years ago and invested the proceeds in residential real estate. I looked okay on paper, but had little cash for extras.

I began teaching a night class to relieve a cash flow problem. Going back into the classroom at the age of 59 was tough. I returned to something I had left 11 years earlier and remembered keenly why I quit then. The night hours and the low pay of part-time teachers left me wishing for some event, happening or circumstance that would require me to quit. The boat trip looked like a personal passage to adventure and a good writing and photographic opportunity.

The thought of realizing a dream aboard a boat gave us new life and the enthusiasm to pursue it, even though it meant taking courses in the evenings and hundreds of hours of planning.

Two crabby people, eager to change their routines and willing to take risks, joined in a common endeavor to make a dream happen. Many people talk about following their dreams, and don't. We were intent on putting our Nikes on and doing it. We had a healthy amount of fear, but it was never greater than our confidence in our abilities to overcome obstacles.

Our limited boating experience taught us that operating a boat requires a fair amount of coordinated movement and athletic ability. There were lines to handle, emergency moves to make and quick decisions to execute. There is a time in one's life when the steep curve for learning new tasks such as navigating, piloting and handling a boat, can be managed. Tomorrow might be too late. We opted to grab the brass ring now.

We were afraid to be on the east coast during the hurricane season and with the knowledge that it is cheaper to "go with the flow", as in the Illinois and Mississippi Rivers, we opted to do the loop counterclockwise. The plan was to leave Florida in February, follow spring northward up the Atlantic Intracoastal Waterway to New Jersey where we would do an open ocean run to New York Harbor. We would go on up the Hudson River to the St. Lawrence Seaway and arrive at Montreal, Canada, in early summer. The Ottawa River flows past the capital city where the Rideau Waterway begins the run to Kingston, on Lake Ontario. A short way southwest is Trenton, and the beginning of the Trent-Severn Waterway where the dream was born three years earlier. Lake Huron and Lake Michigan would be our passage to Chicago, and by September we would cruise the Chicago River into the Illinois River. Motoring down the Mississippi River to the Ohio River and the Tennessee-Tombigbee Waterway to the Gulf of Mexico and back to Florida we would complete the loop before Christmas.

When Eva attended Amy's graduation at the University of Washington in Seattle, she used her free time to research the kinds of boats that would be appropriate for coastal cruising. She concluded that the Pacific Northwest's Inside Passage was a protected waterway just like the Atlantic Intracoastal Waterway, and the same boat type could be used, so she had brokers usher her aboard various vessels, disguising in her demure way, that the coast she intended to cruise was across the continent.

We looked at boating magazines on the library shelves and subscribed to some so we would have a regular supply of current information coming into our home. A wealth of information was discovered in free tabloid-type boating publications that we picked up at boating centers and marinas. We wondered about types of boats and kinds of engines. We didn't know displacement from planing hulls at that point.

I surprised Eva one day with a copy of *Chapman Piloting, Seamanship & Small Boat Handling* by Elbert S. Maloney, which I picked up at a discount store. I suspected that this was a significant book; but it was the per pound value that convinced me. At $18.95 for a ten pound book, it came out to only $1.89 per pound. That's cheaper than a steak, and a lot more to chew. Neither of us realized that I had just bought the "Bible of Boating." The inside back jacket flap contained a paragraph about the United States Power Squadrons' boating courses and an 800 phone number. We called and were soon connected to the commander of the local United States Power Squadron twenty miles from our home. They had a public Boating Course in progress; but we could join and catch up, which we did. We also heard of the United States Coast Guard Auxiliary, and by sleuthing (the names and numbers were not easily available in our area) got information about their courses. We signed up for their Boating Skills and Seamanship class and arranged to have it meet in our church. Soon we had a small network of boating friends and instructors. Many of the people had a lifetime of experience they were eager to share.

We were about as ignorant as they came, but beginning with a blank slate is probably why courses with the Coast Guard Auxiliary and United States Power Squadrons meant so much to us. We joined the local Costa de Oro Power Squadron, and continued with their series of courses.

The company of people in this U.S. Power Squadron unit was a great combination of talent, experience and congeniality. Many of its members were Vandenberg Air Force Base engineers. They loved the technical aspects of boating and navigating, and many were lifetime boaters. Sailors, we learned, were engrossed with piloting, navigating and electronics, and some in our group had sailed half-way around the world. They couldn't

believe that we were serious about this endeavor with our lack of experience, but Bill Schultz, the Squadron's Education Officer, set up courses for
us and we'd knock 'em down like milk bottles at a county fair. After their
basic course we took Seamanship, Piloting and Advanced Piloting. We even
squeezed in a course on Engine Maintenance. I wouldn't call Eva a grease
monkey, but she learned enough in that course to be meddlesome.

Eva was a kindred mind to the engineering heads of the squadron. She
loved studying the charts, reveled in calculations, and thoroughly enjoyed
doing the homework and cruise exercises. When the administrators in Ra-
leigh, North Carolina, graded her final examination in Advanced Piloting,
they wrote, "Congratulations on having written an excellent examination.
As you continue...we hope that you will share your expertise with your
fellow members as an instructor..." and... "Excellent examination with particularly good understanding of use of Tide and Tidal Current tables...(Blah,
blah, blah)."

On my test they wrote, "Difficulties with one of the major concepts of
AP—current applications. Review with your instructor." which I interpreted
to mean, "We have never received a grade as low as yours, work done so
sloppy as to suggest a disturbed mind, and still you qualified for the certificate. You ought to be ashamed."

"Look," I said to myself, "a certificate is a certificate. Mine looks just
like hers."

While the courses were taking place, we scouted boats and schemed
how to finance our escape.

We gained more ideas and information by looking at boats in the San
Francisco Bay area where we have kids, in Houston where we don't have
kids and where it was rainy and cold in January, in Miami where it was hot
and muggy, and in nearby Los Angeles and Ventura. We nosed around boat
yards and asked stupid questions while owners worked on their boats. Never
were we turned away; rather, we were treated as inquisitive people interested in something really cool. We expanded our association with the great
fraternity of boaters.

Every aspect of boating is fascinating to a boater. Couples dressed in
surgical smocks filled pocky depressions in the hull...and sanded...and
filled...and sanded, with the interest and attention a mother attends a sick
child. Guys covered with oil and grime crawled out of holes looking like
victims of violent crime, but through the drudgery was the assurance that
someday their boat would transport them to worlds unknown.

Soon we were spouting terms that made us look at each other and say,

"Ooooh, you really sound like you know what you're talking about." It was wonderful to go through this growth process together. Eva was more avid about the learning and the prospective trip, but I tried not to be a wet blanket. This was going to be a joint affair.

We decided that if southern Florida was the best starting place for the boat trip, it would probably be the best place to buy our boat. The search went on with an elderly salesman who worked for a brokerage in Fort Lauderdale. He sent BUC listings of boats that were close to what we wanted.

When he mailed us photos with the listing on a Kha Shing Spindrift 40, we knew we had found our boat. She was a double cabin, sundeck trawler with twin Volvo diesel engines. We wanted the twin diesel engines for maneuverability and resale. A walk 'round queen size bed in the aft stateroom with head and shower looked very accommodating, and there was room for our laptop computer and bubblejet printer in a cabinet designed as the lady's vanity. Forward was the galley and guest quarters which consisted of vee berths and another head, perfect for guests. The accommodations were good enough to provide civilized quarters, but not so good that they would stay indefinitely. In the galley was a propane stove and oven, microwave and refrigerator/freezer. An 8.5 kW diesel generator was sufficient to run both the fore and aft air conditioners, the hot water heater, Grunert cold plate freezer and refrigerator and all the electrical outlets. It had everything to make us comfortable. Above the aft stateroom was the sun deck covered by a hard roof, and forward of that was the upper helm with front isinglass and covered bimini.

Two large anchors, a 45-pound stainless steel plow with 200 feet of chain, and a 35-pound Danforth with 150 feet of heavy braided line, plus an electric windlass, assured us of adequate ground tackle. Teak decks, a blessing to some and a curse to others because of their high maintenance, made excellent non-skid surfaces. All of them were in relatively good condition.

Our great odyssey was designed as a one-year affair. Do the trip and sell the boat. California's rugged coast was not our kind of cruising country, and we were not prepared to own a boat of this size for an extended period of time. We made our offer with contingencies, and it was accepted. We flew to Florida to finalize the deal.

We looked over the boat and rode along to the haul-out location. Seeing our dream boat in the slings with her undersides exposed was like seeing your lover naked. It was love, possession and pride. We were getting married.

We went back to California with the full survey to take place the following day, in our absence. The report was seven pages of minutia—nothing that couldn't be fixed for a couple thousand bucks we figured. We approved. The brokerage's handyman was asked to proceed with the necessary repairs.

If we got the boat out of Florida in 10 days after the closing and did not return for at least six months, we could be exempt from the sales or use tax. Since we were going to be on the move constantly, we felt justified in taking advantage of this legal loophole and delayed the closing until the day before we began to cruise. For the time being we had "bought" (or nearly bought) a boat and everything looked rosy.

The boat's name was *Annandale,* possibly a combination of some previous owners' names, and we didn't want to keep it. We'd heard the superstitions connected with changing a boat's name, but we didn't believe them. "There's a tradition to name the boat after the captain's lady," I said. "How about your middle name, Imogene?"

"Well, my daddy used to call me his 'Little *Genie* Girl'," Eva said.

We received a lot of help with name suggestions from friends and family, but in a dream one night Eva sat up in bed and said, "Ron, I've got it. How about *Dream O'Genie*, like in the old song, 'I Dream of Jeannie...'?"

"Swell," I said with the enthusiasm of a somnambulist. "Now go back to sleep."

Eva also came up with a solution of what to do with our home when we were gone for a year. We learned that friends who had joined the Peace Corps would be coming home early. They'd sold most of their furniture and household possessions and needed a place to live. We contacted them and they agreed to live in our house and take care of things for reduced rent. Lynne was also a technologist and had worked at the hospital in the past. She was rehired temporarily to cover some of the available hours.

Eva completed the paperwork for her leave of absence and I quit my teaching job at the end of the semester. We prepared to empty savings accounts and draw on our home equity loan, sold our late model truck and fifth-wheel travel trailer, and started the progression of boxes to Fort Lauderdale. We turned our keys over to the Peace Corps returnees who were happy to move into our furnished home with full cupboards and sheets on the bed. We briefed them about managing the rental properties and forwarding our mail. The saga had begun.

CHAPTER 2

READY, SET, GO

We flew to Miami on February 1 and took a room in a two-story motel on a busy thoroughfare in Fort Lauderdale. It was cold and raining. Our rain gear was in the UPS boxes coming across the land so we ran between cloud bursts and bought umbrellas at the nearby variety store.

After the first night in the room above the city streets with sirens wailing and garbage trucks announcing the dawn, we decided we'd had enough. We found a little motel off the main streets displaying a vacancy sign. A small Korean woman showed me a glossy-white room up a flight of uneven stairs where small dime-store pictures of flamingos and palm trees were placed close to the ceiling. The furniture looked like Goodwill throwaways. I returned to the rental car to have Eva look. I had parked next to a puddle, so when she got out of the car she stepped ankle deep in water.

She agreed the room was awful, but it was on a quiet street and it was cheap. We returned to the car and discovered that we had locked all the doors with the keys inside. We called Dollar Rent-A-Car and they sent out The Flying Locksmith. While waiting for the locksmith, Mrs. Kim agreed to take us back to our first hotel to get our luggage. She pulled a shabby Cadillac out of the driveway. Mirrors hung from the doors like broken hands. A sagging headliner brushed the top of our heads. Dials and cables clicked like old clocks. Shock absorbers, weary from plunging into pot holes, made the Caddy yaw and pitch like a boat in swells.

Mrs. Kim spoke broken English and I speculated that she took STOP signs to mean—*It's the custom in this country to stop, but if you're from somewhere else you can follow the practice of your native land.* She hardly slowed. Eva and I took turns saying, "Oh, we just went through a stop sign,

Mrs. Kim."

"Oh my, there's another one."

"Don't you stop for stop signs, Mrs. Kim?"

"The light is turning red, Mrs. Kim. WATCH OOOOOUUUT!"

We had traveled only three blocks and she had piled up seven transgressions. She swerved and weaved around corners like a thief with hostages. I giggled at the prospect of being totally lawless without accountability while Eva was in the back seat sucking air.

After only a day at Mrs. Kim's, we went searching for another new place to stay. The need for a telephone in our room and the nocturnal wanderings of her winter clientele, brought us to this decision. Mrs. Kim was disappointed. We found a little mango-colored motel on the Intracoastal Waterway called the Wish You Were Here Inn. We used our time at Wish to acclimate to the ICW like a swimmer dangles his feet in the water before diving in.

The next day we drove to Deerfield Beach to see the boat again. It was thrilling to see her there, so full of promise, so (seemingly) ready to take us on a fantasy ride to the far corners of the Great Loop. We saw her as a veritable magic carpet.

We brought her down from Deerfield Beach to Fort Lauderdale with Randy, the brokerage's handyman acting as captain. He taught us the elements of handling a forty-foot boat — how to turn the boat without using the rudders, how to do fast stops, how to deal with the wakes created by super-charged cigarette boats that kept the ICW rocking. The experience was new, fascinating and scary.

It took about four hours on the Intracoastal Waterway to travel to Fort Lauderdale. At numerous places, road bridges lifted to let us through. Waiting for the bridge required us to "tread water" and keep the boat in one place. It was tricky, with wind, current and waves buffeting us but I was beginning to get the feel of the twelve-ton boat.

We slid into Bahia Mar Marina and Randy had us dock into the slip stern first. I didn't have a notion what I was doing, so he instructed, screamed, grabbed the controls and we tried again and again, until I was frazzled. It felt a lot like the first hours in a small plane when I was learning to fly. Finally the boat was in the slip. We handled the lines like we were trying to recall textbook diagrams of marlinespike.

The brokerage assured us that in the next two weeks we would go out frequently to practice. "We will not send you out there cold," they told us.

The weather was tropically sultry with hints of the Caribbean. We settled into the routine of boat care and life on and near the water. In the evening we sat at Cafe Europa on Las Olas Boulevard sipping capuccino while a parade of babes and hunks strolled by. It felt like vacation.

Even though the boat was not officially ours, we had the brokerage's approval to begin the task of cleaning and getting her ready to go. After shipping fifteen boxes of goods from home, we still needed more housewares and supplies. We bought linens, glassware, lamps, a television set, stereo, bike helmets, fire extinguishers, charts and cruising guides. We shopped 'til we dropped.

Eva put her creative hand to the aft stateroom with rugs in blue, ivory, and beige and a quilted comforter on the bed. Small lamps at the headboard cast funnels of light on the pillows, and the warm teak interior gave the stateroom the coziness of a cabin.

Outfitting and repairing the boat was exhaustive. The pop-off valve on the water heater and the generator exhaust elbow had to be replaced. The bilge pump switch was inoperable, the seacocks frozen. All the batteries were exchanged, hoses were replaced, the oil changed and a new holding tank macerator installed. I didn't realize there were so many systems and

Our magic carpet gets a new name, Dream O'Genie.

so many parts.

We purchased a new GPS (Global Positioning System) to replace the non-functional Loran and added a radar because we were sure we'd run into fog along the way. Whenever an item added to our safety or appeared to improve our chances for success, we bought it. A Heart Inverter, that converts 12 volt DC to 110 AC, was installed. This was not safety; this was pure convenience. Our Visa was screaming, but we didn't care. We charged ahead. The outfitting discount at Marine West and Boat/US saved us a bundle, but the $5,000 designated for startup costs (including repairs, maintenance, and miscellaneous expenses) had nearly doubled.

Getting the boat ready wasn't anything like our dreams. It was like the health problems of an aging person. Everything seemed to be going or gone. We understood from commiserating boaters that this is the essence of boating. We spent a lifetime in the engine room while we envisioned long sunsets with margaritas on the aft deck. We smelled of diesel fuel and mildew, an intoxicating combination that we thought of packaging for old boaters who have given up life on the water. With only a sniff they could be transported back to the good old days.

I pleaded with the brokerage for some cruising time so I could practice piloting the boat. "Soon," they said.

We realized we had gotten into something that would require much more money than we had allocated and vast amounts of time. We had virtually separated ourselves from regular income, except for accumulated paid time off and some income from rental properties. We were beginning to see the bottom of the pot and hadn't yet left the dock. Eva still had her long, red nails, albeit with oil and grit beneath, but nothing that a little nail polish wouldn't cover. What we didn't have, or what we were losing quickly, was our friendly dispositions. The weight of bills and the threat of yet more expense made us crabby. This is the mental state we thought we had left behind in California.

Before we began this trip people asked us, "You're going to be together on the boat for a year?" This was said with raised eyebrows and a cynical look, as if they knew that this would be difficult. Maybe impossible. We knew folks in the Power Squadron who sailed around the world and then came home to finalize a permanent split. But we resolved to do this boat trip, stay together, forgive and go on when tough situations arose.

Eva and I hadn't been apart for more than five minutes since we left, and we loved it. But honeymoons with people, and with boats, are short. The days wore thin, the romance of boating and the newness of life together twenty-four hours a day called for stamina, patience and endurance. We asked our friends to pray for us.

The days wore on. I still didn't have any additional practice on the boat since we brought it down from Deerfield. "Maybe tomorrow," they said.

One day, as the calendar moved toward the time of our departure, the brokers made different murmurings. They said that I had shown such dexterity, such coolness and extraordinary savoir-faire, that they were sure I didn't need any additional practice. They thought that my four-hour run from Deerfield Beach showed that I was made of the right stuff and that I was going to be able to handle the boat just fine. I argued vehemently that a four-hour run did not a captain make.

I began to see their ploy. By assuring me I was Cap'n Ron, even before I was, they could forget their pledge. They were not going to provide me with further instruction.

The day of reckoning was close at hand. The boat seemed about ready, although Randy, given a long list of work to do for us, demonstrated the height of inconsistency and intemperance. He'd start on a job, then disappear for the rest of the day. A follow-up survey requested by the insurance company revealed a number of tasks still incomplete. A grudging seacock wouldn't open, but Randy, enraged when confronted, showed that he could do it. He lunged at the seacock coming up with a broken handle in his hand. We faced yet another night in the bowels of the boat where the sun never shines.

We felt twinges of homesickness for our California country home and reminisced about our last night there in the hot tub with the call of coyotes in the foothills.

There was a series of weather fronts that brought cold, rain, high seas and a string of small craft advisories. We delayed the closing and leaving, and continued to work on the boat.

A break in the weather was forecast. The brokerage arranged to have Randy go with us the first day. This was their way of "...not sending you out there cold." Randy admitted he didn't make all the needed repairs. The rest of the chores would have to be done along the way.

Eva began looking at the charts, getting ready to lead us along the ICW going north. We listened to the VHF radio to get an idea of what was happening on the waterway. We had never used a radio. We had never charted anything (except in class). We had never gone solo. We were virgins at sea and tomorrow was our wedding day.

CHAPTER 3

THE ODYSSEY BEGINS

We left Fort Lauderdale at about 7:30 a.m. with winds and frequent showers still battering us. The forecast was for clearing skies later in the morning and moderating winds. Handy Randy helped me pilot the boat out of the slip without hitting anything, but it wasn't a masterful exit and I felt very shaky. Nobody booed either (they were all sleeping). We headed out of the marina and into the ICW.

Every time I started the engines from that very first day until long into the trip, I had that uncontrollable urge to leave the bridge and visit the head. I thought of a captain's catheter, a device that a guy could hook himself up to as he began each day.

Later in the morning we filled with diesel fuel along the waterway. Spiders and other critters had made their home in the air vent hoses, plugging them and giving Randy a snout-full of diesel fuel. He screamed for water and detergent so we could clean up the deck and disperse the fuel before it entered the waterway. There are heavy fines for spilling and polluting. We dug the little critters and their debris out of their hose warren with wires until air exited and fuel flowed, ringing up our first fuel bill of $238. Ouch!

At Del Ray Beach the landscape became more natural, with preserves and the softening aspect of forested hummocks and mangrove habitat. The boat traffic decreased considerably and I sighed with relief. The weather had turned gentle after a stormy night and Eva and I took turns piloting the boat with Randy sitting by attentively. There were many bridges across the ICW and we frequently had to stop and wait for them to open since our clearance was 17 feet to the top of the anchor light. Some of the bridges opened on the hour, some on the half or quarter hour. We tried to relax and experience the pleasure of cruising.

Lake Worth is truly a lake, but only 7 or 8 feet deep. The Intracoastal Waterway is continuous from Key West, Florida to the Chesapeake Bay. I was beginning to understand that it connects rivers and lakes by man-made canals. There are inlets to the sea and some travelers go "outside" as they travel north or south, but we chickens stayed inside, protected by the barrier islands that separate the ICW from the Atlantic Ocean.

After practicing anchoring, we dropped Randy off at a dock at West Palm Beach. It was a nerve-wracking landing. I had to nose the boat in at a 90 degree angle between several docked boats, stop when the bow touched the dock, let Randy jump off, then reverse in wind and current without hitting anything. My first attempt was aborted when I was unable to bring the boat in at the right angle. Randy grabbed the controls impatiently, turned the boat in the channel with a lot of noise and churning water and headed us back into the dock. He handed me the controls and dashed to the bow. I tensed, took the boat in, slowed, slowed, stopped. Randy jumped off. I slipped it into reverse, gunned the engines, and we were back in the channel going north. I was shaking like a leaf. Eva and I looked at each other and I said, "Well, Toots, it's you and me. There's nobody around to help us. I hope you're good."

We both knew that we had bought more than we bargained for. My fear was that at a crucial moment I would lose my cool and gun it when I should be shutting it down, or reverse when I should be going forward. With no foot controls and separate throttle and forward/reverse levers for each engine, my head was a fire storm of neurons talking to each other.

Randy had called ahead and made a reservation for us at a marina in North Palm Beach which was about an hour north, so they were expecting us. We entered the marina with Eva handling the lines and fenders. Dock hands were ready to receive us and I slowed the boat to a crawl. No doubt there was something in the way we looked that told everyone, "These people don't know what they're doing. Be ready for anything."

I made an easy slide onto the dock, bow first. Eva threw a line to the waiting dock hand. A little kick on the port engine in reverse got the stern in. The dockmaster commended me on my slow approach. "You can't do much damage if you're going slow," he said. The first day was behind us, and behold, it was not too bad.

The second day dawned bright and promising. People were sitting on the decks of their boats having breakfast, reading the paper and basking in the pleasure of their waterfront "homes." We too had a moment of satisfaction, but there were miles to do that day so we were ready by 8 a.m.

We were pinned between boats fore and aft and rehearsed our exit in my mind. With twin screws we could swing the stern out by reversing the starboard engine, so while Eva pushed the bow away from the dock on the starboard side, I put the starboard engine in reverse and timidly applied the throttle to get the stern moving into midstream. Then I had to figure out how to keep the bow from continuing the swing into the boat behind. I put both engines in reverse and came out of the slip straight toward midstream, skimming past the neighboring boat whose skipper looked like he had just swallowed an egg. Once midstream, I turned the boat around, forward on one control, reverse on the other. She pivoted just like she was supposed to do and we were under way in the ICW going north.

North Palm Beach looked like country compared to the south coast. The dominance of condominium domiciles was replaced with parks, lagoons and uncluttered horizons of trees. Pelicans were diving in the water and fishermen were angling for the same. This was fun and for the first time the hot and smelly tasks we endured the last two weeks seemed worthwhile.

Just before we reached Jupiter Inlet we heard someone call us on the VHF radio, "Captain (I love it) of the *Dream O'Genie*. This is *Yellow Brick Road.*"

I looked at Eva and said, "What the hey is *Yellow Brick Road?*"

"I don't know," she said. "Maybe it's a boat named *Yellow Brick Road*. It's probably behind us."

"Well, talk to them, Eva."

"No, you talk to them. You're the captain."

I fumbled for the hand held VHF radio which we had NEVER used and which was fresh out of the box, and replied like a wimp (not at all like a captain), "*Yellow Brick Road*, this is the captain of *Dream O'Genie.*"

"Go to 72, *Dream O'Genie*," he came back.

I thought, "Well, you go to 72, Buster. I like it right where I am." After what seemed like 17 hours Eva and I concluded that he wanted to TALK on channel 72, but by that time he was back on channel 16, saying, "Captain (I love it) of the *Dream O'Genie*, let's go to 72."

Scrolling up on our NEW, AND NEVER USED VHF, for what seemed like another transport through time, while steering our forty-foot trawler around fishermen and other small craft, I finally got back to *Yellow Brick Road* and we talked. He wanted to know if we had clearance for the next three bridges. This required several things of us: knowledge of the charts, the height of the bridges, and familiarity with our boat. I thought, "This guy has a sense of humor." I was still learning port and starboard and he wanted to know the height of our anchor light on the radar arch.

We got to know *YBR* pretty well, and because he was a resident of Florida and St. Augustine to the north and had been up and down the waterway, we decided to follow him instead of lead. We slowed and fell behind him, traveling in his wake and mimicking his movements around shoals and across the Jupiter Inlet. The incoming tide churned the channel waters into strong cross currents that moved us around and set us diagonally across the waterway. I could see what was happening to *YBR* so when we got into the inlet's stream I anticipated the effect of the surges. When we finally signed off I said, "This is *Dream O' Genie*, FUC 666091, out", when in fact our temporary call sign was KUS 666091. You can see how confused I was. "I want to be institutionalized," I muttered. "This is too hard."

Eva was sure that the FCC was going to come down hard on us for this infraction so I scanned the horizon for Federal helicopters and sinister-looking agents. "I'm really sorry for this and promise I'll never do it again," I said, looking heavenward.

Eva noted that *Yellow Brick Road* was flying the stars and stripes from her stern flag staff. She stated that our boat, without any flags or burgees, was virtually naked, like leaving the house in the morning without putting on earrings. I had trouble identifying with that.

The area north of Jupiter was very beautiful, with piney woods, palmetto palms and mangrove swamps. This is a good look at what Florida is, or was, naturally, a sub-tropical wilderness of great diversity and beauty. I longed to get off the boat and walk the trails through the preserves and state parks that line the Intracoastal Waterway.

There were many protection zones for the manatees between the Jupiter and the St. Lucie Inlets. We hoped to see them, but had no luck. This was our first day at work. The cameras were out; the bird book open; we had time to dawdle as we observed the world at 8 knots, and often, in no wake zones, we'd poke along at 5 knots. We were doing great.

Sandy Beach on Peck Lake is a thin strand that separated us from the open ocean. We saw crashing breakers over the beach from our fly bridge. This was the prettiest section of Florida so far, with homes situated in woodland settings similar to what you see on northern lakes. Egrets congregated in rookeries in the mangroves near St. Lucie Inlet.

We moved into the Indian River which runs northward to Cape

Canaveral and beyond. Day marks in the form of green squares marked the right side of the channel and red triangles designated the left side. The water was very shallow, only a few feet deep outside the marked channel, and the deepest was only 10 feet.

Eva was at the wheel when we spotted dolphins. She immediately slowed and began to steer away from them. "Stay on course, Toots," I called out to her. "They'll get out of your way. Maybe they want to play in our wake." And they did. Four of them porpoised in and out of the wake and launched themselves into the air. I was amused, but it was hard for Eva to concentrate on piloting while I was hanging overboard photographing them.

We decided to spend the night at Vero Beach. Eva read in the guide book that they had moorings for much less than the dockage, so I asked her

Jumping dolphins frequently accompanied us in the ICW.

if she was game to pick up a mooring. "No way, this is only our second day. I have no idea how to do that."

As I approached the dock, engaging the dock master for docking instructions, our battery-powered, portable VHF went dead. Stopping midstream because of incomplete instructions, we wondered what to do. "Honey, go to the downstairs helm and use the wired-in VHF." Eva looked anguished. "I've never used a radio before," she whimpered. "Well, then you stay up here and I'll go down," I said. "No, I'll go. I can't run the boat."

And in that uncomfortable state she left the flybridge to have her first experience on the VHF. She did fine. She got the instructions, put her head out the door and shouted orders to me. Soon we were close to the dock and she was on the fore deck messin' with lines while I fumbled with the controls. Somehow we brought the boat in and completed another day without mishap.

Vero Beach Municipal Marina was a lovely place with a congenial group of boaters, some sail, some power. Chicagoans Bob and Julie invited us for cocktails on their 36-foot sailboat, *Plastikos*. We were in the company of seasoned boaters who were simply adding another chapter to their boating lives. We were alone in our greenness. They treated us like the novices we were, giving advice on equipment and routes. The next morning Julie gave us pages of hand-written notes which outlined their favorite places along the ICW, through the Chesapeake, to the Hudson River, and Canadian waters. Their kindness was exemplary, and a warm realization that other boaters were there to befriend us. This early lesson in friendship was the strongest, most enduring benefit of cruising the inland waters. We didn't have much to give at this point, but lessons of thoughtfulness and consideration were being learned.

Osprey nested along the section of the Indian River north of Vero Beach. More dolphins played in our wake and Eva had her chance to watch them. They jumped over the bow wave like jet skiers, then dove down and swam even with us, rolling over on their sides to look at us.

We tried to set the anchor in the channel near the town of Cocoa. A sailboat was already there and the skipper was fully involved with a martini when we pulled nearby and tried to get some idea where to anchor and what the tides were like. We asked a lot of questions and hoped for some help, but not all boaters are nurturing and helpful to beginners and we were left to our own abilities. The anchor wouldn't hold so we pulled into a marina on the west side of the channel and prepared to celebrate another day without incident. Little did we know what surprises awaited us.

CHAPTER 4

TROUBLE IN "RIVER CITY"

In the morning I dropped into the engine room to check the oil and water levels. The floor and pan under the port engine were covered with coolant. I called up to Eva, "We've got trouble, Toots."

The port engine had been running a little warmer than the starboard engine but we had been checking the levels in the morning and watching the gauges throughout the day. Everything seemed to be okay up to this point.

We called the dockmaster and asked if there was a reliable mechanic nearby. He referred us to Whitley Marine and their contracted service.

Mike, the mechanic at Noah's Ark Repair, came aboard. He took one look at the bleeding engine and suggested we move the boat to a dock at Whitley Marine where his tools were handy.

Mike removed the port heat exchanger and discovered that the housing was badly corroded by sea water (replacement cost — over $900) and the part wouldn't be available until the Volvo dealer found one — somewhere in the U. S. ...or Sweden.

Mike asked about the condition of the starboard heat exchanger, but removal of that one indicated that its housing had previously been replaced. Both exchangers' cores were full of gunk and debris and needed a thorough cleaning so they both came out and were laid on the dock like a pair of vital organs. We wondered why the former owner hadn't replace both of them at the same time?

While I was in the engine room experiencing a personal moment of grief and contemplation, Eva flushed the electric head in our stateroom and I heard water running down the engine room wall. The sewage line to the holding tank was leaking. This was an unpleasant little diversion. The line ran out of sight through a locker in the salon, so as we searched we removed all the stowed items and laid them out on the cushions until the boat looked like we were having a garage sale.

In desperation, Eva went to the manual head near the galley...and it didn't work either. You couldn't even budge the gear-shift-like-thing.

When the manager of the marina walked by, I said, "Hey, Charlie, give us an idea what's going on with these heads." After some time he surmised that our holding tank must be full. So we thought, "Well, the toilets must work, that's good news. The bad news is there's no place to go with the stuff."

The marina didn't have a pump-out station and the nearest one was 15 miles north at Titusville. With both engines apart, we resigned ourselves to using the marina's washroom. We thought disdainfully of mid-night potty runs along the pier.

When you're on a roll (down hill) all kinds of things seem to happen; you pick up speed in a pell-mell, free-fall to oblivion.

When Charlie was poking around looking for the head problem, we posed another question to him. "Charlie, the boat's water looks like the Red Sea. Our white wash cloths are becoming totally orange. How can we clean the tanks?"

Charlie stopped, and with an ashen look said, "Oh, I hope you don't have those cheap Taiwanese stainless steel tanks with the crappy welds that rust and leak." We said we sure hoped not, too, but how could we tell.

"Are the tanks under the bed?"

"Yes."

"Do they have two bolted inspection holes on top?"

"Yes, why do you ask?"

"Because last year I had a guy in here with a boat just like this whose water was rusty because of degrading welds. His tanks were leaking and we had to take them out. Ran him about $2000. Yours aren't leaking, are they?"

A peek was all that was necessary. The inside welds of those cheap Taiwanese "stainless steel" water tanks were as rusty as a sunken warship, and they were leaking. The surveyor missed it and we missed it, until now. Around the edge of the tanks underneath the bed was a dark, wet zone, almost imperceptible, but now glaring to our searching eyes. And do you think you could buy those 150 gallon water tanks out of the Sear's catalog? Or any catalog? Get serious. Those babies needed to be custom made, and even if we ordered them that day it would take several weeks for them to be made.

Two-thousand bucks was serious money and a huge dent in our budget. We began calling around to find a less expensive solution and found smaller, ready-made polyethylene tanks in the West Marine catalog. We ordered them over the phone, saving about $1,600.

We were not in Orlando with Epcot Center and other national attractions where a lay-up could be turned into a mini-vacation. We were in "River City" (Cocoa) where *Dream O' Genie* lay hog-tied against the dock with her innards all over the mechanic's floor and gas fumes rising like hot air in a mirage.

A major concern was that we had to have our boat out of the state in a week. We dodged the Florida sales tax by buying the boat through a Delaware corporation. The state of Florida isn't happy with boaters who register their boats in other states and then use Florida as their cruising grounds, so we had to pledge that we would skedaddle out of Florida. If we stayed over the limit, we would be required to pay the tax plus a 100% penalty, which totaled almost $11,000.00, and THAT would put us out of business. (Florida now has a new law extending the 10 day limit to 90 days.)

Eva seldom cries, but that morning she could not hold her disappointment and frustration any longer. She slumped into a pathetic little bundle of confused and broken humanity. The *Dream O' Genie* had become a nightmare. It was depressing thinking what tomorrow might bring. Two years of the best-laid dreams and fantasies were coming to a grinding, smelly halt, with visions of winged dollars fluttering skyward and us on a landlocked boat without a pot to...

We called the state and told them our tale of woe. Surprise! They were sympathetic. Told us to be cool. "Get it fixed. Call us when you're ready to go."

"It may take a week or more," I said.

"No problem, so long as you're laid up in a ship yard with Problems."

That's Problems with a capital "P" and that rhymes with "T" and that stands for Trouble. I imagined their office staff in a half crouch chanting like a New York stage troupe from *Music Man*, "Trouble, Trouble, Trouble...".

The water tanks came out. It took three guys over an hour to pull those tanks the size of coffins from under the bed and through the narrow doorways. We set up fans to dry the wood before the new tanks arrived. We were without water, our septic tank was getting more septic by the hour and our engines were dissected like cadavers. To top it off, I flossed a crown off a molar and the jade setting fell out of my wedding ring. We were on the road to degradation. We both spent considerable time in stupefied trances of depression and wonder.

From the outside we looked brown and outdoorsy, and with our bike helmets and Florida tans you'd think we were absolutely normal and having a good time. Inside, we were rotting.

On Sunday we biked to the nearby Methodist Church; we needed to be recharged. Our boating odyssey had become a test of faith.

As our stay in Cocoa, Florida, lengthened, we were soon on intimate terms with everyone at Whitley Marine inasmuch as they all worked on **Dream O' Genie**, now unaffectionately dubbed, **DOG**. Hank, one of the wrench-hands, took us out on an airboat to the headwaters of the St. Johns River where we became ecoterrorists, "flying" through swamps and onto small islands where we met other airboaters who were hunting wild boar. The hunters sat around in a loose circle sluggin' beer, and didn't look anything like a prayer group. A couple of hounds slept, their work for the day over. The quarry was "hog-tied", with visions in his piggy head of slow rotations over an open fire. Talk about depression.

We explored the headwaters of the St. John's River in an airboat with Hank.

We played tennis with Susan, the marina's employee who ordered our parts and sympathetically listened to our worsening tale of woe. We ordered BBQ chicken dinners from church fund raisers who worked the marina population. We did our part to relieve the recession in Cocoa. It seemed that passing our Visa card to someone was as natural as presenting a business card.

We hoped to leave on Wednesday of the second week, but not all the parts had arrived so we waited and did a myriad of things that needed to be done. We pulled 200 feet of heavy anchor chain out of the chain locker and removed corroded links and painted ten foot markers for easy reference. All the hand and toe rails needed refinishing so we began that year-long task.

On Friday new polyethylene water tanks went in and we filled them. In fact we overfilled them and water gushed everywhere from under the bed where the tanks lay, soaking all the wood we had so carefully dried. It was back to drying the wooden floor under the new tanks as best we could, until we finally adopted the attitude that nothing is perfect and close is as good as done. Besides, in Florida, dry means damp, damp means wet and wet means you're under water.

Saturday the last of the parts arrived. The mechanics went to work in the afternoon, but by 11 p.m. one mechanic was still in the engine room wrestling the heat exchanger into place for the fourth time, and Mike, the owner, who was baby-sitting, was in the salon with his daughter on his knee. Leaks of various kinds showed up, and the thin metal of the access covers on the exchangers cracked which could be fixed only with welding. At midnight we sent them home.

On Sunday everything went together, but we waited until Monday to test it.

The mechanics came aboard at 8 a.m. and after starting the engines, heard a rattling noise in the starboard engine alternator; so it was replaced. Later in the morning we did a sea trial. Everything seemed go.

I hadn't been at the helm for two weeks and I felt like a beginner again. We thought everything was going smoothly from the fly bridge where you can hardly hear the engines. Mike, (who had a habit of squinching his eyes whenever he presented us with bad news, so we called him *Wink*), and Hank, his helper, (who was big and kindly with drowsy brown eyes earned the nickname of *Pooh*), were checking things out in the engine room...and heard something new. *Wink* called me down while *Pooh* came up to the fly bridge to run the boat with Eva, (nicknamed *Dopey* because she had been very sad of late). *Wink* revved the engines and had me, (called *Grumpy* by everyone who knew me because I was such a grouch), listen to a whine of the turbo charger on the port engine. The verdict from *Wink* was that the turbo charger was "fried" and needed to be overhauled. He said that if it disintegrated and oil was lost, we could destroy the engine.

We thought back to the Engine Maintenance course with the U. S. Power Squadrons and couldn't remember fact one about turbo chargers. So much for book learnin'. "Maybe," Mike said, "we can have it done by the end of the week."

Dopey looked dopier, *Grumpy* was even grumpier, and *Pooh* looked mellow and unconcerned because he was not paying the bills. I wanted to be like *Pooh*. They removed the turbo charger and *Wink* shuffled off to get the work started. *Dopey* and *Grumpy* slipped into deeper despair.

We settled into a daily routine.

Grumpy (me) went down to Wink's repair shop and flailed on him about how long it was taking for the turbo charger to be repaired. *Wink* explained that the turbo repairman was very good, but also very sensitive (did you ever hear of such a thing?), and if we pushed him, he could quit and tell us to take our business elsewhere. "We've got to be gentle with him," *Wink* said, "but I'll see what I can do to hurry things along."

Then we had breakfast.

Grumpy thought of jumping ship and running for city council. We had become community members, like it or not. *Dopey* went house hunting. We thought we may as well move here and do some day trips with the boat when it was finally fixed, if that time ever came. We got sick of the boat and spent more time around town so we didn't have to doctor our *"DOG"*.

Next day, a repeat. *Grumpy* went down and pounded on *Wink* for some action. *Grumpy* wailed and cried and carried on while *Wink* winced and winked. They drew a crowd; it was pathetic.

Then we had breakfast.

Dopey found a beautiful home on the waterfront and laid plans to drown our "Hound".

Next day, *Grumpy* went down to *Wink's* repair shop and repeated yesterday's performance. The histrionics, the blood-in-the eye rage, the offensive affronts that left *Wink* winking, were shameless. And...it was very INEFFECTIVE! *Wink* was doing what he could. During these episodes *Pooh* would hunker off to a corner of the shop and clean something.

Dopey said she bought a new car in a fit of depression, and three sticks of dynamite for the boat. Said she was never going to step back on *DOG*, so help her GOD.

The verdict on the turbo charger was that it couldn't be cracked, so it had to go to Orlando to a diesel turbo shop. They got it, took a look at it, ordered replacement parts from Virginia, which were made of pure gold according to Volvo's specifications, and didn't promise a completion date.

We settled in, again, and thought of pleasant ways to bide our time. Cocoa was, after all, a pleasant place to be stuck. It reminded us of our home town of Arroyo Grande, California. It had a small historical village, a great hardware store, friendly merchants and good mechanics. Cocoa is not to be confused with Cocoa Beach, that glitsy strip along the ocean where Ron-Jon's Surf Shop panders for tourist bucks like a brothel beckons weak men. Cocoa is modest and wholesome, a town with a library as big as its churches, and a place where workmen produce essential services.

Cocoa is near Cape Canaveral. We were on the fore deck when the space shuttle, Columbia, took off. It was a spectacle, a veritable orange torch screeching into the sky. The sound was better than a dozen low riders in Miami on a Saturday night.

Cape Canaveral and the Kennedy Spaceport were just a few miles away beyond the bridge on Merritt Island, and so were the Merritt Island National Wildlife Refuge and Cape Canaveral National Seashore. These sanctuaries are the wild and natural side of Florida. We decided to take a

Pelicans pose for the camera at Jetty Park near Cocoa Beach

look.

We rented a car and drove the short distance to Titusville and then to Cape Canaveral. We walked and motored through much of it and photographed thousands of birds and reptiles that find sanctuary here. We watched pairs of shoveler ducks upending their little bottoms as they foraged for food in the lagoons, while nearby a Great Egret with showy plumes hunted small fishes.

One hundred thousand coots winter there making puddles of black bodies with white-tipped bills. As the flock grazed the duckweed, they strung out in long continuous beads and connected from one pond to another. This is also a winter haven for 14,000 gulls, 3,000 raptors and a myriad of song birds.

Oaks draped in Spanish moss spread their beams over a foot trail through a palm/oak hummock. The understory of palmetto palms caught the mottled light from the forest canopy like out-stretched hands. An armadillo rustled in the brush, enough for us to catch a glimpse, then was gone as an owl flew from an overhead limb.

Bob and Jane, on a neighboring boat (*Brass Ring*), befriended us. They shared their budget-wrecking boating experiences and buoyed us with tales of endless summers aboard their boat. They gave us cruising maps, information on where to go and restored our hope.

Relatives of friends back home, who live in Cocoa, invited us to their home and loaned us their car.

One day, when the sun was shining and the thought of going somewhere in the boat was as probable as a snow storm in Miami, *Wink* and *Pooh* showed up with the rebuilt turbo charger. They held it like a mother holds her newborn. They pulled back the wraps and let us see. It was beautiful. Then they submitted a bill that was greater than last year's part-time teaching income. We decided to call our boat an investment so we would feel good about all the money we were putting into it.

The next day we had another sea trial. Everything worked. The boat was seaworthy, but the weather was being obstreperous again. We had to wait until the threat of high winds and marauding squalls made our passage less exciting than our past. We wondered how much more we could endure.

CHAPTER 5

ON THE ROAD AGAIN

We did leave Cocoa late one windy day in March, separating ourselves from that place as though it had suction. It was good to be moving again after being tied-up for over three weeks. Crabbers were working the waterway for clams, raking the channel bottom with 15-foot rakes. They'd pitch the rake off the end of their skiff, then with a tugging motion rake the bottom, letting the muck and debris filter out. As the rake approached the stern of their boat they'd pull in their catch. Clams were sold by the sackful to local restaurants.

Crab-pot markers appeared, frequently within the boundaries of the waterway channel.

We decided that the fifteen-mile run to Titusville would represent a trial run, so we spent the night where manatees drink from running water hoses and great blue herons hunt off the docks all night.

In clear view of the Vehicular Assembly Building at Cape Canaveral we did our first big-time shopping on the bicycles. We rode a half-mile to a supermarket and loaded up. We were aware that our bicycle packs had limited storage, so we bought cautiously; but still there was a gallon of milk, soft drinks, frozen meat, canned goods, fresh vegetables, two big bags of cookies and the sundry things that wind up at the end of the checker's conveyor. We brought the bikes into the store and jammed the packs until they were bulging. The rest were hung from the handlebars. We wheeled the bikes outside and mounted our mules, heavy and unbalanced. Eva got ahead of me, weaving around but making progress.

At a stop light we got off the bikes and walked across the street, but half-way through the intersection my pack, loaded with canned goods, milk and cookies, came off its hooks and fell into the spokes, making movement impossible. I picked up the bike, now weighing 50 pounds, and returned to the curb while Eva rode off into the sunset unaware that I had broken down. Never lose sight of the guy with the milk and cookies, is a lesson she learned the hard way.

The shuttle landed at Cape Canaveral while we were there. Everyone in the marina was out on their boats awaiting the sonic boom, hoping to catch a glimpse as it glided to earth. We were in Cocoa when Columbia lifted off several weeks before and in Titusville when it landed. It did 27 gazillion miles, we did 15.

The Indian River north of Titusville is as broad as a lake. We took the man-made channel into Mosquito Lagoon, a heavily forested area that was wild and primitive. Crabbers were tending their pots and pelicans and laughing gulls hung around the boats reading the menu. A hunting osprey nearby had a fish in its claws. Fishermen were everywhere. If the ecosystem is in trouble, at least here things looked healthy and abundant. Oyster beds are cultivated and harvested at low tide when the pickin's as easy as hoein' a tomato patch. This perspective of unspoiled land is lost to motorists on the road.

South of New Smyrna Beach is a section with many fish camps and RV parks. A fisherman was angling on our side of the narrow channel and a large motor yacht coming toward us was passing him on the left, so we moved to his right, bumping aground on the shallow sand bottom. *DOG* rose out of the water like she was goosed, the stern wave crested, slapped her on the butt, and she slid off the other side into deeper water again. The fat man in the fishing boat, jaws agape like a hippo in heat, offered insulting advice about our piloting ability. We had words, too, for the squatter in the middle of the fairway.

Daytona is the Fort Lauderdale of the north, a city landscape of high-rises and condo towers. We docked at English Jim's and it went fine. By the tiniest increments our skills were growing. The port engine battery was dead in the morning so we panicked, sweated, became depressed, and then had a level-headed session on switches and chargers. After we had things figured out and switched both batteries together, the engines started and we were off again.

We were beginning to understand and make use of the many appliances and devices of our boat which were designed to provide variety, entertainment and conversation with other boaters at the docks. One of the unique features of our trawler was the Grunert Cold Plate Refrigerator/

Freezer. Traditional boaters know and love the features of this odd-ball, deep-dish appliance. The refrigerator/freezer works like a block of ice. Its cold plates get frostier and colder the longer it is run so you can go hours or days without electricity or the use of the generator. The refrigerator is on one side of the appliance with both a top loading and front loading door. The freezer is next to it with a top door only. Each unit, is about three feet deep and two feet wide. A tray half-way down is the (singular) convenience feature. If you want something from the bottom of the freezer, and you have things stored on the (singular) convenience feature, you have to re-move the tray and everything on it, then stand on your head to reach the bottom where everything is piled on top of everything else. The bottom looks something like an arctic fissure which has swallowed an expedition.

With counter to floor depth, getting to the bottom for Eva, who is only 5 foot tall, required an upended position to find things. Sometimes I would see her in the freezer (well actually, I would see only part of her because her head and shoulders would be IN the freezer) and her bottom would be on the counter with her legs squirming and kicking. It was a strange sight and I didn't know whether to help or play.

Then there were the cabinets in the kitchen that were designed for big people, and Eva had to push her little blue step stool like a hockey puck beneath the upper cabinets and reach up blindly to tip the dishes toward the edge, catching them in mid-air. Getting them back onto the shelf seemed to work best using the basketball free shot technique, which resulted in a num-ber of rim shots, missed shots and air "balls".

Another prominent feature was a cellar-like cabinet in the floor which touched the bilge water so when you pulled it out and set it down on the floor you left behind a bilge slick. We stored potatoes, turnips, pumpkins, carrots, rutabaga, jerked beef, hog jowls and wine down there. Yes, we did eat good.

Two stainless steel sinks were so deep Eva looked like a draped towel when she did dishes. She said it was going to make her flat-chested if she did too much of this, so I became the dishwasher.

The staircase to the galley, from the salon, was extremely short and steep. We advised everyone on board when descending to be sure to hold onto the built-in grip that was attached to the wall, and never walk down in stocking feet.

The forward head had the unique feature of being a shower and potty simultaneously. You could stand while you showered or you could sit on the toilet seat. Landlubbers are bewildered by this, but boaters realize the savings in time and energy by performing all toilette functions in one great cleansing. Problem is, the toilet paper got soaked, because the entire head became the shower. Drains in the floor carried the water to the waste water sump, where it was pumped overboard. We eventually created a plastic drape to hang over the tissue holder and other parts of the head, which brought clinging plastic sheets up against wet bodies. The plastic sheet, the shower on the toilet seat position and the frail dribble of water from the shower head led many of our guests to go dirty or seek washroom facilities at the marina.

The shoreline north of Daytona is untrammeled wilderness. This is Florida of the 16th century. Small wooded islands support hummocks of oaks, palmetto palms, cedars and pines. It was strikingly beautiful and a great relief from the domicile domination of southern Florida. North of Flagler Beach the channel cut through limestone strata with palms and scrubby oaks on one side and pines on the other. "Why don't we live here?" I said to Eva.

We smacked bottom again on an encroaching sandbar. Just a temporary moment of fear and hysteria, then we were free. It was one of those episodes when the nervous system sounded all the alarm bells, the heart began racing, and the episode passed. The physiological tide washed over us in wasteful readiness.

The Sheraton Palm Coast Resort and Marina appeared on the left side, in the middle of paradise. The Palm Coast has extraordinary beauty with many preserves and tall palms. Close to the inlet of the Matanzas River is the original Marineland of Florida.

The ICW is separated from the ocean by a thin strand of sand which attracts homes and crowds and barren landscapes trodden by the pounding feet of sun worshippers and beach-goers.

The entrance into St. Augustine Harbor appeared obvious to me so we pulled into a large central basin and began looking for slip B7 that the dockmaster assigned us, but we couldn't find it. Eva said, "Call the dockmaster again and ask for some directions." I slowed and fumbled with the radio while current and a strong southerly wind carried us toward docked boats. Taking care of two tasks at once was more than I could handle and *DOG* drifted toward the docked boats. I raced the engines and stirred the water in a frantic effort to be clear again. The dockmaster gave additional directions to go around the outside of the marina to the far north side where a dockhand waved us in.

Finding a home after a day on the water in new environments was always a time of anxiety. You don't park a boat like a truck and trailer. We discovered that as soon as we stopped the props and forward movement ceased, we were vulnerable to the forces of wind and current.

I was so new at docking that everything I did was done irrationally and without purpose. Nothing was second nature to me like the immediate actions and reflexive responses that motorists use after years on the road.

We dream about places to live and retire. St. Augustine is one such place after you get past the touristy historical district. Oak-canopied city streets ensconced quiet neighborhoods with sprawling homes among azaleas and dogwoods. Out of the sub-tropical climate of southern Florida, there is a serenity and grace not found in many places.

The Spanish were a dominant presence in America in the 15th and 16th century. Ponce de Leon arrived in 1517 and gave Florida its name and Pedro Menendez de Aviles founded St. Augustine as a city in 1565.

The English, who were establishing Savannah and Charleston in the 1600's, came down from the north and did their best to burn and pillage the Spanish stronghold, and so did the French who were camped out near the headwaters of St. Johns River. In 1695 the Spaniards got tired of the stinging, pesty English and French and constructed Castillo de San Marcos, a fine coquina stone fort that absorbed many canon balls and proved to be virtually impenetrable. It still looks that way today, but the Spanish conceded to the English, and eventually to the American Revolutionaries. On July 10, 1821, the Spaniards lowered their flag from the top of

St. Augustine, established in 1565, burned many times. An old schoolhouse is a rare surviror.

Castillo de San Marcos, circa 1695, is the only permanent Spanish fort on U. S. soil.

the fort for the last time and the stars and stripes were raised. It is now a great historic monument to the occupancy of foreign powers who fought to make America a satellite colony.

Henry Flagler, the railroad builder, left many turn of the century monuments around town including the Flagler Hotel, now Flagler College. The collegians live in splendid quarters where stone toads and fish spout in ponds and fountains; but open windows with drying clothes and blaring music announce a new era of collegiate informality and clutter.

I bought "blooper" tee shirts (3/$10) with images of florescent shells, sea horses and surfing dudes on the front, and "St. Augustine" stamped on my left arm. I didn't think I'd ever do anything as tacky as that, but I had ruined so many clothes in the first month of owning the boat I didn't have anything respectable.

The views from the waterway going north from St. Augustine were natural and beautiful. There were few homes, no cell-block condos, and miles of native woods and salt water marshes. It's big sky country with long vistas over Edenic landscapes.

Despite pejoratives associated with salt marshes like filth, despicable, low and worthless, we found them to be romantic and artful. The sky is a moving carpet over them, casting shadows across a monochromatic landscape of waving grass and soft river bends. We traveled along places with poetic names like Sawpit Creek, Black Hummock and Pumpkin Hill.

From her assortment of guide books, Eva identified an idyllic anchorage in the middle of a vast marshland north of Jacksonville near Amelia Island. We were intent on learning how to hang on the hook and not pay the usual 50 to 85 cents-a-foot marina tariff. We took a small detour up Alligator Creek and found a spot in the middle of nowhere with miles and miles of horizon and centipede grass and occasional islands of hardwoods. We swung *DOG* into the wind and dropped the 45 pound plow with its all-chain rode.

Actually it wasn't that simple. As we were choosing our spot, a mother storm developed and the winds picked up. Eva, who was swaying on the bow of the boat, sweated and stewed about where to drop the anchor while I was under cover on the fly bridge (because I was the captain) trying to persuade her to drop the darn thing. Finally she did, and it reeled out like it was being dropped from the sky, so great was our backward movement in the wind. But finally the anchor was out....and set. In fact it set so hard it nearly knocked her down. She took bearings, then waited to see if we were moving and, voila, we were not. We thought we may NEVER go anywhere again.

Then the wind huffed again, an ugly cloud dumped on us, and the weather turned beautiful and calm. We decided to set another anchor off the bow Bahamian style. I got the dinghy ready, lowered the 35-pound Danforth anchor into it, attached Ye Olde Wizard (air-cooled 5.5 hp engine, made by Western Auto in the sixties — no reverse, no neutral; when it starts, you're gone), and went upwind in the dink to drop the second anchor. Now we had two irretrievable anchors in the muck.

So taken were we with our success, we decided to go for a ride in Alligator Creek in our dinghy. It was very romantic. Eva lounged in the bow like a goddess while I putted the Wizard through marsh grass until *DOG* was a toy boat in the far away. Then I shut the engine off and we floated through a vast wilderness of centipede salt grass and sky and warm winds after a storm, where no sound is made but the call of wild creatures and the breath of porpoises on still waters. It was an idyllic moment of animal sounds and pastel sky...and little sand gnats (called No-See-Ums by an ancient Indian savage, no doubt, or Tiny Little Biting Sons of B...'s, by us moderns) that were stabbing us and making us slap ourselves silly.

But once back on the boat, with alcohol running freely through our veins and enough insect repellent to ward off mosquitoes and No-See-Ums for miles around, we sat on the aft deck and watched the sun go down, congratulating ourselves on the savings of $38.50 (which we had paid each night in St. Augustine) and the good fortune of a beautiful night in a matchless setting. No more marinas with hot showers and nearby grocery stores and telephones for us. No siree. We were going wild from here. Our inverter converted the boat battery's DC to AC so we were good all night without ever having to run the generator.

Eva walked the decks in the moonlight and came in to tell me that the two anchor lines were hopelessly wound around each other and the wind had picked up again. *DOG* was taking a new position in Alligator Creek. The good news was that we were set for the night. The question was, were we set for a lifetime. We thought our new address might be:

Alligator Creek
Somewhere off the ICW
Florida/Georgia Border

CHAPTER 6

"I WANT TO LIVE HERE"

Soft mist hung on the moor at Alligator Creek and the sun reflected across the water like the moon at twilight. After breakfast we walked to the bow of the boat and examined our lines.

We did, in fact, have our two anchors hopelessly entwined. I had to take the line to the Danforth anchor, which is 3 miles of nylon the size of beef tongue, and gather it in my hands and arms and pass it through the guard rail and over the chain anchor where Eva had to hold it over the gunwale, tipping her nearly into a shoveler duck position (bottoms up) and then take it back from her and pass it through again and do this several more times and return this humongous pile of line to the deck and try to pull up the Danforth by hand. It had seventy pounds of black muck on it which made it heavy as a "mothah" so that I couldn't lift it. The thought of using the warping drum on the windlass to pull it in came to mind; and in less time than it takes to fly from here to Europe, we had it in.

I went to the flybridge to ease DOG forward as the big plow anchor with its 160 feet of heavy chain came up. Eva stood on the bow of the boat shouting commands to me, "FORWARD. STOP. BACK. STOP. FORWARD. SLOW! STOP!!. STOP!!! STOP!!!," all the while operating the foot control for the *Silver Toad* (windlass) which was gulping chain like a chainavore — gulping, gulping, gulping the whole thing in one endless string (you would hope so) until I thought the poor thing would choke. Finally the plow broke through the surface of the water like a prehistoric monster. Caked with clay, it approached the bow, wobbled on its rollers and settled into place like it was giving up the ghost.

Now we had two anchors decked, heavy and gray with globs of mud, which gave DOG a down-in-the-mouth appearance as if she had the morning blahs. (Much later in the cruise we developed a crude washdown technique.) Then we were off again into the murky, misty low country of endless marsh prairie and winding trails, gliding like a great white swan. Gwak, gwak.

The smell of jobs and industry hit our nostrils. A nearby paper pulp mill sent its plume of acrid pollutants across the waterway near Fernandina Beach, Florida.

By mid-morning we were in Cumberland Sound, an awesome body of water, open to the sea and full of commerce and activity. We were warned that submarines at the nearby naval base may emerge from the water in the sound as they return from sea, creating waves like a tsunami, so we thought about wearing fins, masks and snorkels; but none appeared, and we made it across to the other side, albeit nervously.

We really wanted to spend some time on Cumberland Island, now a national park and open only for day use and camping. This was the home of the shamelessly rich at the turn-of-the century, but their estates have returned to the wild, and feral horses have joined the indigenous wildlife amidst the wooded hummocks of pine and oak.

We followed the shoreline of Cumberland Island into St. Andrews Sound, one of the largest, shallowest bodies of water we'd seen. The buoys were over 2 miles apart and in the haze we couldn't spot the next one. We knew we needed to head out seaward. We became anxious that we had missed a buoy and would end up in Bermuda.

We hadn't learned how to set waypoints in the GPS yet so we reverted to our Power Squadron training. Eva spotted a tower on Cumberland Island and a tank on Jekyll Island, both identified on the chart. She took readings with the hand bearing compass and plotted them on the chart, assuring me that we were still on course. Soon the elusive buoy was within sight and we pivoted around it and headed for Jekyll Island.

Jekyll Island was a favorite spot for blue bloods in the 1800s, now operated by the state of Georgia as a National Historic Landmark District. It is a wonderful island-world of historic seaside estates, communities of single family homes, and resorts who lease their land from the state. Development has stopped, commercial advertising is curtailed, and the island demonstrates the best in environmental planning.

The state of Florida required proof of our exit from their state, inasmuch as we waived the payment of their sales tax, so we bought fuel at Jekyll Island, using the receipt as proof of passage. The ten day period for escape was obviously violated, but we had given them notice of the time DOG was tied-up in the boatyard getting fixed so we didn't anticipate any problems.

We rode our bicycles from the marina into town, picking up the bike path that passed through woods of pine, palmettos and magnolia. Some of the trail was paved, some was made of the duff of the forest floor. The perimeter of the island was open and uncluttered, and a 20-mile bike path circled the island. We spent a day bicycling, visiting old cemeteries, walking the beaches and following the winding paths through woods and marshes where alligators lay in the sun.

A residential community north of the historic district had simple homes in rustic settings. Tall pines, wisteria, azalea and dogwood gave it a dressed-up look. Beyond the small airport, with an elevation of 12 feet, were the Presbyterian, Baptist and Episcopal Churches, clustered together ecumenically.

All the trails and roads followed the idiosyncratic curves of the island. They wove around marshes and woods and gave us a continually changing view of the landscape. Nature loathes straight lines, and so did the original trail and road builders of Jekyll Island. I said to Eva, "I want to live here."

Giant oaks draped in Spanish moss graced an ancient cemetery. On the gravestone of an early islander is written:

Our bitter tear shall fall
above thy grave like autumn rain
Yet we not thy spirit call
back to these scenes of care again
For blessed is he, and doubly blessed
who nobly all life's paths have trod
content to find his final rest
within the bosom of his God.

April 27, 1850, Joseph Dubignon, in the 38th year of his age.

Industrialists of the 19th century had awesome wealth, and the families who owned Jekyll Island were reputed to represent one sixth of the world's personal wealth. Men like William Rockefeller, J. P. Morgan, Richard T. Crane and Joseph Pulitzer built cottages the size of hotels and ate communally at the Victorian Club House, a giant affair with ballrooms, meeting rooms, parlors, dining rooms and 60 guest rooms for select friends who didn't own homes on the island. It now operates as the Raddison Hotel. None of the "cottages" were built with kitchens because members of the club were expected to socialize at mealtimes. The club raised its own beef, had its own dairy, grew its own vegetables and cultured its own oyster beds.

The croquet greens are still in front of the hotel, and the clay court tennis club and golf courses continue to be attractions. Golf was the new pastime of the elite in the late 1800's. The extravagant use of acres of cultured fairways and greens to pursue a little white ball, was both absurd and the height of fancy. Jekyll Island's 63 regulation holes made it the center for golf, and is still the largest golf resort in Georgia.

The depression, changing tax laws and the reversing fortunes of some of its members brought about the decline of Jekyll Island Club. During W.W.II, the island closed temporarily, then permanently, as the next generation of wealthy turned their back on Jekyll Island as a stodgy place from the past and ran off to new hot spots like Palm Beach and the Riviera. Following the war, the island fell on bad times and stately cottages sagged in old age. The State of Georgia reclaimed the island as a historic reserve and maintains it.

At our marina on Jekyll Island we observed millions of jelly fish. They swing with the pendulum of tides trailing their tentacles and pulsing in slow rhythms.

St. Simons Island is nearby and we moved to an anchorage in a cove for the night. The weather turned raw and cold. Eva stood on the bow like a flag in the wind while I positioned Dog for a favorable place in the lee of the island. We dropped the hook and went to bed.

An ebb current of two knots and winds to 25 mph made for a disturbing night. In our sanctuary, which from the outside appeared besieged, we were quiet and calm. We didn't know if this complacency was the mark of seasoned cruisers or sheer stupidity, but when we pulled the blankets over our heads we felt safe. The rolling on the water and the gentle turning was reminiscent of prenatal life. We rocked in the warmth of the unconscious, secure and unconcerned.

In the morning it was raining relentlessly. I got up to observe neighbors who were anchored near us in a 44-foot motoryacht with their three kids. Somehow they braved the elements to weigh anchor and be on their way. Wussily, I went back to bed and pulled the blankets over my head to find fairer climes in the images of my dreams.

We spent the day on the boat, reading, writing and catching up on chores while rain poured and wind swung DOG around like a toy. We had a luncheon date, but without a phone and the bay waters too disturbed to go in, we couldn't cancel. The day brightened as it wore on and we dinghied to shore. Taking bicycles in the dinghy was out of the question, so we had no transportation and attempted to thumb a ride into town. In this part of the country those who stand on the side of the road with their thumbs in the air are derelicts, bums and thieves. No one stopped, so it was back to the boat. By evening we sat on a mirrored bay with an ink-black sky overhead.

There are a hundred miles of marshlands and barrier islands on the way to Savannah from St. Simons and we picked our way through small creeks, rivers and sounds that comprise the ICW. Numerous range markers guide ships like sights on a rifle. Sometimes the ranges are to the rear and when you have your boat on course in the channel, they line up.

There wasn't anyone on the water except an occasional boater and crab pot waterman. From the high position of the upper helm we had exceptional views of the countryside. Our flybridge was outfitted with a canvas bimini top and front windshield but only partial side curtains, so we were not fully protected from the wind and sun and were often chilled. Land temperatures are always 10 degrees warmer and less breezy than life on the water. We lived our life outdoors until the engines stopped, then retreated to the inner salon and aft stateroom.

Our speed of travel was about 8 knots, which meant that to travel to Savannah, a distance of 100 miles, we needed two days at the helm. We could drive that in a car in two hours. This makes boating appear archaic. We were, in a sense, pioneers again, experiencing every bloody inch of the way, feeling the land, swatting the insects and naming every laughing gull and fishing osprey that became an intimate encounter. Some of the travel was repetitious, some of it tedious and some of it luxurious in the time we had in one place.

We anchored half-way to Savannah in the desolation of sky, marsh and biting gnats. The evening sky turned a gauzy pink and we maneuvered DOG off the ICW into Buckhead Creek in the lee of Pine Island, a refuge from strong southeast winds. We dropped the hook, closed up shop and let our cares slip by.

We were beginning to anchor without histrionics and near marriage-wrecking dialogue. We felt a bit more relaxed with each other's performance and were beginning to understand the other's development, or lack thereof. I ran the boat and Eva handled the lines when docking or anchoring. She had the tougher tasks and I volunteered to change with her, but she was not comfortable running the boat so I got the easy job and she was down on the deck doing the grunt work. Fortunately, a childhood on the family's South Dakota farm made her capable of anything. She lifted, pushed, handled lines and ran around on wet surfaces to keep us safe and undented. And in matters of navigation, there was no one better. I was like a blind man. She pointed. I moved.

She had an ideal for the perfect boater's body. It would be a tiny person who could get around like a basketball guard, gargantuan arms 7-8 feet long for reaching lines and fending off boats, eyes on all sides of its head for repairing things in tight places...and in high places...and in places that are hard to reach; ears big enough to hear the first default of a dry bearing before the engine self-destructs. Each hand would have two thumbs and two index fingers for holding the multiple things that need fixing; webbed feet for the times of being pitched out of the boat or dinghy. A huge skull with a marvelous brain that could remember charts and bring them to recall immediately, compute waypoints, and do dead reckoning on a dead run. This mind would know what's for supper and have a grand scheme for making money, because those who boat, spend.

The problem is, what captain would like to have *IT* for a first mate. I was glad I wasn't experiencing her dream evolution as the trip progressed.

On a few occasions I won her approval for piloting the boat, but she began to understand that she was stuck with a klutz who sometimes was hot and sometimes was not. There was no doubt that we were both getting better at what we did. Her margaritas became legendary.

That night, in Buckhead Creek off the ICW, I prepared a meal of grilled pork chops with horseradish sauce, scalloped potatoes with sour cream and onions, summer squash and farm-fresh broccoli. "Not bad," she said. "If only I could pilot the boat like I cook," I thought to myself, "I'd be the complete Renaissance man."

Through the night we swung like a pendulum, but so soft was our turning we felt not a thing, and in the morning, we weighed anchor and were on our way.

In the Vernon River, Eva was at the helm and saw something flipping up and down in the water. She thought it was more of the playful dolphins that had been our constant companions so she stayed her course. I was below refilling my coffee cup when I heard her shout. This thing bobbing in the water was a railroad tie and there was no way she was going to avoid hitting it. She swerved and it struck a glancing blow off the bow. She yelled for me to check the bilge and see whether we were holed. Fortunately we took the hit along the length of the tie rather the end and were okay, but she was shaking and scared.

We docked DOG along the ICW during our stay in Savannah as the city waterfront was used primarily for commercial traffic. We were committed to bicycling, walking and using public transportation during our year aboard the boat, a forced discipline which we hoped would reveal our self-sufficiency and point to a simpler lifestyle. We were willing to rent a car if we really needed it, but a bus ran into the heart of the city of Savannah so we walked the five blocks to the bus stop near Savannah State College, a predominantly black co-ed institution. I didn't realize when we boarded the bus, that exact change was required. The fare was $1 each and I only had large bills. I asked the driver what to do. He turned away indifferently and got off the bus to take a break. I asked the riders on the bus, all black, all students at the college, if any could make change. No one could help. I got off the bus to appeal to the driver again; meanwhile two female students fumbled in their packs and came up with our passage, a magnanimous gift considering their economic status as students. Two white *yachtees* received a handout from two black students in the heart of Dixie. We were impressed. The obvious barrier between blacks and whites in the South dissolved in an act of kindness. For a moment, there was peace on earth.

That act of kindness inspired us throughout the trip. Even the bus driver was touched. He became cordial and as we rode along he pointed out sights and recited historical facts. He got off the bus at our stop and pointed in the direction of Mrs. Wilke's Boarding House where we were having lunch. On days following, we saw him in his bus as we walked through the city. He'd wave and we'd wave, and at the end of the day we would catch him for the last run of the day back to the campus.

Savannah, established on a bluff of the Savannah River in 1733, is a magnificent museum city. Georgia, the 13th and last British colony, was chartered by General Oglethorpe in the name of King George II. With him were 144 English men, women, and children, which makes you wonder why everyone doesn't speak with an English accent. He laid out Savannah in a prescribed grid system, with public squares for use by those living in the country to take refuge in case of war. Churches and civic centers occupied strategic places in and along these squares. Azaleas, dogwood and wisteria were blooming, and the numerous fountains and statuary in the squares, magnified by the many restored homes, made it stunningly beautiful. I said to Eva, "I want to live here."

General Sherman stayed in town during the Civil War and spared Savannah the wrath he bestowed on Atlanta. Lucky for us. If there is an American city with European splendor, Savannah has to be it.

We walked through Savannah, rode through Savannah in horse-drawn carriages, and photographed it until we were exhausted. We toured the regency-style Owens House, one of many historic homes preserved from the past. On some homes, opposing winding staircases arise from the street level and meet at the top, symbolizing the "welcoming arms of the South." Purportedly, the propriety of the South forbade a man to follow a woman up a staircase lest he catch sight of the seductive turn of her leg. A lecherous glance was as good as an offer to marry.

Under the front porch, in an underground cellar, ice cut from northern lakes and rivers was stored and utilized on hot Savannah afternoons for mint juleps, a gentle person's drink of bourbon, finely cracked ice, sugar and sprigs of mint.

A group of travel agents was touring the 1920's Oglethorpe Hotel, a den for Mafia gangsters in the '30s and '40s before it became reformed into the respectable Sheraton Savannah Inn & Resort. Its island isolation made it ideal for surreptitious underworld characters; and now, for couples and families wanting insular luxury. We boarded the faux paddle-wheeler *Magnolia*, that was docked near our boat, and motored over to the island.

We had never been piped to dinner, but this group got the king's treatment. As we neared the dock of the hotel, a waiting Scottish bagpipe band welcomed us. We fell in step and marched off, following dutifully to the oyster roast where we dug the little guys out of their houses using long-handled, short-bladed knives. Fresh pineapple, strawberries, wine and cheese, got us satisfyingly sated; but then the band struck-up and again we followed like French Legionnaires after a night on the

The curved stairases of Savannah's elegant homes symbolize the welcoming arms of the South.

town. The crisp walking-in-step degraded to a shuffle as fattened sheep were led to the slaughter. Some slaughter. The grand banquet room was a culinary den where more food passed beneath our belts and the world of Savannah looked splendid.

We satisfied our need for a quiet night on land by taking a room at the Gastonian, a beautiful B&B in a pair of restored 1868 three-story brownstones owned and operated by runaway Californians, Hugh and Roberta Lineberger. Under a peach satin canopy we slept in a bed that must have been filled with whipped cream and sifted flour. It didn't rock, nor did waves lap against our bow or wind slap the halyards of neighboring sailboats. It was wonderful. In the morning we didn't even think about raising our anchors. We just walked downstairs and dined on southern-style French toast filled with cream cheese and pecans, covered with whipped cream, bananas, strawberries and crowned with Georgia peach preserves. This is the way we want to live.

While in Savannah we received word that Eva's sister, Cora, was diagnosed with colon cancer and was given a prognosis of two months to two years to live. This was a severe blow to the family and raised the question of continuing the trip. To stop here meant to cancel all of our carefully laid plans, including the purchase of the boat. We decided to go on as there was nothing we could do at this point. We opted to make frequent calls back to South Dakota to keep informed.

After our stay in Savannah, it was tough for me to get back on the boat and drift in the uncertainty of the tides, but Eva was content to be in our home on the water. The day was warm with fluffy clouds and once back in the ICW things became comfortable. I steered with my feet and sat back, relaxed.

We took the ICW toward Hilton Head, but stopped at Defauskie Island instead, opting to see a barrier island with its maritime forests before it is transformed to golf courses and housing plantations. The maritime forests are a rich variety of oak, pecan, loblolly pine and cedar. The Gullah-speaking black people occupy this island and remnants of their time are here in school houses and domiciles. But their time is going. The developers are making the crooked plain, and the rustic splendid. The "insect infested marshes and sloughs" are becoming sterile ponds with clean edges in the middle of fairways.

Gullah is a dialect of West African and English and is nearly as indecipherable as the language heard at most southern diners and truck stops.

We stopped at the island's only dock. The night was cold. It was April

1st and the temperature was down to 37 degrees. We ran the ship's reverse cycle air/heat in the morning and warmed up the boat before we ate a hot breakfast. The maritime equivalent of a school bus pulled onto the dock at Defauskie just before we left. Students on Defauskie take the passenger boat each morning for classes on Hilton Head, a few miles away.

We skipped Hilton Head and Harbor Town Marina and the civilized developments with golf courses and tennis clubs, and went right on to Beaufort, South Carolina.

"I want to live here."

Beaufort (pronounced B'you-fort) is small and charming with many historic homes set along the marsh grasses. These areas are only a few feet above sea level, and frequently suffer storm damage. In 1993 an isolated storm wiped out their docks and tore up boats on the waterway. There have been times when storm surges brought water to the second story levels of the homes.

The servants' quarters of the 19th century homes were always on the ground level where it was either hot and dusty or likely to flood. The head of the manor and his family lived on the top floors where breezes entered the windows and they were safe from floods.

Hurricane Hugo was so devastating to these coastal communities in 1989 that they use time references like BH or AH, Before Hugo or After Hugo. Many of the large trees of the hummocks, and the great trees of the cities, were toppled and split.

Pat Conroy wrote many of his books in this setting — *The Water is Wide*, and others. The movies, *The Big Chill* and *Prince of Tides*, were filmed here, and the cast and crew of *Forest Gump* finished filming just prior to our arrival.

Before we dinghied back to the boat, which lay at anchor, we stopped at Emily's Restaurant for her delightful She-Crab Soup, a delicate blend of soft-shelled crab, cream, onion, garlic and spices. Female crabs are supposed to have a more delicate and rich flavor. I think it's more of the South's adoration of things feminine.

Beaufort was all decked out for Easter. On Saturday at St. Helena's Episcopal Church, local parishioners were scurrying about filling window sills with Easter lilies, sprigs of dogwood, magnolia and azaleas. Each window was decorated by a different family. The place was a happy melange of people and large bouquets.

As we arrived at St. Helena's for Easter Sunday service, the ancient cemetery that surrounded the church was buzzing with parents and kids.

The Easter egg hunt was about to begin. All the children were corralled behind a starting line which ran between the cemetery and the entrance to the church. At a given signal the children, looking like sun flowers and butterflies, ran through the gray tombstones, giggling and gathering eggs. It was the symbolization of the resurrection.

Inside the church decorum stifled laughter and conversation; worshippers knelt and became still; acolytes got last minute instructions while cherubic priests in flowing white garb walked from one side of the chancel to the other, genuflecting to the cross as if it were a magnet. Their pink skin and thick glasses suggested years of study, prayer and devotion. We felt like street-persons—ruddy and wind-blown.

The rich symbols and gestures, the fabrics and flames, the incantations and posturing, the up and down and sidewise looks to moving symbols, transported me back to earlier churches...to England's Anglican Church...to the Holy Roman Catholic Church...the Apostolic Church. Eva kept us in order with the bulletin following it like a navigational chart; she knew when to sit, when to rise, when to hold them, when to fold them and when to walk away...

There is talk about southern hospitality, but these Episcopalians were not warm and fuzzy to us. The Anglicans seem to be a "closed to new members" club, while the splinter Methodists are a class-less society that

Wide verandas catch the summer breezes along the tidewaters of Beaufort, S.C.

embraces everybody.

St. Helena Episcopal Church spans the time from before the Revolution when everyone was loyal to the queen, and British soldiers and families comprised the parish. It was established in 1712 when it was still the Anglican Church, the Church of England. When the revolution was complete and Mother England no longer revered, the Anglican Church in America became Episcopal.

Among the dead in the church yard were two British Revolutionary officers from the Anglican period and three American generals from the Revolutionary period; and at the entry to the church was a tribute to soldiers from a third era: "...to our honored dead of St. Helena's who wore the gray and fell in the service of the Confederate States 1861-65" ... a long list of names. The oldest grave was marked 1724.

The way to Charleston from Beaufort was through more marshlands and not much different from the geography we experienced since northern Florida. We expected to eat more of the "low country boils," the feast of seafood: crab, shrimp and oysters.

Osprey use the day markers for nesting sites along the waterway. The two-faced metal markers are 10 feet off the water and the birds build idiosyncratic nests between the uprights. The day markers provide a safe place to nest, an easy escape and a good vantage point. We didn't see any chicks, but the season was right for another brood.

The most prevalent and bothersome animal of the lowlands was the sand fly. Also known as *punkies, can't-see-ums* or *no-see-ums*. These nearly invisible hypodermic needles have the bite of a dragon and the venom of a snake. You can immediately feel their serrated-edged beak cut through the flesh. They're not easily spooked, so it's SPLAT! A rather dry SPLAT, because they're so small. But there's a backup of another million waiting to fill the ranks. It's endless. The venom of their bite is more irritating than a mosquito's and the bites itch unmercifully for days. Our bodies were a disgrace of red welts, particularly our ankles. So much for southern hospitality.

The long expanse of marshlands from the Coosaw River heading north is as broad as the eye can see. We moved from marker to marker, each about a mile away, feeling like a conestoga wagon on the endless prairies of the plains. This may be one of the last frontiers, still wild, untamed and savage.

At the Fenwick cut in the ICW we met a tug heading through, pushing two huge barges. We heard his SECURITY call and were prepared to meet him, but suddenly he was there, churning and pushing his unwieldy barges and blocking the entire way. There was not room for two of us so I pulled into a cut on the right side and asked him on the radio if I was out of his way, or was he coming in my direction? He thanked us for standing by and assured us we were in a safe spot.

Some tows and their barges were so long that we saw the barges before the captain saw us and it was necessary to take immediate action to avoid a collision. Pleasure boats never win against tows and barges, and we could have been under the barge and heading for the tow's props before the captain knew what happened.

We headed through more marshland and places with intriguing names like Scanaway, Jehossee, Edisto and Bowhickett. Bowhickett was an upscale island of cultured golf courses and posh housing tracts. We didn't stop.

Charleston, South Carolina, looks like a city that is confused, growing and undergoing reconstruction surgery. Hurricane Hugo took out the city marina and they were just getting around to renovating it. After a day anchored in Charleston Harbor, we decided to move the boat inside the protection of the city marina. Strong winds and choppy waves in the harbor made the ride in our tender dinghy both wet and perilous.

It wasn't until we had taken a Gray-Line Tour of the city that we began to see the charm and history of Charleston. A bicycle ride in the evening gave us an intimate feeling with the city, its gardens, its *single houses*, ancient churches that date to 1734, the home of John C. Calhoun and St. Michaels Church where both Robert E. Lee and George Washington worshipped. We fell in love with yet another southern city and I muttered to Eva, "I want to live here."

Dates on buildings of 1670 and 1711 struck us as early dates for our very recent civilization, considering that the Jamestown Colony dates to 1607 and the landing of the pilgrims at New Plymouth, Massachusetts was 1620. In our home state of California, the date of 1772 on the San Luis Obispo Mission appears ancient to us.

We bought a bag of boiled peanuts from a black street vendor. They were in a wet plastic bag and looked as if they had been soaking on the bottom of the bay. They were soggy and disgusting-looking, but I dared myself to buy some. We sat on the curb and shucked 'em. The skins were purplish, but the peanuts were firm and salty as if seasoned by a variety of salts. I think they were boiled in sea water. They were delicious.

South Carolina dances to the tunes played in Charleston. There is no

A child enjoys the spray of the fountains at Waterfront Park in Charleston, S.C.

doubt about Charleston's leading force now or in the history of America. The American Revolution had its seed in early uprisings against the British in Charleston when in 1765 the townspeople, tired of the Queen Mother's taxation, sent England's ships bearing the official papers of taxation back to England. This was one of the first instances of rebellion in any of the 13 original English colonies. It occurred 8 years before the Boston Tea Party, which everyone remembers from junior high history, and 11 years before the Revolutionary War of 1776.

The first shots of the Civil War were sent from Charleston against the U.S. at Fort Sumter. South Carolina was the first state to secede from the Union (1860), a major player in the establishment of the Confederacy in 1861, and one of the last to succumb to Union forces. If any people deserve the label, Rebels, it's the Charlestonians.

There are numerous plantations in the surrounding countryside and we had the opportunity to visit the grounds of Middleton Plantation. Union forces burned the main building, but a flanker building remains, as well as the original design of the gardens and farm buildings.

I took m' love for a boat ride one evening in our tender. Our boat's position in the marina was so far from the laundry and washroom facilities, it was easier to use the dinghy than to walk. There was a soft southern breeze that sighed and brushed her skin like the whiff of camellias in the morning. We had libations on board (a tumbler of cheap Chablis), and hors d'oeuvres (the soggy, purple peanuts). She lounged, I rowed. I hummed a tune. She swooned. Waves lapped the hull like the wet licks of a golden retriever.

When we got to the dock, we took our bags of dirty laundry and shyly walked the ribbed walkway to the dock level where an early evening tour boat crowd was standing, dressed in white and smelling like jasmine, and dimestore perfume. We trundled our cargo past them knowing that all eyes were upon us. Step by painful step we walked the plank, their shiny white patent leather shoes visible to our downcast eyes. We ducked into the laundry room as if it was a sanctuary.

We returned to the tender with bags of clean linens for the dark ride back to the boat, during which time m'lady neither lounged, nor did she sip libations. Nay, rather, she hunkered down with her hands between her legs for warmth and said naught a word, but endured stoically until we reached our yacht, whereupon we hauled the laundry up the transom, over the aft deck, through the salon doors and down the aft stateroom stairs where we put away all the stuff.

Thus are the pleasures of doing laundry on a boat, a close second to the water closet experience, which in its primitiveness predates the pit. In the pit it's gone, forever. In the manual commode, affectionately referred to as, *Le Crappierre*, it circulates and recirculates that which you never want to see again, until you cry out in grief and disgust, "GOOD GRIEF, BE GONE ALREADY!" And even then it's not really gone. You've got it caged (holding tank) and now you have to see if someone wants it. Wants it?! Of course, nobody wants it. You have to pay someone to take it off your hands, which as you may or may not know, means hooking up to some great SUCKING MACHINE whereby you get to both see and feel your stuff flow by— again. It's a great relief when it's finally gone. You're tempted to never do that again, but you can't help it.

We had a brutal day on the ditch (ICW) after leaving Charleston. A strong nor'easter blew at gusts to 30 mph making our way slow and uncomfortable. As we left Charleston Harbor the waves sent DOG pitching, coming up in time to dive into the next wave. It was the first time that spray came over the bow and covered the plastic windshield on the upper helm, a distance of about 15 feet from the water. We leaned into the wind like pedestrians on the streets of Chicago. Gusts shook the canvas of the upper steering station and rattled us like a dog shakes a rag doll. After hours of abuse we retreated to the lower helm and the protected interior of the boat's salon; but the threat of running aground forced us back to the upper helm where the wind whistled and cold air sucked body warmth from us until we were cold and depressed.

When we approached McClellanville we were exhausted. Safe harbor is a concept that has special meaning for boaters. A lone sailor in his sloop stopped short of town, dropped anchor along the channel of the ICW and let the day go on. We went by him and radioed ahead to Leland Marina in McClellanville. No answer. Another call. Still no answer.

We turned left into Jeremy Creek and approached the 18th century town of fishermen and shrimpers. Large oaks and pines broke the fury of the wind and there was an immediate transformation into quiet. Comfortable homes appeared as if pages on a book had been turned. Gaggles of shrimp boats rafted together like a great brotherhood of workers, their raised bows and many-eyed windows mugging all newcomers.

We searched for Leland Marina amidst the working docks and the wholesale fish suppliers. A Texaco Star suggested a possibility, but there was no business name or evidence of dockhands. We continued upstream where I spotted some fishermen working on their boats.

"Hey fellas, where's Leland Marina?"

"Yu'llpasseditbackdere." (They speak Gullah.)

So I threw DOG into reverse, did a 180 degree turn in the middle of Jeremy Creek and headed back down to the Texaco sign. Still no sign of life. I made an approach toward the dock which sometimes brings life to the wharf. A worker on a shrimper saw us and left his work to take our lines. Only then did Jimmy Leland appear, apologetic and exceedingly attentive. By his side stood his dog, Jeremy, a Jack Russell terrier with teeth like a shark, head like a horse and short, peg legs that put its belly close to the ground.

Jimmy gave us the lay of the land—the retail fish store where we could buy the local catch, the grocery store a half-mile away and the offer to use his car if we needed it.

We took the bikes down and wandered on terra firma, past 19th century homes with large porches and vacant lots that remain vacant because there is no urban sprawl here, no pressure to subdivide, no inclination to erect a condominium, nor the least impulse to consider a planned unit development. These people have their wealth in shrimp boats and their bank accounts are the yet-to-be-caught nets of shrimp.

Hugo was there in 1989 and flooded them. They retreated to the attics of their homes, and the school which they considered the safest place. When the school flooded, they placed their smallest children on the heating ducts close to the ceiling, and fathers held older children on their shoulders while the waters rose...and finally subsided. The town is back to normal, but Jimmy verified that Hurricane Hugo created a new reference point for these people just inside the marsh grasses along the Atlantic Coast. The ancient oaks stood the test of time and flood and continue to give McClellanville an air of dignity and grace.

We rode our bikes to the Carolina Seafood Company where we bought shrimp and scallops, then to T. W. Graham Mercantile—cafe, groceries and general merchandise, all in one store. The local gentry gathered on creaky chairs in the front window arguing local and political issues, welfare and the disgrace of food stamps, and what they would do if they were in the state house. The shelves contained one or two of everything, the smallest denomination of canned goods, baked goods and utilitarian goods I have ever seen. One person on a serious shopping expedition could wipe them out. They provision as if everyone has only three things on their shopping list.

We headed back to the boat with our loot in our bike bags, and prepared our catch of the day in the galley of the boat—sautéed shrimp and scallops in butter, garlic, onion and wine. The sun set and a pack of smiling

19th century McClellanville is a refuge for watermen and a port for shrimpers.

shrimp boats beamed at us like a portrait of workers at a company picnic.

The following day, boaters from Charleston made McClellanville their day ride and tied-up behind us. As boaters often do, stories were swapped and friendships begun, and we decided to have dinner together. Jimmy called the Crab Pot Restaurant on the outskirts of town and made arrangements for them to pick us up. At the appointed time, a waitress using her own car, showed up and took us to the restaurant and waited our table. We ate cheap and good and she brought us back again.

Dave Gallup pulled into the marina to have his boat repaired on Saturday. We got to talking and he invited us to the worship service of their Episcopal church in the old 1768 brick church in the country on Sunday. "Twice a year we lock the doors of our town church and hold our service in the old historic church with the box pews," he said. "Afterwards we have a picnic in the church yard with tables of food. Gets people to church who haven't been there all year, probably because it's as much a picnic as a service; and the food is great. If you want to taste southern cooking, you ought to come out." This sounded too good to miss, so we asked him to pick us up in the morning. If they had this event every week, we'd probably say about McClellanville what we've said about many charming southern towns, "I want to live here."

CHAPTER 7

THE FINAL LEG OF THE INTRACOASTAL WATERWAY

Cars were parked everywhere along the road and parishioners flocked into St. James Santee Episcopal Church on Old Georgetown Road, which they affectionately call *The Old Brick Church*, circa 1768. Parishioners who are seldom seen in church show up for this coming-together-service in the country that takes place on the Sundays following Easter and Thanksgiving.

They clambered into box pews with friends and family, side-by-side and vis-à-vis, penned like sheep in a fold. The pew's four-foot walls made of unfinished pegged cypress boards had bench seats all 'round so that worshippers, huddled under blankets in the winter, faced each other and the carriage heater which sat in the center. They rented their pews from year to year, but public pews were available to parishioners who did not or could not rent their own. The pulpit stood in the center/front. The curved ceiling carried the sounds well to all sections of the sanctuary without amplification.

Before the service, a trustee of the old church drolled in honey-tongued phrases about the need for a caretaker home because the church had recently been vandalized. His talk was as smooth as the swaying of moss on the live oak trees. Hurricane Hugo had put a financial strain on everyone and his appeal, which could have been as grating as a dry screw in a hard oak plank, was as convincing as asking parents to buy shoes for their kids.

The service was taken from the 1662 Book of Common Prayer of the Church of England, a service that would have been conducted in the late 1700s. All the hymns were in use before 1740 and sung without accompaniment, such as Isaac Watts', *O God, Our Help In Ages Past*. A common chalice (circa 1750) was passed from person to person at the rail. The shuffling feet across the creaking wood floor created an historic mix of treading clatter and priestly incantations while the priest administered the sacrament.

After the service everyone spread their food across a 50-foot table in the side yard next to the cemetery. It was the largest bounty of southern dishes we had seen. Eva pointed to things she recognized as particularly coastal and southern: black-eyed peas, red rice, shrimp and grits, shrimp in tossed salads, shrimp with

everything including a beef roast stuffed with shrimp and crab. The desserts were equally creative and lavish, saturated with taste and as pretty as hydrangeas. "Praise God from whom all blessings flow." It was a day to remember.

There's a distinction between "Been'eres" and "Come'eres". Anyone not born and raised there were "Come'eres". It was obvious to everyone that we were not "Been'eres". "California?" they gushed. "Well, you're a long way from home."

We were within the fold, worshipping and eating with them, but we were really outside. The south has an invisible wall that demarcates the heart of Dixie from the Yankee otherworld, and California was probably perceived as the distant rim of the otherworld.

In the side cemetery were the remains of Daniel Huger, born 1651 in Turenne, France, who avoided the persecution of French Huguenots and fled to South Carolina. King Louis the 14th revoked the Edict of Manse that spelled death for heretic Protestants. Turenne and thousands of others fled France for the new world. Turenne's plantation was called Wambaw, and this cemetery plot and the place of St. James Santee Episcopal Church were part of that original plantation. The church began as a parish of the Church of England and changed to Episcopal following the War of 1812. Turenne married Margaret Perdria with whom he had 12 children; only two survived him. He died in 1711.

The countryside has many historic plantations and stately homes, some used as hunting clubs, some as private reserves and hideaway retreats for the wealthy and famous. Along a country road we saw the Georgetown canal, a seven mile straight-through-the-woods trench, hand-dug by slaves in the early 1800s which was used to transport rice raised on the antebellum plantations to markets at Georgetown.

From McClellanville, it was a short run to Georgetown, South Carolina. We pulled into the channel that runs by the town, dropped anchor in the middle of the harbor and dinghied to shore. The city dates back to 1721 when it was declared a royal province by Prince George of England who later became King George the 2nd. It's a living museum town of wide avenues, sleepy streets with historic homes and Norman Rockwell idealism. We walked the town, took a jeep tour of the city, and visited old churches and ancient homes dating back to 1737. Back at the waterfront we toured the rice museum in the Town Clock/Old Market building (circa 1835). The wealthiest rice plantations in America prior to the civil war flourished along the rivers near Georgetown. Only Calcutta, India, shipped more rice around the world than Georgetown. This wealth built a rich southern gentry who resided in the Carolina low country and gave the south its aristocratic separateness.

The scenery changed dramatically north of Georgetown. Along the Waccamaw River the sameness of marshland evolved to maritime woodlands of cypress and hardwoods. At first there were small islands of trees, then dense forests in swamps with pines and oaks filling the upland slopes. Hurricane Hugo ripped through these forests and stumped many of the old giants. We thought that the monotony of endless sea prairies and pestiferous gnats might be behind us. The tannin of the cypress trees turned the water a dark coffee color and their tapered trunks and willowy limbs cast artistic reflections along the waterway. *DOG*, and all the other boats, wore a brown mustache from plowing through the dark waters.

The marshland grasses are the nursery of shrimp and South Carolina protects these waving fields of grain. The Ecuadorians and Chinese are raising shrimp in controlled aquaculture habitats and are giving the Carolina watermen a challenge.

After a day of travel on the ICW we stopped at Barefoot Landing, a free dock for boaters along the waterway provided by the merchants of outlet stores at North Myrtle Beach. Several boats were tied beneath the restaurants lining the waterway. We were the side dish for the guests at the Alabama Grill Dockside Restaurant who watched us come in. I nosed *DOG* into the dock and Eva jumped out to secure the bow. I set the stern and she tied that, then I jumped off and we strung our spring lines. Hot stuff. It was probably the first time we docked without the need for an apology from me, a review of what went wrong and pledges to do it better next time. And it was in front of an audience. We were very proud. I swaggered like an old salt who had done this a million times. The little boy in me, however, was jumpin' and grinnin' and doing high-five's and nearly ruining the act.

Intermittent showers and wind gusts got everyone off the ICW by evening. The dock was full. It was surprising how comforting it was to be able to walk through shops and lick an ice cream cone and have dinner at a local restaurant with immovable earth beneath us. When we have a series of anchorages where we never set foot on land, it's comforting to be tied to the earth again. Prenatal life in the amniotic universe is something from our past. We needed the dependability of solid land to stabilize our watery legs.

When we went ashore I discovered that I'd adapted to the constant uncertainty of boat balance, and I would tip unconsciously standing still. It's a little unnerving to sway and stumble while singing in church, or crash into a urinal at a restaurant while standing.

The gypsy in us had us moving like migrants, bored when our stay on land went beyond three days, but crabby and fatigued when we were on the hook too long. Worrying about the boat, tending to maintenance tasks, sleeping uncertainly in anchorages that are subject to weather, wind and currents eventually degraded us to gray automatons that needed a land furlough. We don't understand sailors who are happy at sea for weeks without sight of land.

Our anxiety in traveling by boat was steadily declining. It was always high when we were leaving or approaching a dock and low when we were underway through long stretches with few obstacles; but when crossing obscure bodies of water out of sight of land, we were anxious again. Our increasing comfort level was both welcome relief and concern. There are inherent perils in boating and unless we paid attention we could get into trouble.

We left Myrtle Beach with most of the boats in the morning, many making their way north after a winter in Florida. Northward, the uplifted geology reveals small cliffs of shale and clays over an igneous bedrock.

The ICW is very scenic as it enters North Carolina. There are still intermittent marshes, but it's mostly woodland. At Cape Fear we entered the Cape Fear River and headed up stream, then along the intricate canals of the ICW. We stayed the night at Carolina Beach State Park Marina and had time before dark to walk trails through woods and swamps. Boggy conditions are right for sundew and Venus flytrap, two insectivorous plants that trap their victims and digest them. Eva was looking for a man-eating plant like in the play, *Little Shop of Horrors*, but alas, they were the size of a fingernail and required getting down on our hands and knees to see. Nevertheless, they worked and we saw them in action.

The ICW approaches the ocean at some points with a thin strand of land between us so that we could see the ocean breakers...past Wrightsville Beach inlet, and northward through the LeJeunne Marine Base to Swansboro where we spent a few nights at Caspers Marina. The wind blew and formed tiny breakers on the shallows of the marshes. Swansboro is another southern town with an English beginning. Robert Swan was a major for King George during the time when America was a British colony.

We were ready to leave Swansboro for Beaufort, North Carolina, when we heard NOAA, the National Oceanic and Atmospheric Administration (pronounced Noah) give their typically wordy and sometimes confusing weather report...." Southwest winds will continue for southeast North Carolina and northeast South Carolina with speeds to 35 knots, changing tonight to southwest in the north central part of North Carolina and the northeast sections of South Carolina, and then east-northeast in the northeast section of South Carolina, then shifting to the north-northwest in southern North Carolina and northern South Carolina by late tonight and Sunday. Variable winds from the north, northwest, southwest or east in central and northern South Carolina, may spread to the southeast sections of North Carolina and eastern North Carolina."

This made us reconsider our plans to move on, and we continued to stay tied up in the southeast corner of North Carolina. It was all kind of up in the air.

When the wind stopped, we headed for Morehead City and Beaufort, North Carolina near Cape Lookout. We spent a day in Beaufort, (pronounced Bo-fert, in contrast to South Carolina's Beaufort, pronounced B'you-fort). This Beaufort was named for Henry Somerset, Duke of Beaufort, England. It was surveyed in 1713 while Queen Anne was on the throne. When she finished, the town became incorporated (in 1722), which sets a new record for anyone sitting on the throne during a town's incorporation. There are a number of things associated with Queen Anne, including a style of house, which I'm sure you know, and a bathroom fixture (the throne) which you probably didn't know.

The town has a wonderful water-front dock and board walk, and nearby is the maritime museum and historic homes dating to the early 1700's. We biked, walked, picked up our mail at the post office, and sat in the park on a beautiful sunny day, then went back to Town Creek Marina to use their courtesy car to grocery shop at a large supermart a few miles away. The yellow zephyr, a belching, hissing 1974 Chevrolet wagon, was a bit hesitant about the prospect of moving, but after we let it warm up, it slumped into gear and we were off in a great cloud, wallowing around like a boat in a following sea, heeling over and sliding around curves as if in water. We knew exactly how to handle it. Having a courtesy clunker was a nice service to boaters who often find that the waterfront is where taffy and tee shirt shops are, but real stores with useful goods are miles away.

Getting to know these Beauforts, the one in South Carolina and this one in North Carolina, were like brief love affairs. A few hugs and kisses and we were saying good-bye again. We longed for a more intimate encounter, but we threw the lines off and promised, like watermen have always done, that we'd be back again.

We hit bottom again. We were at Oriental for a night's rest after a day's run and pulled into their itsy-bitsy harbor packed with shrimp boats. The search for the town dock took us to the end of dead-end channel where we found their dinghy-sized dock. We had to spin on a dime and get out of there. Every night we entered a strange harbor with tight twists, that sometimes led to heavenly docking experiences and sometimes to oblivion.

We decided to hang on the hook in their designated anchorage, an area designed to produce laughs for the locals and needed work for the boat yards. The Waterway Guide said there was 6-8 feet of water, but while we were circling around and feeling our way in with the depth sounder, the sounder began to scream showing 5 feet, then 4 feet, then 389 feet, which it does when we have NO water. *DOG* slid to a stop. Dead in Oriental. With the revving of the props we got off and floated freely again, and found a place where there was a meager 5 feet (our draft is 4 feet). Eva's tidal calculations indicated we'd be okay, but we're never sure. As low tide arrived, we wondered if we'd be hung up and laying over; but we made it fine and the next day headed into the biggest body of water on this trip so far —

Pamlico Sound.

Before this odyssey, a *sound* was nothing more than a wide body of water, now it's a word that brings fear and anxiety. A sound is where a river empties into the sea. It is usually wide and shallow because of the sediments carried by the river. Both current and wind play a part in a sound's wave formation. If current is opposite the direction of the wind, there are usually formidable waves and tricky currents. The object is to cross them at slack water, with no wind. This requires a coordination of tides, winds, weather and divine intervention. Eva had been able to dodge all kinds of nastiness through her thorough preparation and serious fretting. When we got in trouble, it wasn't because anything got by her.

That night, Eva and I got up to speed on the Garmin GPS (global positioning system) and Raytheon Radar and were ready to put in waypoints through the sound so that even if we were out of sight of land for times, we would be "on instruments", using the screens of the GPS and radar to follow plots and graphs, going from point to point until we were back in the confines of the ICW channel.

With the GPS electronic signals are sent by satellites in space. The signals are then computed by our receiver and our place in the universe displayed in latitude (N-S) and longitude (E-W), along with our course and speed over ground. Taking readings from the GPS we could determine exactly where we were on the charts. The radar, which was interfaced with the GPS, displayed all this information and showed our waypoint, the configuration of the land, and any ships or buoys on the water. It was like an arcade game.

The sounds are shallow and often shoaled near the mouth of the river. In most cases you have to go to sea some distance to find deep water, then come back in again on the opposite side.

These vast sounds look like small seas but have depths of only 15-18 feet. The consequence is that winds over an extended period of time create waves as the upper water rolls over the deeper layer. This happens in a very short time and winds over 15 mph can be a problem.

Another hazard in the sounds and bays are the ubiquitous crab pot markers. The buoys bear the signature of the watermen who own them. Some of them are color coded, some numbered or initialed for its owner. Many are white or orange and crudely constructed, but some are designer crab pot markers with exotic colors like purple and silver and topped with a knobbed staff for plucking them from the water. They often edge the navigable channels because the bays and sounds are so shallow (deepest in

Pamlico Sound is 17 feet). If you run over one of these buoys, the line to the crab pot sitting on the bottom can become wrapped around the props. Then it's time to dive overboard and cut them off or call out a towing service and do a haul-out. Meanwhile, you're incapable of maneuvering the boat, which means you may run aground, so you do everything you can to avoid these things. That kept us from day dreaming or sightseeing.

The time to forget about crab pots and markers is when you tie up at the end of the day; then you can think about crab cakes, crab imperial or crab sandwiches at the local restaurants. From here through the Chesapeake, crab is king.

Coming across Pamlico Sound we passed the mouth of the Neuse River then cruised up the Pongo River to Belhaven. The Pamlico and Albemarle Sounds are vast bodies of water which aren't any bigger than an inch on a national atlas but on a slow moving trawler represent the better part of a day to cross. We stopped for fuel at Rob's in Belhaven and wished we could have filled some auxiliary tanks. The price was 94 cents a gallon. It would have been 91 cents if we paid cash. 'Turns out, this was the cheapest price for diesel fuel anywhere on the Great Loop.

This is scenic country with sculpted shorelines and a variety of marsh grasses the color of hay and autumn leaves. There are no cities and towns and we felt as if we were crossing one of America's last unspoiled frontiers.

At the upper end of the Pongo River the man-made Pongo River-Alligator River Canal shoots through the East Dismal Swamp to the Alligator River. The day was wearing on and we thought about dropping the hook and making the next day's run up Alligator River and across Albemarle Sound. Weather reports indicated that doing the Sound in the morning would be a safer bet, so we pushed up Alligator River until we passed the East Lake Swing Bridge and tied up at the Alligator River Marina.

The next morning we headed out into Albemarle Sound and had a pleasant time crossing it. Lucky for us. Boaters crossing later in the day had high winds and 10 foot seas.

Mid morning we passed two dirigible hangars on our port side, purportedly the largest wood buildings in the world and the manufacturing site for two blimp building firms. Several blimps were in the air doing maneuvers in what appeared to be test flights. At the far end of Albemarle Sound and up the Pasquotank River is Elizabeth City, a charming English town with historic homes and exemplary courtesies to boaters.

Elizabeth City is at the entrance to the Dismal Swamp Canal and to induce boaters to stop (and stimulate their economy) they offer free dockage at their Mariner's Wharf.

As we approached the docks we sized them up and had trouble imagining how to come in along the spring poles heading toward the bulkhead. Our beam was 14 feet and the poles were 14' 1". We approached in strong winds, chickened out, turned around, approached again and caught the attention of a boater on shore who watched us flutter and squawk. He shouted instructions and placed himself at the head of the widest slip, encouraging us and guiding us. Funny, how a helpful hand on land can ease the apprehension of landing safely. We eased in, chafing the rub rail on the boat and glancing off the spring poles, using them like bumper poles, which is what they are. When we shut the engines off and Eva disconnected the GPS, the visual record of our confusion was recorded, a series of zigzagging lines that finally ended at our landing point.

Years ago two old guys with a yen for doing good in the world decided to greet boaters each day and present them with a rose from their gardens. Stop and smell the roses was their idea. Since then they have been called the Rose Buddies.

Their hospitality has been legendary with boaters up and down the ICW. One of the initiators died a few years ago, but Fred Fearing, now in his 80s, continues the tradition, driving up in his golf cart around 4:30 in

The Rose Buddies greet cruisers at the docks of Elizabeth City, N.C.

the afternoon with good tidings, news of the town, a newspaper and an invitation to a wine party (when there are four or more boats). On the days we were there Fred invited us to his home a few blocks away, and on the front lawn spread tables with wine, cheese, nibbles and informational booklets. Local merchants stop by to keep him supplied with food, wine and beer. Fred waves to everyone who rides by his home like they were relatives (some are). The Rose Buddies party was an excellent way to meet other boaters and to swap tales and information. Fred is a member of the local United Methodist Church and we went to services with him on Sunday.

Elizabeth City residents continue this cordiality, picking up boaters on the streets and taking them to supermarts and restaurants around the city. Eva and I were picked up twice in one day by motorists. We found that arms full of groceries, a weary trudge and a desperate-for-a-ride look, works very well. We applied this technique in other places also, and it works.

"They done it. They done it. Damned if they ain't flew." This was the shout from Johnny Moore, the sixteen year-old who photographed and witnessed the first manned flight by Orville and Wilbur Wright. The place was Kitty Hawk on the barrier islands surrounding Albemarle and Pamlico Sounds. We had to see, so while in Elizabeth City we rented a car and drove the fifty miles through farmland to the outer banks and Kitty Hawk and the Wright Brothers Memorial and Museum. The National Park Service Rangers perform an animated

The Cape Hatteras Lighthouse warns boaters away from the Outer Banks of North Carolina.

history lesson in front of a mock-up of the original Wright Brothers plane. The Wright Brothers were bike builders and it's amusing to see how many sprockets, chains and hubs from bicycles were used to build the first powered flight of about one minute and 852 feet. Actually it was Orville Wright's flight in the morning of 12 seconds that made history. A machine under its own power carried a man into the air and landed at a point as high as that from which it began without any reduction in speed. It was the dawn of the age of aviation.

Eva had a wish to see the Cape Hatteras Lighthouse, so we did another fifty miles on the outer banks, through Nags Head and Cape Hatteras National Seashore. It was depressing to see such rampant development and honky-tonk commercialism along the Outer Banks. Summer homes are perched perilously a few feet above sea level, fully exposed and vulnerable to the next hurricane with spring tides. The national seashore preserve, in contrast, is pretty, windswept and beautifully adapted for high salt winds and occasional flooding. It's mid-way along the Atlantic flyway and a feeding and resting area for many species of birds.

At Nags Head Woods Ecological Preserve we visited the Nature Conservancy's remnant maritime forest. Red maple, sweetgum and pine compose a dense forest that flourishes in the sweet water of the back dunes just beyond the searing salt winds of the fore dunes and beaches. There's a comforting aspect to the covered canopy of a mature forest, like being under the blankets during a storm.

During our last night in Elizabeth City our sleep was disturbed by flashing light. Eva and I jumped up and looked out the aft stateroom ports. A tug pushing four empty flatbed barges with wooden stake sides was churning up the Pasquotank River. By the time we were ready to leave in the morning, that same tow had four loaded barges with logs, bound for the mills. We heard his conversation with the Coast Guard and there was some discussion about a train bridge that he had nicked.

We had a choice to continue north along the ICW from Elizabeth City on the Pasquotank and into the Dismal Swamp on the Dismal Swamp Canal, or follow an alternative route around Camden Point and into Currituck Sound, following the Chesapeake and Albemarle Canal to Norfolk, Virginia. The Dismal Swamp Canal had the reputation for being shallow and full of stumps, but outstandingly scenic. It was worth a gamble we figured, so we set out along the Pasquotank River into the Dismal Swamp.

This is the most mysteriously beautiful section of the waterway from Miami, Florida to Norfolk, Virginia. The river is dark from the tannins produced from the cypress trees and the images of cypress and the reflections of dogwood, sweetgum, red maple and pine are stunning. The river winds tightly so there is a continuous view into the heavy forest, and the boat's wake and prop-wash leaves a winding trail of bubbles that makes your past as interesting as your future.

The Pasquotank narrows and the manmade canal begins beyond a lock that raises the level to eight feet. It was our first locking experience on The Loop and we were a little nervous. We had to wait next to a "dolphin", a ring of huge pilings that were too big to get a line around. We did the best we could to secure ourselves while the lock was emptied, then proceeded inside when instructed to do so. The locksman was helpful and eased our anxiety, and we locked through without mishap. One down, 144 to go.

We came to the railroad bridge that was the subject of the tow's conversation with the U.S. Coast Guard. It appeared that the swing bridge was closed so we let loose on the horn to alert the watchmen that we wanted it raised. No response. More horn blowing, then calls on the VHF. We idled in the Pasquotank thinking we were going to be unable to continue. On a whim, I moved *DOG* to the right side of the channel and discovered that the bridge was drawn and open to traffic. It was very obscure and very tight for a boat our size. Then we remembered that the tow with his four barges had maneuvered this section. It was not surprising that the tow with his ungainly train had trouble negotiating this passage which even forty-foot trawlers traverse with the greatest caution.

We stayed one night at the Dismal Swamp Canal Welcome Center near the border between Virginia and North Carolina which serves as a highway and waterway tourist information station. Boaters provide a novel diversion for highway travelers who were curious how we got there. Free dockage allows boaters to linger a while and take the dinghy further into the swamp.

Here we met a couple from British Columbia on a small trailerable sailboat who began their cruise in Jacksonville, Florida. They were roughing it without most of the creature comforts we had and seemed much happier. Makes you wonder about the relationship between possessions and happiness. They left the next morning before we did, held the lock for us, and we locked through together. We got to know them better in Norfolk where they made plans to return to Jacksonville to retrieve their boat trailer and tow vehicle.

As we motored through the swamp, a great blue heron rose from along the shore, beat its wings in pendulous thrusts out over the water and headed straight ahead of us in the canal as if to guide us, landing along the shoreline a quarter mile ahead. Approaching, it took off again, repeated its same pattern of entry into the unobstructed mid-channel, loping along the waterway, finding a hiding place, exiting again and leading the way. We couldn't tell it we meant no harm, but there's no doubt we were an intrusion. We spotted many water snakes in the river. Small bogs and bayous made the river appear undisturbed and powerfully primitive.

There are many straight canals throughout the reserve that resemble a city plat. The man-made cuts are uninteresting and a curse upon this beautiful land. George Washington was one of the first opportunists to exploit the swamp. He saw profits in the pine and cypress trees, as did many who followed. Most of it has been logged several times and much of it drained before it became a national refuge. Only recently has it received protected status. Keeping it deep enough and snag-free for boaters is costly and debate goes on about its future accessibility.

We ought to know. As we approached the Norfolk side of the swamp we hit a deadhead, or submerged log. Immediately the boat began vibrating and the port prop began making swishing sounds. I was sure we had done some damage to one or both the propellers. We locked out of the swamp and headed for Portsmouth on the Elizabeth River, calling ahead to a marina that did boat repairs and had a lift large enough to haul our boat. The evidence was there as the boat came out of the water. A branch had wound around the port prop and was not about to get off without assistance. We unwound it and that was all there was to it. There was no significant propeller damage and the boat went back into the water after we replaced the zinc plates (which prevent damage to other metal parts due to stray electrical currents in the water).

We stayed a night at Norfolk's Waterside Marina, a large waterfront area with a giant undercover food fair, piano bars, shops, touring schooners and party boats. Norfolk and Portsmouth have giant ship building and repair yards for ocean-going vessels and the river is alive with working tugs pushing ships and barges. Nearby, shipyards sent sparks flying as they repaired and refinished hulls of large vessels, including naval aircraft carriers, submarines and destroyers. It's a strange juxtaposition of heavy commercial traffic, repair outlets and the playland waterfront park of Norfolk.

We had exhausted the ICW. From here we would explore Chesapeake Bay and its miles of shoreline and historic villages. There was no prescribed way of going anymore, no magenta line that would take us from one place to another like in the ICW. My navigator was a little nervous. If it was up to me, I'd head in the general direction of the next port and dodge the crab pot floats, but my navigator was one who sweated and stewed and did it perfectly. I relaxed and awaited instructions.

Norfolk, Virginia
to
Montreal, Quebec, Canada

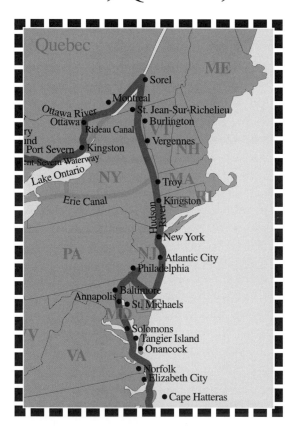

CHAPTER 8

CRUISING CHESAPEAKE BAY

Norfolk was the biggest and busiest harbor we experienced at this point in our trip. We felt like a minnow in a pond as we cruised through the chaotic traffic of tugs and cargo ships and made our way into Chesapeake Bay.

Eva had a nervous day navigating because many of the floating markers that showed on the charts did not exist, and some markers on the water were not on the charts. She was confused and anxious; so we hailed a nearby boat and checked our GPS against their Loran and concluded that we were okay. The buoys had been changed and the charts were out of date even though they were the latest edition.

Fishing Bay was on our chart though, so we pulled off the Chesapeake for our first night along this inland sea and anchored at the mouth of the Piankatank River near Deltaville, Virginia.

There is the eastern shore of the Chesapeake and the western shore, two different worlds, and the towns are some of the oldest in America. The eastern shore, detached from the western edge by this vast estuary remains rural, pastoral and quiet, everything Annapolis and Baltimore are not. Their separation from the mainland is so complete (save for the road bridges near Norfolk on the southern tip of the Chesapeake, and at Baltimore in the north), that they are given separate status — the realm of DELMARVA—a peninsula comprised of DELaware, MARyland and VirginiA. The name Delmarva is used everywhere. Their kinship is bound by geography along small rivers, fertile farm lands, and separation from the rest of the world.

There isn't much evidence of the native Americans that lived along the Chesapeake Bay, just the names of rivers that bear their names—the

Pocomoke, Rappahannock, Wicomico, Potomac and others.

I don't know what you've heard about the Chesapeake, and if you've read Michener's *Chesapeake*, you have his notion of the area. Our impression of the bay is that it was big, mysterious, windy, cold, full of crab pots, ugly, threatening, charming and a playground for boaters in the summertime.

When the last glacier receded, it flooded the Susquehanna River basin forming the largest estuary in the U. S.. The river is still down there, eroding into the bedrock where you can find depths to 95 feet. During high tide, the Susquehanna fills with returning sea water, while the upper levels remain brackish, a mix of salt and fresh water.

The Chesapeake is tremendously productive and yields 23 million pounds of crab each year. Oysters were prolific at the turn of the century, but heavy harvesting of oysters and continuous trapping of crab all through the Chesapeake, along with the pollution and runoff from cities' businesses and farms, has many experts concerned. There is much talk about limiting crabbing, outlawing crab pots (also because they are a serious threat to navigation) and curtailing farm erosion.

Stink potters (power boaters) like ourselves calculate every move based on wind and weather, and the message as often as not was "stay put." If we were in some charming place eating crab cakes and biking village streets, and we heard that bad weather was coming the next day or two, we'd leave immediately, cruising on the "good" days and saving the "bad" days for ports. We wore more rubber and wool than was decent, smelling like an old sheep dog who had come in out of the rain. Thank goodness our boat had a heat pump or we'd have been miserable.

The middle of the bay was our least favorite place. The bay is a small ocean, but the shoreline communities of the Chesapeake are fascinating. The ride up rivers to 17th century fishing towns was genuine discovery.

We had been looking forward to cruising the Chesapeake. We had an older version of *Guide to Cruising the Chesapeake Bay* and Eva spent many hours poring over the pages, trying to choose the best places to visit. Many people along the way had recommended their favorite not-to-be-missed spots so we compiled an almost unmanageable itinerary. Our path up the Chesapeake was from the west side to the east side, and back again, several times.

One of the must-sees was the town of Onancock on the eastern shore. As was our custom each night Eva studied the charts in detail, covering the area that we were going to cruise the next day. At anchor in Fishing Bay she realized that our Chart Kit book did not include the Onancock River past the entrance. We wanted to go all the way to the town of Onancock, which meant we needed a separate chart that we didn't have. The next morning we tried to contact the nearby marina, but they were closed. A friendly sailor working on his boat that Saturday morning responded. When we told him of our problem he said he had the right chart and we were welcome to come and look at it. We offered to buy it from him but he refused and gave it to us instead. Another example of the great fraternity of boaters. We had the opportunity to pass along a favor immediately when a sailor on another boat at anchor near us was having outboard motor trouble and needed a tow to his boat.

Following our night in Fishing Bay along the Piankatank River, we set the GPS for the mouth of the Onancock River on the eastern shore. Numerous green and red markers lined the river ("red-right-returning") so we kept red to our right as if returning from sea.

The surrounding woods of mixed conifers and deciduous trees were dark and dense, and picturesque homes peeked from the woods through small paned windows. Ospreys occupied the daymarkers and were busy feeding their young who stuck their heads up as we approached. Marsh grass softened the points and places of shoal water as the river wound and got tighter and more intimate with the land. The shoreline was flat, and the sky, big. Clouds and water and the woods beyond were moody and beautiful. This was the Chesapeake of poets and artists.

We passed age-old plantations and two-story frame homes with brick chimneys on outside walls and in every roof quarter there was a fireplace. Eventually we reached the town docks which were in a small rectangular pond bounded by walls. It was so small, so tight and so obscure we felt trapped. Heading into a bight of the channel we searched for an anchorage and touched bottom. A little throttle and we were free again. We found our place and settled in.

The watermen were coming in, their long white work boats slicing the water like a wedge. Men moved on the dock and took lines and threw crates and washed down boats, and it became quiet. We were in the land of Delmarva.

We launched the dinghy, and examined this 1680 English crown port where Main Street runs down to the dock. From the dink we viewed the town upwards like a medical scope examines parts of the body—homes along brick walks, overhanging trees, a woman walking her dog, the town shops, the closed Chevrolet garage, the steeples of the Episcopal and Methodist Churches. On shore we walked crooked brick sidewalks and searched for a grocery store, which we discovered was a mile away on the outskirts of town. We walked out and hitched a ride back with Emily Boice, the wife of the Methodist Church District Superintendent.

That night *Genie* turned with the current and we slept in the womb of the Onancock River, swinging back and forth, without sensation, a constant cradled movement, her nose unerringly turned into the wind like a pointer.

Sunday morning was dark and cold. Rain fell and the temperature refused to move over 50 degrees. Eva prepared a breakfast of fried grits with butter and syrup, bananas and grapes and hot coffee. She'd gone native, inspired by the southern cooking we had along the way in the Carolinas.

We dressed for church but the moment we launched the dinghy, rain fell hard and we retreated back inside. Indecisive, we stood looking out. Eva looked at me with eyes that said, "You need to be redeemed. We ought to go." I looked at her and said to myself, "Church could help you." With a mutual impulse, that some would call the prompting of the Holy Spirit, we took off our Sunday-go-to-meetin' clothes and dressed (again) in rubber and wool. The dinghy was a floating puddle so we bailed and dried the seat, pulled the Wizard into action and headed for the docks. By the time we reached the church, a half-mile away, we looked like the boat people we were. We squished into the entry leaving puddles where we stopped. Shaking ourselves like wet dogs, we searched for a place to drop our rain gear and umbrellas, then went inside.

After church the Boices invited us out to lunch and showed us around their pretty town, explaining some of the unusual architectural features of the Eastern Shore Virginia homes (big house, little house, colonnade and kitchen). Back at the dock we again met Harry and Margaret, the couple from Canada aboard *Phoebe*, and decided to travel together for a few days.

The weather cleared by afternoon and we fired up *Genie* for the short ride to Tangier Island situated in the middle of the Chesapeake. On the way we passed Watts Island, now uninhabited, which was occupied at the time of the Revolution (1780's) by a colony of British Loyalists who were driven off by Tangiermen. So much for freedom of expression and affiliation.

The channel markers brought us through shoals to an island that appeared to be without land. There were piers and docks and sheds but they were all on pilings and unattached to land. The channel ran between them, a boulevard of boat houses and packing sheds. Still no evidence of land, yet there were so many piers and docks it resembled a corral on a ranch. We saw the church steeple at the end of the channel through the maze of gates, pilings and docks.

We finally reached the shoreline and a dock. *Phoebe* was already tied up and our friends waved us in, taking our lines and introducing us to the dock master and his daughter-in-law who took our fee and acquainted us with the marina's slim provisions.

There was a desperate quality to Tangier Island. It appeared to be a bog, with hardly a tree. Its elevation is only a few feet above sea level. A dirt trail led from the marina to a paved roadway 15 feet wide. Small frame homes with postage stamp lawns sat behind cyclone fences. Everything was miniature. There are no automobiles or trucks on the island so everyone uses either a bicycle or motor scooter.

At the Methodist Church we observed a hundred bikes parked along the road and leaning against the fences. The lights of the church were on and we heard the sound of music. Eva walked to the church door and eased it open. Music poured out like water. She beckoned to me like someone sharing a secret. We stepped inside and entered the religious life of seafaring people. A preacher that looked like Garrison Keeler was at the organ and, with the piano player, was leading the congregation through hymns we hadn't heard for years. A section of the congregation came together as a choir and sang many verses of a familiar hymn where everyone joined on the chorus. We sang it again and again until the words and feelings permeated us, and the message was inscribed in tablets of the soul.

The organist became the preacher, introducing the Ambassador Quartet, four watermen with tanned skin and callused hands. They sang and the preacher invited the congregation to kneel at the altar and surrender to the Lord. Believers flowed to the altar and the kneeling rail filled until there wasn't room for one more, but they kept coming. It was like the indomitable march of lemmings to the sea. They came with heads stooped as the preacher implored the Holy Spirit to fill the place. There were confessions, needs expressed, admissions of dysfunctional families, and hardships brought about because boats and equipment were lost in storms. There was crying and praying and singing and touching, and special prayers given for people with real hurts.

The service ended with more singing. The Tangierites went out into the night and pedaled home on all those bicycles parked outside. Eva approached a woman and asked her how she handled her flying skirts and high heels astride a bicycle. In language that carried the dialect of her Cockney ancestry, she smiled and showed Eva it was not difficult at all. Then she rode away with the others, a flock of bicycles and flowered skirts and men in starched shirts and creased pants, until they turned off to small homes behind cyclone fences and the streets became empty again. We found ourselves standing alone in the dark, spellbound by ordinary people living simply and meaningfully.

We looked at ourselves—rubber boots, sweaters, jackets and caps. We looked like watermen. They went to the Lord's house in the best they could afford, and we went in work clothes. We felt irreverent, but we wouldn't have missed this chance to worship with them.

The next morning we rode our bikes through town and had lunch at the Islander Restaurant where we ordered the soft shelled crab sandwich. We were anticipating a wonderful crab sandwich on homemade dark bread with avocado and onion and butter lettuce with chunks of white crab meat in a "to die for" sauce. Instead we got two slices of Wonder Bread with five little crabs, their tiny legs peeking beyond the crust like fringe. There was no tomato or lettuce or pickle, not even a rosette radish or sprig of parsley to adorn the plate. I lifted the bread. That was a mistake. Five WHOLE crabs the size of silver dollars, their legs and feet entwined, looked up at me and sang in chorus, "You're not going to eat us, are you?" Four of them occupied the corners of the bread and the fifth one sprawled in the center.

We wanted to return the plate saying, "I'm sorry, but these look like real crabs. Don't you have the kind with the white flaky meat and drawn butter?" But being the adventurers we presumed ourselves to be, we dove in. It was like having an insect sandwich. Good though. Those five little guys had recently molted so their exoskeleton was soft and entirely edible. 'Said so right there on the menu. We also ordered their crab chowder which we renamed "Turn of the Tide," a watery, gray slop that went down as easy as drinking a barium solution.

We've tried it all—crab cakes, she-crab soup, lump crab cakes and crab salads. In most cases the whole crab is used except for the gills and eyes, which they cut off. Good thing. Can you imagine flossing crab eyes from your teeth in the company of your spouse or friends?

What makes crabs taste so good is what they eat. The watermen at Tangiers, for example, trap the crabs with bull lips, eels and chicken necks, all of which go to the bottom of the bay in traps where they rot. The blue crabs find this delicious, which is why crab gourmets should ask themselves, "Why am I eating this?" If crabs are so non-selective, it makes you wonder why the watermen don't use other unmentionable animal body parts as well.

Having had our "fill" of Tangiers, we ventured into nearby Crisfield with Harry and Margaret who dinghied ashore with us, four crab-filled cruisers seated in the dink like kids in a bathtub. The waves lapped at the gunwales and we all sucked-up to reduce the waterline. Margaret rewarded us with two fresh sticky buns from the town bakery and Eva and I decided we had found a new way to make a buck.

We moved across to the west side of the bay, up the Patuxent River to Solomons, where we took care of essential needs (getting haircuts, doing laundry, filling the propane tank), then back across to the east side of the bay again to Oxford and St. Michaels, old English towns of immense charm, tipping brick walkways and vintage homes beneath towering horse chestnut trees. Trees have the right to grow as they wish, so a roadway or sidewalk is not altered to make it safe. Trees grow, sidewalks bend, puddles form, grass grows in the cracks. It's like the age lines on an old face.

At Oxford, the oldest privately operated ferry service in the United States runs across the Tred-Avon River to Bellevue. Begun in 1683 and still in operation, the Talbot County Court records showed that the court "Pitchd upon Mr. Richard Royce to keepe a ferry," and it has been running ever since. Oxford is a charming town with country vernacular homes that show themselves like a classic doily—carefully made, artistically designed and cherished like an heirloom.

Oxford is one of many English Crown Colonies along Chesapeake Bay.

We left Oxford when the weather was fair, but true to our routine, the weather turned foul by the time we were ready to dock at St. Michaels.

We contacted the dockmaster who instructed us to tie to the giant pilings at the end of one of two long docks that had all manner of vessels along one side. The trick was to stay to the cleared side, barely sliding by the docked boats. But we had a strong beam wind that wanted to push us into those tied-up boats and, to maintain steerage for this extremely tight fit, I kept going long after I was parallel to the dock. Eva thought I would stop sooner than I did so she jumped off the boat with the bow line in her hand, soon realizing I had no intention of stopping...yet. She was running along the dock trying to get the bow line over a series of pilings that were at least six feet tall.

It was an athletic event worthy of Olympic status—run, jump, throw the rope over a piling, yell "stop," break a nail; run, jump, throw the rope over a piling, shout "STop," break a nail; run, jump, throw the rope over a piling, scream "STOP," break a na... Well, you get the idea.

Needless to say, she got my attention (and everybody else's within earshot). I threw DOG into reverse and brought the boat to a stop with the engines whining. The trawler's matronly stern rose and water pushed up in a wave like the landing of a great white swan. Eva breathed a sigh of relief.

If you think she cuddled close to me that night and cooed, "You're my hero, you were great today," you haven't been boating. But the ice did thaw and we stayed together, because she had all the charts and I had the keys to the boat.

Small homes near the water at St. Michaels had flower boxes and shutters on the windows and candles on the sills, which made them look cozy. There is a tradition in these coastal bay towns to light a candle in the window for seafaring men. St. Michaels has an authentic disheveled quality in the homes near the docks which validates it as a living, working town of functional people (in contrast to retirement communities that lose their working vitality).

The Chesapeake Bay Maritime Museum at St. Michaels brings many visitors to this eastern Chesapeake Bay town. It's an easy run from Annapolis or Baltimore and on weekends the place is jammed. The octagonal cottage-style screwpile lighthouse from Hooper's Island was moved there and stands at the harbor to greet all who enter. Many historic boats are restored, or are in the process, and there are excellent displays of all types of water craft used throughout history on the Chesapeake. In the evening we walked to the museum for a concert of sea chanteys by Geof Kaufman, balladeer and musicologist from Mystic, Connecticut.

The sun was up and warm when we left for Annapolis. We thought winter was over, but sure as disappointment follows hope, the clouds returned and we had a cloudy day with temperatures in the 50's. The U. S. Naval Academy chapel dome and the Maryland statehouse dome were dominant skyline features as we approached town and picked up a mooring.

Annapolis is an historic town with Middleton Tavern (circa 1769) and markets clustered around the waterfront dock. Pictures from the 1700's show the dock and town nearly as it is today. The roads of the city come down to the waterfront like spokes of a wheel—narrow cobblestone streets and row houses up to the edge of the sidewalks, their respective entrances only slightly different from their neighbors.

The naval academy is next to the waterfront and midshipmen in the whitest-whites are common sights on the streets. We walked through the campus one afternoon, a magnificent establishment of classic buildings and park-like lawns and trees.

Son Greg and wife Tracy joined us after sleeping outdoors because of a big communication screw-up whereby they waited at Dulles Airport for us to pick them up (but we didn't know we were supposed to), and when we never showed they walked to a nearby park, pulled out their sleeping bags and pretended they were homeless. The next morning I rented a car to pick them up and they rented a car to drive themselves to Annapolis, and we met at the docks with one car too many. We returned one car then went to visit Uncle George and Aunt Joan who lived nearby.

We introduced our first on-board guests to life on a floating home and briefed them on duties and expectations as crew. Navigator Eva billed the ride from Annapolis to Baltimore as easy, close to shore, and about 4 hours in duration, just right for an initiation to cruising life. What she couldn't foretell was the local squall that would hit as we approached Baltimore Harbor.

I could see that there were black clouds in our future as we viewed Baltimore from 10 miles out, so we brought down the plastic windshield and put away cameras and valuables. The winds increased in a continuous climb until the water was whipped and frothy. Waves built to 3-4 feet in fifteen minutes and continued growing.

That's when the Coast Guard came on the air with a small craft advisory, "SECURITY, SECURITY, SECURITY, CALLING ALL STATIONS. THERE IS A SMALL CRAFT ADVISORY IN EFFECT UNTIL 2 P.M. A STORM IS DEVELOPING IN THE BALTIMORE HARBOR. SMALL

CRAFT SHOULD SEEK IMMEDIATE SHELTER. THIS IS A DANGER-
OUS STORM WITH WINDS GUSTS TO 40 MPH. ALL VESSELS
SHOULD TAKE IMMEDIATE ACTION TO AVOID THIS STORM."

Too late. We were in it. *Genie* dug in and went for it, sending waves
over the bow and down the walkways. Greg and Tracy were down in the
galley making lunch. They had mayonnaise and lettuce and chopped meat
in a flotsam arrangement across the counters. I really think they took this
opportunity to play with their food like small kids, but eventually they
brought it up, except that when they stepped outside to bring the food to the
flybridge, the wind picked up the plates and all that was thereon and they
sailed. This brought out the gulls who thought lunch was being served,
which it was, but not for THEM. Well, it really WAS for them, but it was
not MEANT for them.

It was a scene worthy of a serious work of art entitled *LUNCH AT
SEA*—*Genie* pitching in the waves, me grim-faced as Popeye at the wheel,
Eva hanging on while reading the charts, GPS and radar, food flying through
the air as Tracy brought lunch to the flybridge, Greg chasing food like
outfield flyballs, a flock of gulls following the boat, and the Coast Guard
calling over the radio: "SECURITY, SECURITY, CALLING ALL STA-
TIONS...."

Add to that the presence of a GIANT Japanese freighter that made us
look like a bathtub toy boat, and you've got the rest of the picture. This ship
came up behind us like a stealth giant, moving at about 30 knots (in comparison to our 8 knots) and was about to pass us. Of course I insisted he
said "May I", not only because we won the war but also because we **were**
the "stand-on vessel". But being the gentlemen I am with a Japanese freighter
the size of Delaware coming up behind me in a storm, I decided to let him
go by. We thought if we "drafted" him, we might get out of the wind.

We pulled into Baltimore Harbor city docks, which were nearly empty.
Nobody, we figured, would be out in weather like this, which gave us the
run of the docks and prime seats on our back deck over this splendid city of
glass and waterfront restaurants, walkways, museums and water shows.

I don't know what you've heard about Baltimore, but from the water's
edge, it's a marvelous place. They have taken 18 and 19th century docks
and converted them to a water-side park. Behind the inner harbor attractions is the commercial high-rise section connected by elevated walkways
along waterfalls and hanging gardens. Baltimore also has MacArthur Memorial Park and first rate art galleries.

The people of the city recreate on the waterfront. There were school groups everywhere, touring the museums, and noontime concerts and paddleboat rentals. Water taxis ran to points of interest on the waterfront, and city office workers had lunch on the bulkhead and in the market place. Eventually the walk along the waterfront will extend to Fells Point, several miles away. For boaters, it's front row and center stage. Our boats provided some of the back drop and pageantry at the docks and we imagined they were all saying, "Gee, I wish I had their money. Wouldn't it be cool to cruise around the bays and rivers in one of those?" We let them believe it and raised our noses and plastic champagne glasses very high.

Searching for a grocery store, I walked narrow brick streets with brownstone row houses and small neighborhood shops. Baltimore has revitalized its historic markets which are block-long warehouses that have specialty shops selling produce, poultry, fresh fish, groceries, sundries and a plethora of ethnic specialties to satisfy the needs of their diverse citizenry. We walked uptown to the biggest of their city markets (Lexington) and at Faidley's Fish Market and Grill, had a stand-up lunch of the best lump crab cakes we had eaten. Their personable staff sell fish, explain how to prepare it, fillet it if you wish, and even send it on to their grill where they prepare it. It's a noisy, smelly place, but the essence of Baltimore neighborhood culture and cuisine.

We took the water taxi to Fells Point, a maritime neighbor to Baltimore a few miles away on the harbor. Established in 1726, it became the port where over 600 ships were built during the colonial period. The famed Baltimore Clippers were built there as was the U.S. frigate Constitution, on display at Baltimore. Today Fells Point is counter-culture, with antique shops, taverns and unusual restaurants. Baltimore is the mall, Fells Point the Bohemian outlet. They have a cobblestone street named Thames, and a city market right in the middle of Broadway.

From Baltimore we crossed over to the east side of the bay and without benefit of full charts cruised up the Chester River to Chestertown, a still-life town of colonial homes and cobble stone streets. Large, solid two-story homes with brick walls around their gardens face the water, and modest frame homes follow the slight grade to the center of town and the Imperial Hotel. Bill Plummer, retired Episcopal priest, stopped to chat with us, giving us the history of the town and the old churches.

Emmanuel Episcopal Church in Chestertown was the location of the first convention that proposed and adopted the name Episcopal on November 9, 1780. The Church of England was no longer appropriate for revolutionaries who were cutting the shackles of the oppressor, but at the service on the Sunday we were there, we felt the strong ties of denomination and ancestry that makes the Episcopal Church a remnant of England's colonial period.

After church we fired up *Genie* and rode the Chester River back into the Chesapeake Bay and anchored in Fairlee Creek for an overnight stay. Getting into Fairlee Creek was a trick. We knew that there were serious shoals all around the deeper channel and the entrance required a sharp turn into the narrow opening. We hung out and got advice from a local who was coming out before venturing in, and succeeded like we knew what we were doing.

When we arrived it was balmy and calm—the eye of the storm feeling. NOAA's forecast was for changing winds from the SW to the NW and an approaching cold front that would trigger rain, hail and high winds. It was our night to cook so while we rustled up some grub, Greg and Tracy decided to take the dink for a ride. They attached Ye Olde Wizard (no neutral, no reverse, when you start it you're gone), and putted away until they were like small children again.

The first clap of thunder brought them back home. Lightning played across the bay and the air was filled with electricity. Tracy's hair stood on end and we all took pictures. She was just right for Halloween, but it was only May.

We ate supper on the back deck while it was still warm and the sky turned the color of thunder fringed with the lavenders of impending rain. We retreated to the inner sanctum for a night of card playing. The rain came, the wind turned and *Genie* spun on her chain rode and repositioned herself while we slept.

Pilot boats escort pilots who navigate freighters through the narrow C&D canal.

CHAPTER 9

GENIE BIT THE BIG APPLE

From Chesapeake Bay we headed for the Chesapeake and Delaware Canal, an 18th century man-made connection that allows ocean liners to go from Baltimore on the Chesapeake, to Philadelphia on the Delaware River. At Chesapeake City, which is located half-way along the C&D Canal, pilot boats meet the ocean liners traversing this narrow waterway. Insurance companies insist that the big boats have a state licensed captain aboard to negotiate from one state to the next. Local pilots take control of the ships and bring them through the canal which is not much bigger than the beam of one of those monsters.

The little pilot boats attach themselves to the hulls of the liners like Ramoras (shark suckers). They have no means of securing themselves so they snuggle up, their big rubber bumpers cushioning their contact. While the pilot boat holds itself in place, the Delaware pilot climbs a ladder to the entrance into the ship, walks to the bridge, relieves the Maryland pilot coming off, who descends the ladder to the waiting pilot boat. There is disengagement and the transfer is complete. Diners can witness the whole transaction from the windows of Schaefer's Canal House Restaurant and the maitre d' gives specifics on each cargo ship—their destination, tonnage, what they are carrying and their port of registry.

On both sides of the river is the town of Chesapeake City, a stop over for steamers and commercial boats when this was the site of a lock. Between 1921-1927 the U.S. Army Corps of Engineers converted the canal to a straight-through channel without locks. This was a near death blow to the town that depended on stopping vessels, and the town withered. The museum contains the remains of the lift wheel pumping plant used in the locks from 1837-1927.

Today Chesapeake City is just a village with a story to tell and a place to see big ships move through a narrow passageway. Along the waterfront little doll houses with shutters and high peeked roofs look like teenage girls in their first set of high heels.

From the canal we headed up the Delaware River, now a heavy industry river where George Washington crossed with his troops during the revolutionary war. You remember the scene, George looking gallant standing up in a tiny boat while painters on the far shore shouted, "Hold it right there, George. This is going to look great in history books."

We cruised under the flyway of Philadelphia International Airport, then came into the docks of Penn's Landing where we had a reservation. Except that the city decided to delay the season opening for a week and not tell us. They informed their security guard to prevent anyone from docking, and no amount of yelling and gesturing persuaded him to let us in. We were rocking in the choppy waters of the Delaware River with strong winds, light rain and considerable current, trying to find another place to dock on a river front full of old piers and tucked-away marinas. Nobody answered the radio so finally in desperation we entered a marina between ancient warehouses renovated to waterfront condominiums, and tied up.

We walked to town to sample Philly's "culinary" specialty—cheese steak sandwich—a hoagie roll filled with shaved beef, melted cheese, grilled onions and peppers. If we ever get a national health policy, this sandwich will automatically be forbidden. Sinning can be fun and these sandwiches were unforgettable. A further walk down South Street put us in close contact with chocolate, cookies, ice cream and espresso shops for a totally decadent night of eating all the wrong things.

The next day we saw Greg and Tracy off to their home in Colorado. We had several days to explore Philadelphia before Alan arrived from California.

Philadelphia is a marvelous city with many significant historic buildings, statuary, fountains, parkways and public use facilities, and of course, the Liberty Bell. Philadelphia began the free library system in the United States and in many other ways led the nation in providing museums and institutions of cultural enrichment for the populace.

We spent a day bicycling along the Schuylkill River where nearby universities have sculling clubs. A regatta was underway and teams of women and men lined up at a starting line like toothpicks on water waiting for the call, "READY, ALL ROW." Then they were off, rowing in perfect

The peacefulness and natural beauty around the Jupiter Inlet make travel along the ICW pleasant and safer than traveling in the Atlantic Ocean.

Above:
Boaters cruising the ICW have a chance to visit Cape Canaveral National Seashore near the launch site of NASA.

Left:
St. Augustine is a beautiful city with great architectural history. For many years St. Augustine was a stronghold of Spanish occupation.

Left:
Mrs. Wilkes Board-
ing House is
everyone's favorite
lunch spot. People
stand in line for
hours in the rain
waiting for the next
seating.

Below:
Navigating the
shallow waters of
the Dismal Swamp
required Eva to
stand lookout. The
swamp has been cut
a number of times
but has healed, and
it is now one of
America's great
natural areas.

The beautiful waterfront on the Elizabeth River at Norfolk, Virginia, is a perfect stop for cruisers to begin or end the Atlantic Intracoastal Waterway. The United States Navy shipyards make it one of the busiest harbors in America.

Baltimore is an old American maritime city with neighborhood shopping centers like the Lexington Market where locals and visitors spend eventful afternoons. Here we get instruction on preparing fresh fish and crabcakes.

Philadelphia is a beautiful city with numerous squares for the enjoyment of the populace. It was the home of the first Continental Congress and a contender for the designated capital city of the new republic.

Our anchorage was across the harbor from New York City with views of Manhattan and the World Trade Center. The flowing Hudson River carries heavy commercial traffic as well as gaff-rigged sailboats and cruisers making the Great Loop.

Right:
Eva and Barbara tend the lines as the Dream O'Genie locks through the Chambly Canal. The canal was dug around the rapids and shoal water of the Richelieu River in Quebec, Canada.

Below:
The all-wood cathedral of Basilica Notre Dame in Montreal, Ontario, has elaborate wood carvings and one of Canada's greatest organs.

Tall ships from Poland sailed into the Olde Port of Montreal while we were there. Here they lock through the Lachine Locks near Montreal on their way up the St. Lawrence River toward Toronto.

unison while the coxswain steered them to oblivion or glory. It was a great visual spectacle and the whole city was out on roller skates and bicycles to watch. Philly was having one of the springiest days of the season and everyone was relishing it. People all along these parts complained of a bitterly long winter, and warm weather and sunshine were just what the psychiatrist prescribed.

On the way home, and near our marina, we walked through Elfreth's Alley, a national historic street of look-alike row houses with ivy covered walls, shutters on small-paned windows and lanterns along brick walk-ways. This little community has been occupied continually since 1713 and is still home to Philadelphians.

Nearby is St.George's Methodist Church where Francis Asbury was the third minister. He and 39 other preachers used Philadelphia as home base for the next 59 years as they rode their circuits and established societies. They never intended to establish churches of physical structures, simply cells of people who would increase their devotion through methodical study of the scriptures and service.

A peculiar set of circumstances led to the establishment of a church building for the new world Anglican/Methodists. A Reformed group had acquired the land and built a church but they fell in debt and the elders of the church ended up in debtor's prison. To gain release of the elders, the congregation auctioned off the building and grounds. The retarded son of a wealthy merchant was in the crowd and innocently bought the property as the highest bidder. Rather than discredit his son, the merchant took posses-sion of the church, which he didn't want, and at considerable loss sold it to the Methodists in 1767.

In those days, the ruling leaders of the church occupied the front row center seats, all other males took seats in the center section to the rear, women and children sat along the sides towards the front, and blacks and outsiders filled the back. Blacks were not allowed to take communion, and in a few years they began their own church, the African Methodist Episcopal Church. Even Francis Asbury was not in favor of blacks taking communion. 'Makes you wonder how many of our ethical and theological positions reflect the mores of the times. In 1726 the Jews of Philadelphia were given the right to own land and participate in business on a basis of equality with Christians.

One afternoon, while walking the downtown section of Philadelphia, I wandered into Wanamaker's Department Store to buy a pair of jeans. Wanamaker's is a giant merchandiser of home goods like Macy's in New

York and Marshall Field's in Chicago. In the center of this seven-story department store is an atrium that reaches upward, and along the south wall extending to the sky is a massive pipe organ with bass pipes big enough for a pony to stand in. Every day from 11:30 a.m. to noon and 5:30 p.m. to 6:00 p.m., an organist slides behind the console and performs a varied repertoire of popular and classical music. Shoppers stop in their tracks or sit where they can listen.

Built in 1904 in Los Angeles for the St. Louis World's Fair, the original organ had 10,000 pipes, but John Wanamaker, no small thinker, added 8,000 more to adequately fill and vibrate the seven-story atria of his new department store. His critical ear judged it again to be inadequate and 10,000 more pipes were added from 1924-30. Wanamaker became so obsessed with his organ that he had a factory in the attic where 40 full-time organ builders and installers worked until they got it right.

Famous organists like E. Power Biggs, Marcel Dupre and Louis Vierne gave concerts in Wanamaker's Department Store. Today it is a national historic treasure valued at $50 million. So distracted was I by the organ, I forgot what I went in for and came out empty-handed.

Philadelphia, like all older seaports, has a plethora of old docks and wharves left over from the time of square-rigged tall ships and steamers. With the advent of container ships and independent stowage of goods using the ship's hoists and cranes, the required amount of wharfage shrank, leaving the city with a derelict waterfront. These discards are gradually being converted to playgrounds, condominiums, restaurants, dance halls, billiard halls, interactive sport and video arcades, and even a beach. White sand was brought in, a swimming pool set in the middle of it and plastic palm trees situated around an open bar.

We rented a car in Philadelphia and drove to Washington, D.C., saw the town and picked up son, Alan. Having Alan aboard was like having a new puppy; he was positive, energetic, happy and fearless. We saw ourselves as old, cautious and worrisome.

Of course, we were paying the bills and suffering the consequences if anything went wrong so we had a right to be grumpy and uptight, but we wanted to be like him. He ran all over the boat, handled lines, grinned in storms, and variously made himself delightful. When the going got long and tedious, he went down to his room and took a nap. What a guy.

The way from Philadelphia toward Cape May was down the Delaware River into Delaware Bay. This was a long, gray, uninteresting day of cruising past industrial cities like Wilmington, then into the open waters of Delaware Bay.

We had a warm muggy day that was slowly turning sour. The sky began to darken and I sensed a storm coming. The wind picked up speed. Eva, with the use of the GPS and radar, navigated our way and predicted our landfall at the mouth of the Cohansey River, where we planned to anchor for the night. We peered through the mist at the marshy New Jersey shore, unbroken except for a small daymarker in the water that showed the entrance to the river. With flawless navigating, we skirted the sandy shoals and found the flood current of the river in the marsh, a winding course through sea grass that reminded me of the sea islands of Georgia. Three miles away, in a clump of trees, was the village of Greenwich.

The wind increased and we thought it best to drop anchor quickly. Alan got on the bow with Eva, and I faced *Genie* into the wind. We set the anchor firmly as storm clouds gathered. When a cold air front collides with warm, squall lines and high winds can develop. The Coast Guard came on channel 16 of the VHF with an advisory, "...high winds to 60 mph and hail with the possible formation of tornadoes and lightning. This is a dangerous storm and anyone in mobile homes should seek shelter in permanent buildings..." This announcement was followed by a listing of affected counties and we were in one.

A boat is even less secure than a mobile home, and we were in a very exposed landscape with no wind breaks. My instinct was to seek shelter near the town, so we pulled up the anchor and headed inland for the line of trees that could provide protection. Fishermen along the way watched us and waved as we made our maximum 9 knots through the winding waterway. In few minutes they raced by us realizing the storm was nearly upon them, too. The sky blackened and the wind howled. The canvas bimini of the upper fly bridge slapped and flapped, and we became grim. Again. Even Alan looked a little scared.

As we got near town I yelled, "We need to drop the anchor now. The storm is going to hit any second." Alan and Eva got on the bow of the boat and dropped the anchor near the marina. The force of the wind was so strong against the boat that Eva had difficulty tightening the warping drum and setting the gypsy pawl because the windlass was caked with mud from the previous anchoring. Anchor rode kept paying out as they struggled to make it catch. The decks became slippery and the first raindrops hit like shot. The river was deep (over 20 feet) and required considerable scope to keep us secure, but we couldn't swing too far because we were in a narrow river, and boats from the marina were within our swinging radius.

"We're too close," I shouted to them. "Raise the anchor again. We'll have to choose a new spot." They worked like their lives depended on it. It did. The electric windlass motor sounded like it was pulling against a great weight and soon an enormous glob the size of a Volkswagen with tentacles, hair, and three teeth (so Eva said) surfaced. She stomped on the chain until the monster released its hold and the anchor went down again. We reset *Genie* for the third time and dropped the Danforth anchor as well before running for the protection of the enclosed salon.

The rain came in horizontal sheets. We sat at the lower helm, white-faced and terrified. (We practiced this state of mind so we know just how to do it.) I left the engines running because if we drifted toward shore or other boats, I'd be able to power us out of trouble. Maybe. Trees bent; boats tugged at their dock lines like mad horses straining against their reins.

Alan decided this was really cool and was bubbly and happy. We looked at him scornfully, "Get serious, Alan. This may be where the BIG trip begins." He was not convinced.

"Don't worry. Be happy," he chirped.

Did you ever hear of such a thing? In the middle of a storm? We looked at him with the disdain learned from years of parental superiority.

"You're on vacation. Have a good time," he said.

"Not now, Alan."

"Why not? This is fun."

The wind and the rain stopped. I shut off the engines. We had a moment of peace. Without the opposing force of the wind, *Genie* now succumbed to the force of the incoming tidal current, turning to face the new power. The current became faster and faster. Eva heard a rumbling sound and observed the anchor chain vibrating in sync with the rumblings. I looked to shore and took a fix on a solid object. We concluded simultaneously that we were dragging our anchors and heading for the docks. Eva and Alan raced to the bow and began hauling in the anchors while I restarted the engines. Alan had difficulty pulling up the Danforth anchor manually; so I left the helm and helped him get it on deck, full of mud and twigs. I raced back to the flybridge, gunned the engines and stabilized us. Our depth sounder, which read 20 when we anchored, now read 35. When we turned, we swung over a big hole in the river. We looked for a safer place and moved upstream. Near a curve in the river where the current was less strong, we dropped anchor for the fourth time in less than an hour.

Other boaters in the same storm were less fortunate. Later we heard of another trawler about our size that was tied to a dock and pulled out all four cleats, which set it in motion against a neighboring boat. The captain started his engines and attempted to direct his boat's drift, but the dangling lines wrapped onto his props and stalled his engines. The two boats drifted into a third boat, wedging it against the shore. We had much to be thankful for.

Alan decided to make spaghetti for supper and went into the galley, steaming the windows so we couldn't see outside. Just as well. We were feeling our tequila, so it didn't matter much.

I never thought of New Jersey as marshland, but marshes are extensive on the eastern shore of Delaware Bay. It was like our travels through Georgia and the Carolinas—woods, marshes and gnats. This is wild New Jersey, natural and unspoiled.

The day after the storm we cruised southward on Delaware Bay, now full of crab pot buoys, which said something for the state of health of this bay. The weather remained unsettled and there were more forecasts of rain. We pushed on.

We experienced the great black fly uprising. Somehow, in the middle of the bay, pesky varmints came aboard and bit us like we were liverwurst. They were everywhere. These were not your friendly green bottle, carrion-eating flies. These were fresh flesh eating piranhas dressed like flies.

Eva decided to go to war. Every bite brought more vehement swinging and a crescendo of madness on this dull day in the middle of Delaware Bay. She was a flaming fundamentalist on her crusade to eradicate these damnable beasts. She smashed flies against windows, on the tachometer, across my back, on the seats. Alan and I ducked and bobbed, avoiding her swings which had the force of death blows. She was mad and was not going to take any more. The foghorn in the distance went "Oooooh, aaaaaah", and I began to paint in my mind another portrait of life at sea: *GOING MAD ON DELAWARE BAY.*

At Cape May, New Jersey, we docked for the night and anticipated with dread the open ocean run to New York City. Since the inception of the trip this was the leg that worried us the most. In the morning I listened to NOAA, "Winds gusting to 35 mph from the northwest with seas from 4-6 feet. There is a small craft advisory in effect."

I shut off the radio and went back to bed. Later in the morning I observed my neighbors on their sailboat getting ready for departure.

"What do you guys make of this weather?" I asked.

"It's supposed to get better as the day wears on, so we're going out and make the run to New York."

"You mean you're going to make a straight run for New York?" I asked.

"How long will it take?"

"We should be there tomorrow night sometime. We'll sail throughout the night and be there for cocktail hour."

"You're going to sail all night?" I said with incredulity.

"We'll each take a watch. Doing 4-5 knots, we should be okay." I couldn't imagine such a thing.

"We're pretty inexperienced at open ocean runs," I said, "Take that back. We have never been on the open ocean. How do you think it will be out there?"

They gave me assurances that things would improve as the day wore on, with lessening winds and calmer seas. I checked with the dockmaster and he gave me the same encouragement, "If it gets too rough, turn around and come back. We'll keep a slip open for you."

So we decided to go for it. Eva called ahead to the recommended marina while I got the electronics set up on the flybridge. She came back with the bad news that the marina was fully booked, as it was the Memorial Day weekend. I said, "Give me the phone number. I'll see what I can do."

Armed with the knowledge that nothing was available, I used a line that has worked in the past. I told them that I was a travel writer cruising on a boat and needed a place to stay the night. "Just come on in. We'll have a place for you," was their reply.

This was our first day on the Atlantic Ocean, and though it was choppy and rough, it was not as difficult as we had imagined. The waves were on the bow and *Genie* rode through the swells as if she was made for this kind of thing. We had been in much worse than this. Spray covered the decks and reached the windshield of the bimini, but we did fine. Around 5 p.m. we entered the harbor at Atlantic City, tied up at one of the many empty slips at Farley's State Marina near Trump's Castle, washed down the boat and then went to town on the jitney for a look at the famous Atlantic City Boardwalk.

It was depressing. The ride to the boardwalk was through the inner city which is poor and tawdry, a striking contrast to the carnival atmosphere of hotels with pretentious names and decor like Taj Mahal and The Castle.

The boardwalk wraps the city, and I suppose on a warm summer day... "On the board walk in Atlantic City, life will be peaches and cream," but from our points of view, life was listless, dull and insipid.

The next day we went for our second day on the ocean. The morning was gentle, the temperatures in the 60's and the sea like glass. Eva took the wheel, I wrote on the notebook computer next to her, and Alan stayed below to do some homework in preparation for his summer internship with the Department of Agriculture.

I asked Eva if she was bored. "No, I'm on vacation," she said with a smile. "I have time to think; it's quiet, there are puffy clouds in the sky and the sea is pacific, even though it's the Atlantic."

The New Jersey coastline is one huge beach, from south to north. There is rampant development, with one town touching another. Every burg has a Ferris wheel and amusement park, and the entire sandy coast is a playground.

Alan took a turn at the helm late in the morning. By noon winds had picked up from the south. Swells began to build and Alan turned the wheel over to me. By 2 p.m. we were riding swells that would lift us up until *Genie* was on a hill, then she'd surf down the slope, wallow in the trough and ride the next one. These were huge, and growing. *Genie* was hit on the transom at the starboard quarter, which pushed her sideways as well as forward. I was in a wrestling match with her, trying to maintain a steady course in following seas. I tried going faster, but this only prolonged the time the 6 foot swells pushed on us. I tried going slower, and that helped. We let the swells ride us up and down, each passing wave making a breaking sound as it surged past us, but slower meant we would be on the water longer.

At 4:30 we reached Manasquan Inlet on the Jersey coast. We had traveled about 50 miles, but I felt I had been at the helm for days. I was cold, tired and spent. Many boats were coming into the inlet and we followed the locals past the rock jetties, riding the turbulence at the inlet.

Inside the relative calm of the inlet, we searched for the Shrimp Box Restaurant which allowed overnight dockage at their restaurant if you had dinner with them. Fair enough. Usual dockage fee was $30-40 per night, so spending that same amount of money got us dock space and a meal. *Genie* had plenty of water aboard and her own electricity by way of the batteries and generator so we didn't need hookups. The only requirement was that we allow other boats to raft to us if all the dock space was occupied.

We were the second boat to tie up, so we had plenty of room, and shortly after tying up we went inside. I remember vividly the feeling of being in that cozy restaurant after the tough day on the water. I was exhausted, and the warmth and stability of the restaurant environment was coddling and comfortable.

About 10 p.m. a sailboat came into the inlet and searched for a place to tie up at the restaurant. Eva stuck her head our the door, which was as good as a welcome, and a bedraggled sailor called out, "Can we raft to you?"

I was already in bed, but I got up and helped these sea faring strangers tie down. Both boats put out fenders and we pulled the 34-foot sloop next to us, opened our gates and made a passageway between the boats. On board were two old folks who'd just had the ride of their life from New York City aboard their son's boat. Everyone was sick and looked wretched. They were pitching through those same swells, but instead of going with the waves, they were plowing into them like a rocking horse. Their progress was slow and they finished the trip in darkness.

The old folks spoke in Spanish, and the younger couple had to literally carry them off their sailboat. We lay back in bed and listened to them and felt their footsteps overhead on our deck. *Genie* wallowed from side to side as the pilgrimage of sick souls moved across her bow deck and onto the restaurant's dock. Finally they were gone and we wondered if we'd hear them return. We didn't. The boat captain took the old folks to a relative's home and the younger couple came across our decks later in the night with such stealth we never heard them.

In the morning we unrafted from our New York neighbors and headed again to sea, and New York City. We had two days on the open ocean so far, one a little rough, the second one downright uncomfortable. The weather forecast for our third day at sea was very favorable...and it turned out to be perfect—warm, calm, peaceful and no surprises. By 11 a.m. we were eyeing Coney Island and Brooklyn with the Manhattan skyline beyond, and by noon we were looking Lady Liberty squarely in her...toes, because her eyes were way up there. She is not at the entrance to New York Harbor (the lower bay) as we had supposed, but farther up river (in the upper bay), across from Manhattan, and on the New Jersey side. She is not the first thing you see when approaching New York; the World Trade Center is. And then it's all the traffic—ferries to Staten Island, and cruise boats touring Ellis Island and the Statue of Liberty, and tugs, barges and cruise ships. We were busy, but it was fun. We were out of the ocean and heading for inland waters. We were jazzed.

Alan offered to make lunch if we wanted to continue touring New York City by boat, so he went down to the galley and grilled sandwiches. We had lunch at the upper helm while cruising under the Manhattan Bridge and the Brooklyn Bridge in the East River and around Governors Island. Finally, we located our marina directly across from Manhattan, on the New

We cruised at the foot of Lady Liberty, "Give me your tired, your poor, your huddled masses yearning to breathe free..."

Jersey side.

After getting settled in our slip, we decided to get a feel for New York City on land. We caught the commuter train to uptown Manhattan and walked the streets, gawked at the Empire State Building and other skyscrapers like we were hicks from a small town, which we were. We stopped at a visitor's information booth and got the scoop on what to do. Broadway shows even at discount prices were beyond our budget.

Alan left us the next morning via Amtrak to Washington, D.C. As we approached the station, he said, "Mom, you have your driver's license, don't you?"

"Yes, but it's back on the boat. Why do you ask?"

"Because you'll need it as identification when you pick up your tickets to *Miss Saigon* tonight at the Broadway Theatre. I reserved them for you in your name."

Eva dissolved in tears. This poor, working student-intern found enough money to give us a good time in the Big Apple. The play was wonderful and just what we needed.

We spent days walking through New York and sightseeing. We loved the city for its hustle, the goodness of the people, the hawkers on the street, the sidewalk vendors, the noise and smells, the dialects and languages of the 120 nationalities who make New York home. This is a real league of nations existing in controlled bedlam. We ate at the delis throughout the city and had a special lunch at the *Shalom Kosher Pizza & Dairy*. We had kosher okra, kosher flounder in onions, and kosher pasta stuffed with potatoes. Even a kosher Coke. I really wanted a ham on rye, but they were all

Ellis Island was adjacent to our anchorage across from New York City.

out.

Orthodox Jews, with black hats and curly locks ate there. Many of these are the diamond merchants of 47th Street who control 80% of the wholesale diamonds coming into the United States.

Our mail was supposed to be forwarded to the marina in Jersey City, so we checked at the office after wandering through the Big Apple. No mail, but it had been a holiday weekend, so maybe it took longer. The next day we checked again. Still no mail...and another day. By this time we were feeling the pressure to get on with the trip. A call home to our resident tenants indicated the mail had been sent a week earlier. Three to four days is reasonable delivery time for Priority Mail.

On the fourth day we asked the marina office secretary where the post office was and learned it was only about 3 blocks away, so we made the short walk there. Despite our protestations and implorings, the post office could not produce the missing mail. We asked to see a supervisor and another search revealed our Priority Mail package resting comfortably on a skid in a corner of the building. Seems it had been there for three days. We thought PRIORITY meant it got *priority handling*. How naive of us.

Apologies from the supervisors followed and lame excuses given that they were so busy, the regular carrier was sick and there was a substitute, and with cutbacks in their budgets.... "Don't hide behind that," I scolded, "admit it. You just plain screwed up." Silence. We hurried back to the boat, sorted the mail, paid the bills that were due and mailed them, loosened the lines and headed up river.

The Hudson River, one of the most scenic rivers in America, rolls by New York and we were ready to cruise it. We had completed the main course, the dessert lay ahead.

CHAPTER 10

NORTH ON THE HUDSON TO QUEBEC

It was surprising how quickly we left the hustle of the Big Apple as we cruised up the Hudson River. We traveled under the George Washington Bridge and passed Yonkers on the east side, a mere suburb of 2,000,000 souls, a baby compared to *The City*. Steeples of churches poked through the trees and above the homes giving the town a soul and a center.

By the afternoon we were in the palisades scenic area. High cliffs of columnar basalt made the Hudson a narrow channel through uplifted high-lands. City streets lay behind this facade, but from the water's edge it looked pastoral and natural.

Beyond the Tappan Zee Bridge, the Hudson broadened and the foot-hills of the Catskills appeared. Dunderberg Mountain at 1,000 feet was the first step upward, and in the miles to come the Hudson River climbed through the Catskills through a system of canals and locks.

Since the Hudson is affected by tides, we timed our travel to ride the flood current upstream which gave *Genie* a boost to 10 knots, a lightning speed for this 13-ton matron which lumbers at 8 knots on the flat and level. The tides have an effect all the way to Albany, and beyond Albany is the first lock to the New York Canal System.

At Peekskill the forests were deep and dark, a mix of conifers and deciduous trees. Bear Mountain Bridge was ahead where the Appalachian Trail, a continuous foot path from Georgia to Maine, crossed the river.

We reached depths of 116 feet in the river near Bear Mountain, one of New York State's premium Hudson River preserves. Men and boys were fishing from the dock so we anchored in a cove where the water was only 15 feet deep and used the dinghy to go ashore. We hiked the trails that overlook the river and wandered through wooded ravines to a rustic log lodge. Spending the night in a log house in the woods looked appealing but it was simply a wish, and we headed down the trail again to our water bed.

We spent the night in a bend of the Hudson with railroad tracks on both shores and a schedule which had trains passing this point at the same time in the middle of the night. The wail of their whistles, the shriek of steel on steel and the clatter of swaying box cars, along with the simultaneous waves created by a tug pushing a raft of barges, was sufficient to make us sit up and wonder if we had drifted back to Yonkers.

The uncertainty of our position on water while anchored continued to mystify (terrorize?) us; still we slept though the night while guardian angels watched over us.

The next morning as we were preparing breakfast, a fast moving boat left a gigantic wake which rocked us and sent the coffee carafe to the floor, shattering it. For a while until we could replace it, we had to improvise for our morning coffee.

The Hudson wanders scenically north, the population thins, and bluffs appear as in the romantic paintings from the Hudson River school of artists at the turn of the century.

West Point Military Academy was around the bend and we got on the VHF to a nearby marina for instructions for mooring or docking. They invited us to use one of their moorings so Eva got on the bow and pulled the pendant on board and the accompanying lines that held us to a concrete mushroom lying on the bottom. When we got to shore in our dinghy, the marina operator asked us for the 50 cents a foot mooring charge (total charge: $0.50 x 40' = $20). "But, but, but...," I stammered, "we want to stay for just a couple of hours. Don't you have an hourly rate?"

("No, I'm greedy and you're rich. I can tell from the size of your boat," was implied.) "The rate is 50 cents per foot whether you stay an hour or a day."

So it was back in the dinghy, unhook and search for another parking place. The military academy has their own dock and mooring field and we tried to raise someone on the VHF, but after getting no response we started to tie to one of their moorings. A military directive from shore rang out, "NO, NO, SIR, THOSE MOORINGS ARE FOR LIGHT-WEIGHT SAILBOATS, SIR, (NOT FAT TUBS LIKE YOURS SIR), YOU'LL PULL THEM OUT, SIR."

"OKAY, SIR," I shouted back, "I WON'T TIE TO THE SAILBOAT MOORINGS, SIR."

With no place to go, no moorings to attach to and the Hudson River 100 feet deep and running, we chose to anchor BETWEEN the moorings. Nobody screamed. Once more we dinghied to shore and spent the next several hours touring our nation's most prestigious military establishment. EVEN I was impressed, being anti-military and suspect of anyone with white-walls that always says, "YES SIR," and kills for a living.

"Aw c'mon," you say. "There have been some fine human beings that were graduates of West Point, Robert E. Lee and Benedict Arnold to name just two."

"Okay, you have a point." And Dwight Eisenhower was a graduate too, and he was one of their less sparkling students who only tolerated their laced-up attitude and military protocol but made a good commander and a fine national leader.

West Point began as a military post in 1778 when our fledgling nation was just beginning to flex its independence. It became an academy when our leaders concluded that the way to liberty and freedom lay with being strong and prepared militarily. (Place your right hand over your heart.)

Just north of West Point, the American Revolutionaries strung a heavy chain across the river to thwart the English ships that were pillaging and burning, but the English took the chain for their own use and went up river to burn Kingston and other American revolutionary outposts.

The English continued to be a menace through 1814, carrying on raids from Canada. England's loyalists just couldn't get it through their thick wigs that America was going to be an independent nation, so they chipped and picked and burned and made us mad as hornets, and consequently we established a strong military nation with a naval and army academy that became examples to the world. (Keep your hand over your heart until I'm finished.)

The campus is situated high above the Hudson River on a bluff of granite, giving it a Gibraltar character—solid as a rock. The grounds have the appearance of an arboretum with classic buildings, officer homes and athletic fields. Everyone is in shape at West Point and athletics are an integral part of the curriculum. While studies include military courses, a general education can be completed in science, engineering, communications and languages.

The old chapel on the grounds is a favorite wedding place, the men in full dress uniforms and the ladies in flowing white. So popular are weddings at the end of the school year, (cadets can not be married as long as they are enrolled at the academy), that reservations need to be made years ahead of time. Some make reservations even if they don't have a prospective bride in mind, while others make reservations and in the interim change their choice. "When you've got such a beautiful spot reserved for a wedding, it's a shame not to take advantage of it," is the attitude. We wondered if there were some gals hanging around with white gowns in the closet just in case a cadet had reservations and no bride.

By afternoon we were back on the river, catching depths of 149 feet, then 195 feet. Our depth sounder rolled up imaginary numbers when it didn't know what to do with depths so great. "It's too much, it's too much," it seemed to say.

At Poughkeepsie and Hyde Park we observed monumental homes on the bluffs over the river. The magnificent homes that line the Hudson were owned by some of America's filthy rich, including the Vanderbilts and the Roosevelts, who had estates at the turn of the century.

After months along the Atlantic seaboard we had forgotten how warm and comfortable life is away from large cold bodies of water. We had experienced a lot of windy and cold weather, but it was nothing compared to the long hard winter these northeast residents endured. In these parts of New York State they had snow on the ground through April. Everyone was anxious for sun and warmth, and the hint of summer had everyone out celebrating around smoky grills.

Small granite islands in the river support a mix of conifers and deciduous trees which gives the Hudson the look of the north. The river winds upward, gaining in elevation and passing between hills and mountains.

By the end of the day we made landfall at the Poughkeepsie Yacht Club. We wanted to anchor but the river depths were 260 feet in the center, and remained very deep almost to the shore where there were two to four feet ledges, so anchoring was out. We got on the radio to the yacht club who were out in numbers for their spring party. They were good enough to direct us to an unused mooring and invite us to their barbecue cookout and watermelon seed-spitting contest.

Yacht clubs have the reputation for being a clique of rich snobs, but these New Yorkers were simply a group of boaters (sailors mostly) who love boats and the congenial company of other boaters. These folks were altogether delightful and went out of their way to befriend us.

We were going to bicycle to church on Sunday, so we un-hooked from our mooring and came into the dock for the day. I took the bikes off the sundeck of *Genie* and set them on the dock. Both bikes had flat tires. After a lightning-fast patch job on both we were up the steep dirt road that leads from the yacht club through woods of beech, walnut and maples to the highway. We got part way up and Eva slipped and fell. When I looked back I saw m'lady stirring in the dust with her bike wrapped around her. She was wrestling the thing into submission and when the dust finally settled and we brushed her off, it was clear that the bike had won. She was humiliated, wounded, bleeding and in a mental state unfit for Sunday, or any day. We examined her strawberry bruises and went back to the boat for first aid, a body vacuuming and a restoration of her (usual) pleasant Sunday disposition.

Back on the bikes again, we climbed that blood stained road through woods deep and dark and rode the shoulder of Highway 9. Short of town and church we entered the Vanderbilt Estate high on the bluffs overlooking the Hudson. The estate house(s) were stone monuments the proportions of civic centers. The grounds were developed around marshes, waterfalls, wildflower hills and groves of endemic and exotic trees and shrubs. It was a religious experience of sorts.

On the river later in the day, we turned up Rondout Creek to the town of Kingston. The British sacked and burned Kingston in 1777, but it was quickly rebuilt. An 1871 lighthouse marks the beginning of the creek, and boaters were out en masse on this sunny Sunday afternoon, swirling on the water. *Genie* looked like a whale in a school of whirligig beetles.

The waterfront part of town was full of boaters tied to the town docks having late lunches. Cliff Schoonmaker was assisting the city dockmaster by taking lines of incoming boats. When he saw us come up the creek, he motioned for us to go further upstream where he took our lines and tied us to a long pier, away from the pond of small runabouts. He and his wife, both officers with the U.S. Power Squadrons and the U.S. Coast Guard Auxiliary, do dockside inspections of boats and acquaint boaters with safety regulations and educational programs. They came aboard *Genie* and gave her an inspection, making suggestions for improvement, and then gave her the U.S. Coast Guard seal of approval for equipment and procedures. Following our inspection Cliff drove us in his van to stores where we re-provisioned the boat.

On Monday morning we left Kingston. The waterfront was lifeless. We were alone save for an occasional mute swan and formations of Canada geese honking their way along the flyway. Eva pointed to a number of ancient wooden barges left to decay along the shores of the creek. Old vessels and wharves are abandoned; their rotting hulks and timbers becoming river flotsam that catches propellers or tears open hulls.

We approached Saugerties Creek, which translates to "saw mill" in Dutch. Early Dutch settlers gave names to many places along the Hudson. On the right side of the river is the Livingston estate. Robert R. Livingston was one of the signers of the Louisiana Purchase. His home was also burned by the British, but rebuilt and now serves as a state historic site.

Near the town of Catskill and the Rip Van Winkle Bridge is the Frederick Church estate. Church was part of the Hudson River school of artists whose paintings in the 19th century romanticized and gave national attention to the Hudson River Valley.

Beyond Catskill the Hudson got narrower. Sailboats traveling north stepped their masts at the local marinas so they could clear the 17-foot fixed bridges ahead. The river breaks up into separate channels as it drains the Catskills, and the terrain is less hilly than farther south.

Suddenly Albany, the New York state capital, appeared along the shores, out of place on a river that was becoming narrower and more wild. It's a thriving port city with tank farms, shipping piers, high rises and corporate headquarters. It looked like New York City again.

There is still tidal effect at Albany, an observation that Henry Hudson made in 1607 when he was exploring the northwest passage to the Orient for the Dutch. He concluded that fresh water beyond the place where Albany exists could not be a northwest passage, so he abandoned his search and left his name on the river. Of course the native peoples were here first, but do they get credit for "discovering" the Hudson River? Not if western Europeans are writing the history books. Incidentally, Henry also "discovered" Hudson Bay, and maybe you remember where that got him. His crew mutinied, sent Henry and his son afloat in a dinghy (without a Wizard), and they were never accounted for again.

Around the bend in the river lay the city of Troy and the first lock in the New York Canal System. For miles and months we would be in fresh water, a welcome situation for the boat's metal and exposed parts.

We had a clumsy time of it in the lock. I was intimidated by the lock's high walls and had difficulty getting *Genie* up to the wall where Eva could wrap a line around the steel pipe that went from the top of the lock to the bottom. I charged back and forth in the lock trying to get the boat to the wall, but try as I might, *Genie* would not cozy up to the wall. I filled the chamber with black smoke as I gunned the engines and lurched in futile maneuvers with Eva hanging onto the rails looking at me as though I had lost my mind. Finally I got it done, Eva wrapped our lines, and we became pleasant again.

Seldom are there signs along waterways like you see along highways; but at a junction in the river, there was a sign with arrows. If we followed the arrow to the left, we would traverse the Erie Canal to Lake Erie, or use the Oswego Canal (bypass) to Lake Ontario. By following the arrow to the right we would go through Lake Champlain, visiting lakeside cities in New York State and Vermont and traveling to the St. Lawrence Seaway via the Richelieu River and Chambly Canal. This is the way we preferred to go. To do so required us to be able to pass under 17-foot fixed bridges, which we could do with modifications.

The canal system linking the Hudson river with Lake Champlain was begun in 1792, and in 1833 a canal to the Richelieu River at the north end of Lake Champlain was completed making water travel possible to the St. Lawrence River. Crossing the Adirondacks by boat is accomplished by taking eight giant steps upwards through locks, then three steps down into Lake Champlain.

The canals and streams of the headwaters of the Hudson in the New York Canal System are particularly winding, tight and challenging. In many places the channel was blasted out of limestone to create a narrow man-made cut. We were warned to stay within the channel markers and not to deviate a foot. We stuck *Genie's* keel in the narrow slot like a toy car on its track, making sharp turns and keeping dead center between buoys.

Just beyond lock #3 we encountered the lowest bridge along our odys-

Few "road" signs exist on the Great Loop. This one points to Lake Erie or Lake Champlain.

sey, which we were told had a 15-foot clearance. With Eva at the helm, I got on the roof of the sun deck and dismantled the anchor light and radar dome and lowered the antennas.

The lockmaster at lock #2 called ahead to lock #3 and advised him we may have trouble getting under his bridge, so the lockmaster at #3 lowered the water in his pool by letting more water run through the sluice gates into the #2 lock pool, thereby dropping the water level two feet and giving us nearly 17 feet at the bridge that followed his lock. Eva got on the roof of the aft deck and eyeballed the distance between *Genie* and the bridge using a technique we had learned early on. If you can see the **far** side of the under-bridge as you make your approach, you will make it. We just made it.

The charts noted this bridge height at 21 feet, but this is only to prove cartographers have a sense of humor because with our highest obstacles removed, we passed by with less than a foot to spare. We imagine there are a few topless boats out there with captains scratching their heads..."But the charts said 21 feet!"

At lock #5 we caught the smell of manure. It was like homecoming. Eva recalled her childhood on the South Dakota farm, and I thought about how I could relate to manure. Let's see...my father was a milkman, and milk comes from cows and cows produce manure. There, we have it. A few farms along the Hudson touch the canals, and Holsteins, who love to stand with their udders in water, looked homogenized and dumb, their patchwork hides picturesque against a backdrop of pastoral New York.

Beyond Lock #6 little bridges spanned the canal and small homes with flower gardens lined the water. It reminded us of an English countryside. First the smell of manure and now the fragrance of gardens. The bouquet of manure, jasmine, honeysuckle and spruce trees was a tour de nose. It's a travesty to do this stretch of the New York Canal System at speeds any faster than 7 knots.

The cottonwood trees were in heat and a blizzard of cottony seed made it look like a snow storm in June. *Genie* made furrows in water flocked with white.

There are cement walls at the locks where boaters can tie for lunch, overnight stays, or to walk the dog while the lock is being readied. The bollards on the ledges of the walls are painted blue and yellow, like big flowers.

As we approached lock #7 and the town of Fort Edwards, a mother duck was out with her babies, nibbling cottonwood seeds on the water. Mother duck didn't gather her ducklings as we approached and I slowed

Genie's 13 ton hulk through the water and eased into the flock, hoping momma would gather her brood. But alas, one duckling was left on the port side while the rest waddled to the safety of the shoreline on the starboard side. The isolated duckling fretted and swam in restless motion peeping pitifully as we cut it off from the flock, but as soon as we glided past it made its way back to the flock by literally running on water.

The Champlain Canal is a twenty mile stretch that begins the descent into Lake Champlain. We were in the Adirondack Mountain drainage that feeds Lake Champlain and Lake George, and forms the Richelieu River which flows into the St. Lawrence Seaway and eventually into the Atlantic Ocean. The daymarkers changed to green cans on our right and red nuns on our left.

The canal is intricate and beautiful with large granite boulders. The Adirondacks are real mountains, comparable to the California coastal ranges.

This area is the source of New York City water and all the communities who put their straws into the water; therefore regulations in Lake Champlain and entering tributaries strictly control boat waste discharges. They insist that all boat overboard discharge hoses be removed and all valves turned so that the ship's waste enters the holding tanks. Vermont Water Police board boats unexpectedly to inspect, we heard, so I had a memorable night in the bowels of *Genie* wrestling valves and hoses, removing and blocking all discharge hoses except those leading to the holding tank. Through the Great Lakes we discharged only into our holding tank and pumped out at marinas along the way which had been our preference throughout the cruise. What was upsetting was to find that marinas in June were not prepared to service boats. Either they didn't have the equipment or it wasn't ready to use early in the season when we were there.

Fort Ticonderoga was on a high bluff to our left, French occupied in 1755, then taken over by the English in 1776, and finally captured by Ethan Allen (who, as you know started a fine line of furniture) and his Green Mountain Boys. It represents the fighting spirit of the revolutionaries and their firm resolve to become and remain independent from England. This border area between Canada and the U.S. was the scene of constant skirmishes during the Revolutionary period and the War of 1812, England's last-gasp effort to upset the newly established American Republic.

The river broadens as it enters the lake, and the mountains recede to the west forming an escarpment. The broad expanse of Lake Champlain gave northwest winds little resistance and they rose to 25 mph. The rag top of the bimini flapped and spray came over the bow. It was small stuff in comparison to what we had been through in the large sounds along the Atlantic seaboard and in our open ocean run from New Jersey to New York, so our anxiety was barely raised. Several months earlier this would have been cause for heart palpitations.

Fort St. Frederick (circa 1752) was visible on the left side. A pier allows cruise boats to tie up and visit the ruins of the French Fort, but it was lined with fishermen, so again we anchored in a cove and dinghied in. The English came in 1759, smeared the French, and, rather than occupy the stone fortifications of the French, built a new fort up the hill, which became known as Fort Crown Point (circa 1759-73). The ol' US of A dusted their wigs during the Revolutionary wars and sent them north to the cold of Canada. Recently the "Loyalists" have been re-invading us by trying to take over Florida (in the winter months).

We went back to the dinghy after visiting the fort and prepared to stay the night, but 30 mph winds across Lake Champlain built white caps and the anchor began to drag. *Genie* was slowly drifting into the rocky shore-line so we hurriedly fired up the diesels and got out of there, moving to the lee side of the lake under the protection of Fort Henry where we spent the night.

In the morning we awoke to a glassy lake that was ideal for breakfast on the aft deck. The local bird population joined us, leaving their despi-cable signatures on the rails and decks, which was not very ideal. Eva had a second cup of coffee and I was at the computer writing. We were in a place we loved—rested, sated, happy, the lake as quiet as a reflective pond, a full panorama of the lake and a picturesque town on the hill. Sailboats reflected off the water at their moorings and we painted in our minds an-other portrait of life at sea.

The urge to move again took over after an hour of sweet indulgence and Eva hauled up the anchor and 80 feet of chain, picking off the weeds as it came. Our anchoring "language" had become fairly sophisticated; she pointed in the direction she wanted me to go and I moved *Genie* around. I got to the point where I could anticipate her directions, watching her and the lay of the line.

"It's dirty," she cried. She brought out the bucket tied to a bow line, threw it overboard and hauled water onto the deck to wash down the anchor and chain. She worked the windlass by the electric foot control, rinsed a little, cleaned a little, picked, picked, rinsed a little...and finally called, "It's up."

It's unfortunate that Eva got stuck with the job of hoisting the anchor, but she felt unsure of her abilities on the bridge so I was at the helm while she did the grunt work. Her preparation for this was life on a South Dakota farm. I am the beneficiary of a girl raised on a farm without modern plumbing who was given the task of hauling water. I can't imagine her as a small girl with two pails hanging from her hands. She's a little doll now and her nails are painted, but she can haul water like a peasant.

Each time the anchor surfaced, we'd smile with relief because it had been sitting on the bottom all night keeping company with old logs, sunken ships and large boulders, all of which wish to hold it and keep it. We're never sure we're going to see it again. So far we had retrieved a tree stump and clumps of weed and mud. I always considered going down to see what the life of an anchor was 20 feet below the surface.

The water got deeper as we crossed Lake Champlain. According to the charts we were at 300 feet, then 393 feet near Essex. Our depth sounder had brain seizures again, the transducer sending signals to the abyss and getting no answer. We hugged the western coast to benefit from the protection of the high bluffs. Fishermen were trolling in 168 feet of water using floating buoys off the corners of their boats.

We got off the lake for a ride up Otter Creek to the town of Vergennes, Vermont. The creek entered the lake at a point of land, not a usual occurrence, which made it difficult to find. In fact, we motored by it and had to hail a local boater who gave us directions. The creek was narrow and overhung with trees. We weren't sure we could make it with a boat our size, but our informer assured us that there was enough water for us. *Genie's* keel slid through the deepest groove of the creek with the encroaching shoreline of maples tickling our rails. Fishermen sat in small coves as we came around the bends, their wee boats dwarfed by our hulk. Eva stood on the bow looking for deadheads and gave me instructions. The setting was green and silent, except for the grumble of the boat's diesel engines.

We came to the end where Otter Creek free-falls 75 feet down an escarpment, creating a silver wall. To the left of the falls was the town of Vergennes, the prettiest little back roads New England village along Lake Champlain accessible by boat. It provides free dockage, electricity and water to boaters. Good-will ambassadors came down to the boat with greetings and information on the town's history and shops. Even the police patrolled regularly, assuring us that they would ride by frequently in the night. Thieves were always a concern for us because the bicycles were exposed on the aft deck.

We took the bikes down and rode through town. Red brick homes with wrap 'round porches sat along tree-lined streets. Downtown Vergennes has one of everything, but our focus was the bakery, bike shop (for new innertubes) and the Dairy Queen.

Vergennes was a shipbuilding town during the War of 1812. McDonough defeated the British in the battle of Plattsburgh with ships that were built here, including the paddleboat Ticonderoga.

Burlington was our next port along Lake Champlain, a place we associated with socks, railroads and Ben & Jerry's Ice Cream. We arrived as a sailboat regatta was underway and a weekend jazz festival was in full swing. There were boats everywhere—on the lake, at the moorings, and a raft of them at the bulkhead near the marina restaurant. When they came in from the lake they rafted to other sailboats already tied up. There were boats tied one to another like toys lined up on a store shelf. If perchance someone in the middle wanted to leave, all the other boats had to detach and "tread water" until they could raft up again. This left about 20 boats in the water milling about. The wind was more than 30 knots and sailboats were trying to keep from bumping into each other. The marina crew, comprised of young muscular guys and gals ran across boats trying to unscramble bow sprits from halyards.

We needed to thread our way through this mess because mechanics were going to come aboard *Genie* to repair a starter. The dockmaster waved me through the swarm to a slip, calling on a loudspeaker for boats to make room for us. He complicated things by asking me to back in against the wind because he thought the wind was going to change direction during the night. I slipped *Genie* among twenty milling boats, most of whom had single screws and limited control, and pivoted to make landfall in reverse. It was another time for white knuckles, black smoke and whining diesel engines. The mechanics came aboard, fixed our starter and we got ready to get jazzed in Vermont.

That's almost a contradiction. Priding myself in stereotypes of the world's people, I found Vermonters to be (although my wife and others who are not nearly so perceptive don't see this) tight and clean, inward and bookish. They listen to jazz as though it's a Haydn Concerto. My idea of a Vermonter getting jazzed means guys snapping their suspenders and women softly tapping their Birkenstocks. Eva chided me for such a limited view of New Englanders, "God knows, Vermonters are just like you and me, except colder," she said.

I imagined that after a long winter making socks and ice cream and reading historic novels by yellow lamps, their coming-out-of-hibernation celebration with a solid week of jazz was like tulips breaking out in full bloom after a winter below the snow. Jazz was everywhere—in the parks, in concert halls, even in church. We went to the Congregational Church Sunday service and the Onion River Jazz Band began with a mournful prelude of *When The Roll Is Called Up Yonder*, and ended with foot stompin' Dixie Land jazz that had Vermonters looking like Holy Rock 'n Rollers.

As we walked down to the wharf following the service, we saw our friends from California, Ben and Barbara Horner, who had just driven in from Montreal to be with us. We kept their rental car for the rest of the day and sampled two of Vermont's attractions, the Shelburne Museum and Ben & Jerry's Ice Cream. It was a chance to go wild and sample the flavors that we didn't want to buy in a pint carton.

The Shelburne Museum on the outskirts of town is an impressive as-

Call it a tourist trap; call it "a find."

semblage of Americana. There are 37 exhibit buildings of quilts, decoys, weather vanes, cigar store figures, carousel animals and tools. Even the Ticonderoga, a steam-paddle boat that plied Lake Champlain, is here. In each building, docents give accounts of the inventory in each. The Shelburne Museum contains the personal collection of Electra Havemeyer Webb who used her family fortune (Domino Sugar) and her husband's fortune (a Vanderbilt) to buy 45 acres, erect buildings and buy anything she wanted.

Burlington is a fine port city, with many outdoor cafes, historic buildings and a thriving

Eva promises Ben, "I'll never do it again," at the Shelburne Museum.

economy. It was a good place to provision the boat and get jazzed before moving north on Lake Champlain and into the Richelieu River.

We fueled up at Gaine's Marina at Rouses Point, New York, our last stop within the U.S. before entering Canada. Mr. Gaines said that the winter of '93-'94 froze Lake Champlain and the Richelieu solid when 60 days of below zero weather turned everything into a block of ice. Frequently the temperature was -40 degrees. The marina was just now getting its docks repaired and ready for the short boating season.

The next day of travel took us through Canadian Customs and to Fort Lennox, an 1871 British fort. We tied to their dock and toured the ancient facilities, encountering a segment of American history seldom mentioned in the history books, or in our memories.

The city of Saint Jean Sur Richelieu was our first encounter with the Canadian Quebecois. The transition from English-speaking to French was immediate. Some shop keepers and folks along the waterway had difficulty speaking English or could not speak it at all, but they were kind and did their best to communicate with us. We heard reports that there was genuine hatred for Anglophones among the Quebecois and an arrogance about their French-ness so we tried to learn some common French phrases.

"Ou est le champ de courses?"

"Puis-je predndre rendez-vous pour jeudi?"

"Pourquoi riez-vous? Monfrancais est-il si mauvais?"

We chose these phrases for their full and juicy utilization of the French language, not because they were useful or meaningful. After several days using these phrases, Barbara checked the French phrase book and discovered we were saying:

"Where is the race track?"

"Can I make an appointment for sometime Thursday?"

"Why are you laughing? Is my French that bad?"

When we arrived at Saint Jean Sur Richelieu on Tuesday we expected to lock into the Chambly Canal which leads past the rapids of the Richelieu River, but they weren't operating the locks on Tuesday and Wednesday so we had a day to soak up French culture and learn what Frenchmen do from 11 p.m. to 3 a.m. on the river front.

When the French arrived in 1535 to hunt and fish, they kept their French time and never reset their watches. To this day French Canadians live in another world and another time. The end of the work day is 5 p.m. just like Englishmen, but they don't have supper until late in the day, and then they party until 3 am. Every night of the week is like Saturday night. They seem to live to eat and party.

When they were ready to go to bed, they screeched their tires and hollered as loudly as they could, "Ou sont les toilettes?" which does not translate to, "Good night and good will to all, until we meet again," but really means, "Where are the toilets?" That was surprising because teenage Quebecois were doing it in the streets and behind the bushes (we heard them) all night. I realize that this is another example of a malicious stereotype.

By 4 a.m. we were falling asleep when the city workers arrived in their garbage trucks, street sweepers began to tidy up the city waterfront, and backhoes arrived to dig for the new city sewer system. Needless to say, this late night madness and early morning industry drove us to drink (French wine), eat snails and stuff ourselves with French pastries.

Thursday morning the locks opened and we entered the Chambly Canal, a narrow elevated water course through neighborhoods and countryside that skirts the rapids of the Richelieu River. Bicycle paths paralleled the canal, and bikers and joggers traveled alongside. It is a linear canal through 10 locks, eventually joining the Richelieu River. By 3 p.m. we had gone through the last lock and continued through insufferable heat to the St. Lawrence River town of Sorel. These folks had days of Arctic cold in the winter but in June of '94 they endured equatorial heat.

We docked at a marina in Sorel on the St. Lawrence River which is part of a hotel. We took our drinks and snacks and sat by the edge of the hotel's pool, slipping in regularly to stay cool. Electrical hookups allowed us to run the ship's air conditioning and to cover the late night noise of Frenchmen at the hotel.

The mosquitoes were as big as dragonflies. Barbara did an excellent mosquito interpretation, screwing up her nose with the look of the devil in her eyes and whining like a helicopter from hell. 'Drove us crazy. One more week and she'll be history. Ben relieved me of the chore of running the boat, and he was a good replacement. Better than me in some regards, Eva says. He watched the charts closely, listened to her (the navigator) and seemed entirely involved in what he was doing. "Why can't you be like him?" was the implication.

Barbara replaced me in the galley, which left me double blessed and nearly indolent. In truth, we didn't want them to ever leave.

The next morning we left Sorel for the upstream run in the St. Lawrence River to Montreal. "Maybe with a little effort we could loosen up and become a Francois viveur," we thought. "They seem to be having the time of their lives."

Montreal, Quebec, Canada
to
De Tour Village, Michigan

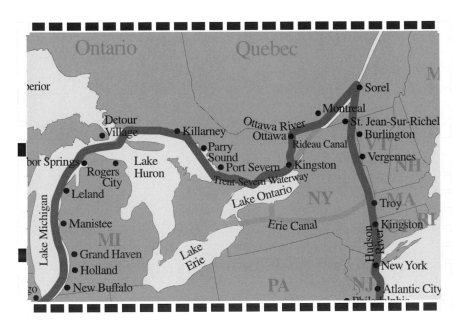

CHAPTER 11

THE FRENCH CONNECTION

The St. Lawrence River carries a two knot current to sea, but it wasn't significant as we left Sorel and turned upstream toward Montreal, a day's run at our monastic speed of 7-8 knots. The Seaway is broad with farmlands on its shores and many islands where Ring-billed Gulls have rookeries. There were thousands of birds covering the islands, spaced as evenly as bungalows in Cicero (Illinois).

Pleasure craft were on the river and we continued a lookout for large commercial ships, but on this day there wasn't much doing, and it was a leisurely trip. The hot, muggy weather was still with us. The river was like glass. We charted our way along the designated small craft channel on the north side of the river and had a nearly boring time of it, powering up a seamless river that was broad and wide and misty.

Inasmuch as the St. Lawrence carries all the water of the Great Lakes to the sea, it also carries the toxic burdens of American and Canadian cities. As a result, it is not prime fishing grounds.

By 4 p.m. we entered the waters around Montreal. There were raging currents near the bridges, and a green buoy in the water was leaning over until it was nearly occluded from view. The water was running at 5-6 knots so our way was reduced to a crawl as we inched past the green buoy in the water and under the bridge. If we had gotten sideways in current this strong, we could have been turned around and sent back downstream or up against a bridge piling; so I hung tight as if our lives depended on it. Finally, after a half-mile of currents that nearly matched our cruising speed, we entered the shelter of the lagoon that leads to the Old Port of Montreal.

Dockhands took our lines as thunderstorms approached. Lightning cracked, thunder rolled and we hastened our pace, brought in the instruments, zipped in the plastic windshields at the upper helm and made tidy our stay. The storm came, the rain poured, the sun shone, we wilted and gasped in 90 degree weather and 100% humidity, and got ready to do Montreal.

The dock at Montreal is situated between old warehouses on the north and south sides. On the west end is a wall and beyond the wall is a park and promenade. Musicians, acrobats and magicians free-lance their talents along this walkway overlooking the harbor. Following the storm the musicians unpacked their instruments, artists set up their easels, acrobats re-assembled their equipment and the sidewalk shows began. It was free, unless you felt inclined to reward a struggling street entertainer. Some of them were excellent, and even the mediocre ones deserved credit for bravery. We had ringside seats from late morning to early the next day. We were on French time, which meant a late beginning and a late end, with the height of activity coming between 8 p.m. and midnight. Eva thought this was how we should live. She hates to get to bed on time.

Two women sang operatic arias, unaccompanied. I heard a man call to his buddy, "Hey, Fred, tell them to hang it up!" I gave the women a token. There were French folk musicians. A couple had a tightwire act—she was on the wire, he played a fiddle. A juggler tossed garden and patio barbecue implements. The variety was endless. After a winter under snow Quebecois come onto the streets for sunshine and outdoor living. Outdoor cafes line the streets and alleys, and the waterfront parks are full of people.

Restoration of the old port began in 1981. Fifty-four hectares (133 acres) were converted from ship warehouses and railroad switching yards to recreational use. Waterfalls and reflective lagoons surround a park amphitheater. Paddle boaters wander through small lakes and under lighted bridges. Everyone stays up late, eats and laughs and walks and eats and sits and eats. There were more tongues wrapped around ice cream cones in Montreal than any other city we visited.

On a weekend evening, Benson & Hedges sponsored a half-hour fireworks display across the river at the Expo grounds. It began at 10 p.m. and lasted for a half hour, a boisterous display that appropriately went up in smoke. It had everyone gushing with appreciation. Who says tobacco companies are up to no good? And they did something that was not bad for our health.

Two tall ships joined us in the harbor, a square-masted sailing vessel from Poland and a sister ship. It took them 17 days to cross the Atlantic using power and sail, and they were finally drying out. It was an educational voyage designed to teach young people the ways of boats and the sea. They were a rag-tag lot, but congenial and shy. The first mate's son, a boy of 12 years, was the most gregarious, coming aboard *Genie* for a look at how we Americans cruise the continental waters. He poked in all the corners and lifted hatches and was very relaxed as we talked about ships and travel. He was really cute. We thought about making him a stowaway.

Choosing the hottest day of the year, we set off one afternoon for the St. Laurent street fair, a trudge up the hills of Montreal toward Mount Royal. We passed through the layers of Montreal's cosmopolitan neighborhoods, each with its own atmosphere, sidewalk vendors and cafes — the Polish neighborhood (sausages and fresh baked bread), the Indian neighborhood (pita, curry and lamb), the Jewish neighborhood (kosher beef on rye), the red light district (haute cuisine), and Chinatown (egg foo yung).

We tramped until we dropped, settling into a chic air conditioned restaurant where svelte looking chicks in baseball caps and tight shorts hustled food out to the patrons. I have forgotten what the food was like. We walked to a market to buy provisions, then took the city bus back to the boat and spent the afternoon by the marina promenade listening to street musicians.

Eva had her heart set on seeing a laser show on the other side of town which began at 10 p.m.; but I was beat, crabby and obstinate and didn't want to go. She was determined, and threatened to go on the subway alone. I couldn't see her going by herself on the subway at night, so out of a magnitudinous spirit, which some would call selfless and noble, I went with her (and had a really good time, but I'm not telling her). The school of architecture set up computer-controlled laser beams around a public square and ringed it with theatrical smoke-making machines. The light cut through the mist, creating images—walls and tunnels and ceilings, a randomly built house that metamorphosed continuously.

On Sunday I persuaded my fellow travelers to attend Basilica Notre Dame which we had seen briefly on our St. Laurent walk. It's a giant frontier cathedral, built of wood, with elaborate wood carvings of the saints, a chancel of carved minarets and a backdrop of midnight blue. The impaled Christ was on a monstrous white pine cross. The service was in French, of course, which gave us time to drink in the atmosphere and examine the architecture. A magnificent choir led the audience in ancient chants and a powerful pipe organ roared the dissonance of 20th century organ music.

In the afternoon we took the subway to the Jardin Botanique, the city's botanical gardens. Spring was busting out all over and we saw plants that we don't see frequently in California—peonies, lilacs, snowball bushes and tulips.

The Montreal subway is fast and efficient. The rubber-tired trains quietly whisk people throughout the city and, in winter, is the principal means of conveyance. Subway stations tie into Montreal Underground, the city beneath the sidewalks, so you can live for months on end without seeing the light of day. The underground shops are malls offering a comprehensive selection of goods. For a city besieged by winter snows and freezing temperatures, Montreal Underground is as cozy as the warrens of moles and shrews.

The Montreal of today is a long way from the Montreal of 1535 when the early explorer, Jacques Cartier, met Amerand Indians and paid a visit to the Iroquois village of Hochelaga near Mount Royal on the island of Montreal.

In 1642 Paul de e Chomedy de Maisonneuve constructed a fort and several small homes on a point of the island which he called de ville Marie. Maisonneuve died and so did all the other settlers, because they were mortals. Their remains were laid to rest in the Catholic cemetery next to the frontier church. Through time the original village site and cemetery were covered and lost by consecutive layers of settlements and buildings. When the 19th century Royal Insurance Building was demolished to make way for a new high rise, the original village site and cemetery were discovered. Archaeologists were called to the scene and work stopped. Layers of early city life were recovered and instead of a new commercial enterprise, a museum was built.

We walked underground staircases to17th century city drainage canals, grave sites and village scenes with tools and artifacts. We poked into corners and saw interpretations through hologram imaging techniques. We wandered through ancient city ruins for several blocks, without seeing the light of day, eventually surfacing at the old customs house.

Through the years Montreal has become Canada's principal port. Today more than 40 shipping lines ensure services and commodities to more than 200 Canadian cities.

We were having mail delivered to Montreal, but after several days when it still had not arrived, we decided to take our leave. The St. Lawrence River has rapids at Lachine that only rafts can negotiate. A Montreal tour company has 30 passenger rafts with big motors and they tear through this section and get everyone wet. They all wear rain slickers and huge smiles. But we boats and huge ocean liners lock around the rapids, re-entering the river upstream.

As we waited our turn in the Lachine Locks, we got a call from Old Port Montreal that our mail had finally arrived. Our two-day priority mail from California had made the rounds in the *Canadian Postal System Read*

A tall ship from Poland locks through with us on the St. Lawrence River near Montreal.

ers Group (no, I don't know such a group exists) to determine if we were subversive, i.e. smuggling recipes for cooking with California wines; so we went back to the Old Port, caught the package of mail tossed to us, headed back out and locked through with one of the tall ships from Poland, two sail boats, a runabout and a tug.

We learned a few days later that **two** packages of mail were sent at the same time, but only one had arrived. Canadian Customs was obviously holding our second package and the contents were probably on their bed tables as they read our letters and lived our lives. Eventually the marina at Montreal received it and sent it ahead to our next city dock, making its travel time through the mails and along the waterways three weeks. It was yellow with age.

When we complained at a Canadian postal office about the long processing time, we were told that Customs had full authority to do as they wished and that three weeks was not an unreasonable time for mail to go from California to Canada; so if our friends died or moved we would be the last to know. Canada and the U.S. are in competition for the most hopelessly bureaucratic, antiquated and inefficient mail system on the planet. Haiti's is probably worse. Maybe Bangladesh.

We had to get used to the idea of receiving mail about a month after it arrived at our address in California. Eva was tearing her hair out trying to figure out our bank balance and what we owed on our Visa bill. Sometimes we had to phone our various accounts and find out what was due because the mail system moved things at a glacial pace.

After the second lock on the St. Lawrence, we entered Lake Saint Louis and had the western view of Montreal and the flyways into Montreal International Airport near Dorval. This was where Barbara and Ben had landed and where they would come back when they were ready to go home; but as long as Barbara continued to cook like a French chef and Ben kept buying wine and piloting the boat, we tried to delay their leaving.

The weather turned rotten as we worked our way across the lake. Rain clouds formed, the wind picked up and we slogged through a labyrinth of buoys across the lake. We finally arrived at Saint Anne de Bellevue late in the afternoon where we tied to a city dock alongside a river walk. Teenagers meet here to do the Quebecois mating dance...or have lovers quarrels into the early hours of the morning, or pee in the bushes. The experience left us convinced that Quebec Province really is a foreign country.

At the dinner hour Barbara chased the blues away with another one of her mouth-watering meals while we anticipated the feeding with excessive salivation. Ben poured the wine, the cook emerged from the galley with coq au vin, the weather turned nice and we had dinner on the aft deck, observing the city scenes like visitors at a zoo.

Ben went for his usual early morning run and was in the shower when we heard him cry out, "There's no water." I jumped up from the breakfast table, opened the engine hatch and dropped down to take a look at the water pump. The eccentric arm to the piston was churning like a champ but the little piston wasn't thrusting. "Are you just about finished with your shower?" I called to Ben who was overhead in a naked state awaiting a favorable report. "No, I'm all lathered up and ready to rinse. How about some water?' "Sorry, old buddy," I called up, "the pump isn't pumping. I think there is a broken bolt."

Ben emerged from the shower wet and filmy, like a baby in its first minute of life (okay, an old baby). We offered to rinse him in milk, orange juice or hot coffee, but he didn't think we were funny. "How about jumping in the lake, Ben?" we suggested. He didn't answer; he just sat there in his amniotic sack with sticky skin and stringy hair waiting for something good to happen. We forgot to take a picture, but it was an image that family and friends would pay good money to have. Another portrait of life at sea— Ben sitting in a puddle around the breakfast table looking sour and neglected while the rest of us stared at him incredulously, a slight sardonic smile on our faces, only a snicker away from a hearty, belly-rolling guffaw. Poor guy.

I took the pump apart and discovered the problem. A bolt connecting the motor to the piston was broken. Part of the bolt was embedded in the eccentric and the head of the bolt was on the engine room floor. I left my breakfast in search of an identical bolt. This should not be too difficult, I thought.

A marine supply was close by so I hoofed it over there and asked for help. It was the day before a Canadian holiday and they were not able to spare a mechanic to help me. "Go to the hardware store," they said. So I went to the hardware store a block away and asked for a replacement. "Not like that," they said as they eyed the bolt. "Doesn't the marina have a bolt like that?" I told them I had trouble getting any help out of the marina because their mechanics were busy. I needed to have the broken stub of bolt taken out. They sold me an *easy out* device, and encouraged me to go back to the marina, which I did, and the marina gave me the same curt service, suggesting I go to the local Subaru auto agency.

The guys in the service department of the Subaru dealership were angels. The service manager looked at my problem, called over a mechanic who took my broken part and went to his bench, returning with the broken bolt removed and a replacement bolt custom made to the proper length. "No charge," the serviceman said.

"Give this man the rest of the day off," I said to the manager.

"If you pay him, I'll do it," he said.

"In that case," I said, "I'll buy him lunch," and with that left $10 behind.

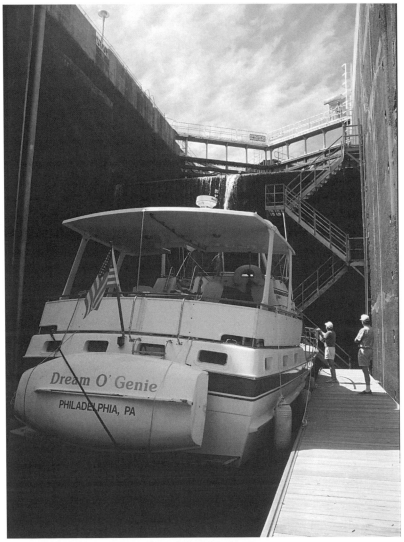

The Carillon Locks on the Ottawa River have floating docks. Neat.

The pump was reassembled, Ben got his shower and we left St. Anne de Bellevue late in the morning. Once again, we were smitten with the goodwill of people, and the French-speaking people of Quebec, although we continue to hear of a quiet war between Anglophones and Francophones. Some Anglophones from the province of Ontario refuse to travel through the French province of Quebec because of the inhospitality of Francophones.

We entered the Ottawa River, leaving the St. Lawrence River traffic behind. They would go upstream to Lake Ontario and the other Great Lakes. We were going up the Ottawa River to the nation's capital, then through the Rideau Canal to Kingston on Lake Ontario, meeting the St. Lawrence River traffic again.

The historic churches along the Ottawa River and on Lake des Deux-Montagnes are the prettiest little things, apparently designed by the same architect. They are fussy Gothic structures, painted silver so that they gleam, and are seen from a very great distance. Every community has one. They're the kind you find under the Christmas tree along with the electric train.

Beyond the lake the land rolls and is the picture of Vermont country-side. Cows grazed near the water's edge and large barns sat on bluffs.

The Carillon Lock lifted us 65 feet to another level of the Ottawa River. This is Canada's longest and tallest conventional lift lock. The weather was windy and cold, but once in the cavernous lock it was warm and quiet. They had new floating docks within the lock so we simply tied *Genie* to the dock and everything rose together.

The lock opened and released us again to the ripping winds and waves. They weren't serious, just bothersome. Depths in the river were up to 308 feet. The countryside is flat and uninteresting, but along its reaches is Le Chateau Montebello, a marvelous 19th century Canadian Pacific Railroad hotel. It's a great log structure with beams and posts of dark wood and a vaulted interior as hushed as a forest. It reminded me of the great railroad hotels of Glacier and Yellowstone National Parks.

The hotel has its own dock and special accommodations for boaters, some of whom spend a season here because of the hotel's immense charm and attractive offerings. Our dock fee was $1.60/foot = $64/night Canadian (U.S. equivalency $1.17/foot = $47/night American, based on an exchange rate of 74 cents on the US dollar). This included use of the indoor swimming pool, Jacuzzi, putting green, golf course, tennis courts, stables, bike rentals and entry to Kenauk, a nearby 100 square mile wilderness. Chateau Montebello is also open through the winter for cross country skiing, curling and snow shoeing.

This is where we said good-by to Ben and Barbara who took the bus back to Montreal. We had 45 locks to negotiate on the Rideau Canal between Ottawa and Kingston, and we were sorry to see our crew leave.

As we approached the capital city of Ottawa we saw bike paths along the edge of the river, and then a great waterfall cascading off the bluffs into the Ottawa River. We were observing the Rideau River in free fall, a spectacle that prompted Colonel By, the engineer of the Rideau Canal system, to name the river "The Curtain." Somehow we had to scale the 100-foot bluffs with a 13-ton boat. We continued around a bend in the river and we saw the solution to our dilemma.

CHAPTER 12

THE RIDEAU CANAL

Eight consecutive locks, spaced as evenly as rungs on a ladder, climbed the hill and entered a break in the bluff. On the hills to the right were the copper-roofed parliament buildings, somber and dark like a scene from a Dickens novel. To the left stood the stately Chateau Laurier, a 1912 Canadian Pacific Railroad hotel, modern and chisel-clean compared to the ancient parliament buildings with their scaly plaques of time-worn soot and stains.

Boats were tied at the blue line and the lock hands were taking inventory as they prepared the first lock for the two-hour ride. There was no room for us to tie up, and a local tour boat was about to leave, so we drifted in the river while lock workers cranked the huge wooden doors open by walking in a tight circle around gears that hinge the doors. Seven pleasure craft entered the lock, shackled themselves to the walls and rode 10 feet to the next level.

We approached the blue (waiting) line and discussed with the lock hands the possibility of entering the locks or staying below for our first night in Ottawa. They said that across the river, the city of Hull was celebrating St. Jean Baptiste Day, a religious observance which usually produced drinking, loud (French) music, buffoonery, debauchery, and various sordid late night activities; and on the Ottawa side of the Ottawa River, they were celebrating French Day, a salute to the French heritage of Canada which usually produced drinking, loud (French) music, buffoonery, debauchery and various sordid late night activities. "Any way you looked at it," they said, "it's going to be *rocque et rolle*. You're best off staying here. The English side (Ottawa) generally quiets down by midnight, but the French side (Hull) keeps going until 3 a.m. The boats going up the locks now and tying along the Rideau River by the waterside cafes near the city parks will be vibrating until midnight."

So we took their suggestion, tied up *Genie* behind the blue line for a couple of nights, and began our exploration of the city. We walked along the locks and watched the boats move from one level to the other. This vantage point gives pedestrian spectators a close and intimate encounter with boats coming up and down. We realized that we would be the entertainment, and if we goofed and flubbered and banged around, which we did when we rode up, we would amuse the summer visitors and be the stars on their video tape. "This boat got one of their fenders caught behind the cable and when they tried to go, it exploded, and one of the dock guys pushed the boat away from the side to free the fender but he was leaning out so far he couldn't get back so he hung from the side of the boat horizontally, fingers on the boat and toes on the dock. Somehow he was able to maneuver to the swim platform of the boat. See him there. The captain of the boat didn't even know he was there. It was really cool. The guy ended up on the back of the boat with their dinghy."

Unfortunately that incident was real, and for the rest of that lockage we had a new deck hand. The process of locking successively through eight locks was not much tougher than locking through one, however. When the lower lock gate closed, the water lifted us to the next level, the upper gates opened, we untied, moved to the next wall and eventually slid into the canal that divides the city. We spent one quiet night at the top of the locks, giving us a different perspective from the previous nights.

The Rideau Canal was built in the aftermath of the War of 1812. The Canadians were afraid that the "predatory Americans" would block Canadian shipping on the St. Lawrence River and along Lake Ontario where the two countries were only a few miles distant, so the queen mother (who owned Canada) decided to build a waterway from the interior of Canada on the Ottawa River to the strategic naval dockyard of Kingston on Lake Ontario.

Fear of American invasion was also the consideration Queen Victoria used for selecting the obscure location of Ottawa as the national capital in 1858, rather than Toronto and Kingston, both of which were located on Lake Ontario and within striking distance of the dastardly Americans. City planner Jacques Greber transformed the city from a rough frontier town to a national showcase by utilizing the natural landscapes of hills, rivers, canals and falls. One historian coined the character of Ottawa as "a struggle between Pittsburgh of the North and Westminster of the Wilderness."

It was fascinating to see Canada's perspective of America in the 1800's. The American eagle was perceived as evil-eyed and opportunistic; but when we were there we didn't sense anything but familial feelings and a mutual feeling of regard.

There has always been a natural water course of lakes and rivers across Ontario from the Ottawa River to Lake Ontario, but in the city of Ottawa the Rideau was a series of shallow rapids that eventually cascaded over the cliff into the Ottawa River. Colonel By and Great Britain's Royal Engineers devised a plan to scale the heights of the bluffs near Ottawa by constructing ascending flight locks and erecting dams around the rapids. Canals were dug where natural lakes and rivers didn't exist and throughout the system, all the way to Kingston, a depth of five feet was attained. Much of this construction required them to blast through the Canadian Shield bedrock.

The Rideau Canal system began in 1826 and was completed by 1832. This was a monumental task given the 49 locks that had to be constructed and the severity of Canadian winters. Irish immigrants were the slave labor and the Scots the stonemasons. The entire lock system was made of hand cut limestone; no poured cement was used. A malaria epidemic wiped out scores of workmen laboring in the sloughs and marshes. Laborers from the tropics brought with them the sporozoan pathogen of malaria. The endemic Anopheles mosquitoes in the Canadian sloughs bit the workmen and transmitted the disease to the next human victim. Entire work crews along the Rideau succumbed to the fatal cycle of fevers, chills and expanding parasites that attacked their red blood cells and eventually took their lives. The cost in human life and dollars made the canal a costly proposition.

It was used for many years as an interior barge canal, but the railroads and the St. Lawrence canal system succeeded it, and by 1850 it was no longer needed. The invasion of the aggressive Yanks never took place and getting materials from Montreal to the naval yard at Kingston was done better by rail and by boat traffic along the St. Lawrence.

Today the canal designed to protect Canada from the U.S., is an historic river route that carries U.S. pleasure craft through Canada. The Canadian Park Systems maintains the canal as a heritage waterway, and nearly all the locks are operated by hand as they were originally.

The five-foot depth keeps bigger boats out of the Rideau Canal, but it was sufficient for *Genie* with her four-foot draft.

Canada continues to lose money on the Rideau. They have increased fees for using the locks and for staying overnight there, but it's only a fraction of their upkeep. Our cost for using the Rideau Canal System was $77 for a six day pass, and staying overnight at the lock stations was an additional $14 per night.

In the winter, the Rideau freezes over, and the section that runs through Ottawa is lowered and resurfaced daily to make it the world's longest ice skating rink, running from the National Arts Center downtown to Hartwell's Lock station at the south end of Dow's Lake beyond the city, a distance of five miles. Government workers ice skate to work on Parliament Hill, carrying their brief cases and shoes. Ottawa has learned to live with long, bitter winters by celebrating Winterlude, a time of ice carnivals, bed races on the ice and other nonsense.

Ottawa is an English-first city where all social intercourse and news media is presented in English primarily, and French secondarily. This is the reverse of the order in Quebec, but Ottawa is bi-lingual and the University of Ottawa offers all courses in both English and French. It is also the capital city with many embassies.

We took a bus across town to view the Royal Canadian Mounted Police Sunset Ceremony. Thirty-two horsemen directed their uniformly colored steeds through a choreography for horse and rider. The Mounted Police are no longer the lone rangers of Canadian wilderness; now they're a showcase group that tours and presents military horse parades throughout the provinces. Afterwards we walked through Baywood Market, an open-air produce market during the day and a late-night hangout after dark. We ate *Beaver Tails,* a local specialty of flat, fried dough sprinkled with sugar and cinnamon or topped with healthful things like veggies and cheese. It's amazing how many regional specialties there are throughout the continent.

Canadians love pomp and ceremony. Of course, it's good business too; and the Americans are right there in line, like we were, to observe the changing of the guard at Parliament, a vestigial ceremony resplendent (useless), beautifully orchestrated (antiquated and wasteful), colorful and heavy with pageantry (aristocratic and a tool of the rich and privileged). But we loved it.

Canadians seem to celebrate governmental power. Parliament buildings are excessive Gothic structures of masonry, darkened with age and heavy with authority. Their love affair with The Queen is striking, also. She's everywhere—on the currency, in statuary and in their celebration of Canada Day (July 1). Only the loon (the Loonie) has surpassed her eminence, but it is only on the one dollar coin.

We attended St. Andrews Presbyterian Church the Sunday before Canada Day and experienced the closeness of church and state and the old world attitude of Canada. It has looked to England for its values and its national style. That's not surprising given the fact that they remained loyal as an English colony and commonwealth state while the upstart American revolutionaries cast off the oppressive mantle of England.

We sang "God Save the Queen" and I think the words were:

"God save the queen
Grand and victorious
Let her lord over us
We think she's glorious
Long live the queen."

Of course, I could be wrong. And then we sang the Canadian National Anthem, *Oh Canada*, like a hymn, softly and reverently.

On a rainy Monday morning we cut our lines from Ottawa and began our wanderings along the Rideau River toward Kingston. Since losing our crew members, Eva and I had to get used to handling the lines and negotiating the locks by ourselves. It was a test of our working relationship. I maneuvered the boat up against the wall of the lock, slowed, then stopped while Eva set the lines. She positioned herself mid-ships so she could loop the line around a cable, then would move forward to secure the bow while I jumped from the helm to tend the stern. She then reached inside the boat to the lower helm and killed the engines and we waited for the flushing to begin. When we left the lock, it was a reverse of this order. Eva started the engines, released the bow line, I released the stern line and got back to the upper helm, then she released the mid-cleat line and we were off. Eva kept our trip accident free, thanks to her agility and good sense.

Sometimes of course, we goofed, or something unexpected happened, or there was a lot of current or wind. That is what made our sleep so deep; the rigors and tensions of moving this hulk through the dynamic media of water and wind kept us on our toes all day.

The curving canal parallels bicycle paths and dome lighted walkways interspersed with woods, experimental farms and Victorian homes. It was strikingly romantic and picturesque, even on a rainy Monday morning. Eva was in full rain gear and I was back in rubber and wool trying to stay warm and dry. The lines were wet and slippery and it was not one of our better days, but the wind was gentle and the rain intermittent. We had a date to keep with daughter, Laura, and her husband, Tim, in Trenton, so it was on to Kingston by the end of the week.

George Hickman, the volunteer lock hand who helped us come up the Rideau locks, sent a message via one of the lock hands that he would meet us with his car so we could re-provision the boat and replace the fender we destroyed. We met him an hour out of town at Hartwell's lock #9. He drove us around in the rain as we bought marine supplies and groceries, then he brought us back to the boat. What a good guy. The goodness and generosity of people we met along the waterways was astounding.

We went through a number of locks in the rain. At the end of the day we passed ferny woods and lily ponds in a shallow lake. There were many small islands and the channel through all of this was shallow but well buoyed. We stopped at Burrits Rapids and met a kind and gentle lock master who, 'turns out, was a defector from the States during the Viet Nam War and was now wearing the uniform (sort of) of the Canadian Parks Service. The lock masters are a casual lot, wearing their uniforms according to personal whim. Their chores around the locks have them maintaining the locks, picnic grounds and washrooms, as well as operating the locks and dispensing information and good will to travelers, so looking as crisp as Canadian Mounties they do not. Their flower beds and grassy lawns are outstanding and they vie with each other for the most decorated and attractive lock. To a person they are helpful, sociable and agreeable.

The Rideau Canal south of Ottawa gave us intimate contact with Canada's province of Ontario.

The day ended as it began, cold and

rainy. We ran the heaters in the boat and got it toasty-warm. We got up early the next day, looked at a dreary world and went back to bed until 9 a.m. The river was beautiful in the rain, curving through marsh and woodlands. This is the quiet and undeveloped part of Ontario, a reserve for the loon and migratory waterfowl and a pleasant respite from cities and cottage lakes.

We had a problem with the port engine transmission and stopped at Merrickville for some advice from a marine mechanic. We didn't solve our problem but got a chance to walk the neighborhoods and admire beautiful stone homes built by the same Scottish stone masons who built the Rideau Canal locks.

Smith Falls is at about the half-way point to Kingston along the Rideau Canal. The two original flight locks were replaced with one 67 foot fully automated lock, one of the few changes made to the original system. The unused locks of 1826 are empty and we saw the sluice gates and the inner working of the hand-hewn limestone blocks.

Smith Falls is the location of the Rideau Canal Museum, a centerpiece for historic memorabilia preserved from the time when Scottish stonemasons and Irish laborers hacked a waterway through stone, ice and swamps. The five-story museum includes working models of the locks and views of the countryside and waterway from its multi-storied observation deck.

What is more important, Smith Falls is the home of Hershey Chocolate Company and the place to fill the larder with the most important supply item after diesel fuel. Those almond bars that either get too many nuts or not enough, are chucked into a basket and set out in boxes in the company store. Lying there side by side, they looked like gold bouillon with the sensual quality of a Tahitian wahine. Their light milk chocolate color and smooth texture made my nostrils flare like a stallion and my heart race. The sane and reasonable Methodist that I usually am, went limp. My hands got itchy and I did in broad daylight what no decent person would do; I reached and... BIT ONE OF THOSE BABIES RIGHT THERE IN THE STORE AND EVERYONE WAS STARING, BUT I DIDN'T CARE!

I hollered to the clerk, "Give me $30 worth of these honeys, and $10 worth of chocolate cherries." Eva, equally addicted and crazed, found my behavior perfectly understandable and joined in the spree. When we walked out of that store pregnant with chocolate, we knew we had done the right thing. We had taken the food budget for the next week and blew it on chocolate.

We rode our bikes back to the boat with bulging saddle bags. I felt like a (chocolate) Brink's guard, suspicious of pedestrians that watched us and wary of vehicles that got too close. We expected a heist and rode with grim-faced determination until we were back on the boat and had hidden our stash in the liquor cabinet. We were rich in chocolate and ready to take on more rainy weather. Every hour or so I'd check our cache, like you do when you've bought something new and you just love to look at it. We could have some whenever we wanted, like when we were depressed, or happy, or when it rained or when the sun shone, or if we were melancholy or had a bee sting...

We left Smith Falls when there was still a threat of rain; actually the forecast called for thunderstorms, lightning, hail and high winds, but we had that forecast ever since we left California so we set out undaunted. Shortly before noon we got to the next lock and had to wait because the lock hands were having lunch, so we tied up at the blue line and had a big chocolate sandwich. No sooner did we imprint our incisors than the wind picked up, thunder rolled, lightning flashed, rain fell in torrents, and *Genie* tugged at her lines. After a half-hour of huffing, blowing and pouring, the front passed, the weather improved and we had a beautiful day in the Lower, Big and Upper Rideau Lakes.

The lakes were reedy along the shoreline and weedy in the channel. *Genie* cut her way through the salad bowl leaving a furrow for the next boat. We wondered aloud if the fresh water strainers were getting choked. Engine temperatures were normal, but that night I checked the strainers and found them solid with weed. Every night I had a new chore. I thought I may have to remove the cover plates on the heat exchangers and clean the cores as well.

We went through an extremely narrow man-made cut big enough for only one boat. Limestone ledges on either side were close to the surface and we kept *Genie* mid-channel. Fortunately we did not meet another boat. Deer flies were pestering us and we were swatting them while trying to concentrate on the narrow channel.

Some of the Rideau Lakes are 310 feet deep, and a number of Provincial Parks along the river provide primitive camping for land travelers and boaters.

The Narrows Lock #35 marked the high point on the Rideau Canal. From there to Kingston it was downhill. This section of the Rideau was very glaciated and there were numerous small islands tufted with conifers and cottages. Narrow channels with random boulders and granite slides made by glaciers creates both treachery and stunning beauty.

At Chaffey's Lock we had dinner at the 1920's Opinicon Lodge, a stately old wooden resort with sagging porches and wicker furniture. White tables with rose patterned table cloths and sturdy high backed chairs graced the dining room. The food was simple, plentiful and tasty.

The landscape became more glaciated with granite drumlins and barren islands as we moved toward Kingston. On other islands, cottages sat amongst pine and hardwoods. The canal curled through narrow cuts, into nestled coves, and around a thousand small islands. We were so close to the cottages, it felt like a ride through the neighborhood. For the moment the weed problem was over.

At Jones Falls, docents live the life of pioneers and give talks about past times from the journals kept by early settlers. The highest dam in North America in 1831 was constructed here of hand cut limestone block by Colonel By and the Rideau Canal builders. The block was quarried 60 miles away at Elgin and transported to the site.

Locking down was easier than locking up. Eva handed off our lines to the lock master, who passed it through the lock's cables and back to her. We were still missing our extra crew members for the locking tasks. When people left after crewing with us for awhile, we asked ourselves whether we'd be able to handle the boat with just the two of us. Of course we did.

As we neared Kingston, the glaciated landscape of the Canadian shield evolved into more productive farmlands of southern Ontario. The ground

The locks of the Rideau Canal are operated by hand.

Eva has bow watch duty as we work our way around the islands on the lower Rideau Waterway.

was muddy, the landscape more agricultural and practical. The water changed from clear to silty and the weed problem became acute again.

At Kingston Mills there was a series of flight locks, four locks one right after the other. The locking crew had to shut the sluice gates that drain the upper locks into the lower locks, but in one of the locks they forgot to do this. As the lock we were in emptied, water from the lock above rushed in to replace the exiting water, creating tremendous turbulence. A pontoon houseboat locking through with us, got free and drifted across the lock, bumping into us. The lock hands shouted excitedly and discovered the unclosed gate. We exchanged names and phone numbers and thought about an insurance claim but the damage was so small, we opted not to do anything.

It was a short ride into Kingston, a fine town with a wonderful waterfront marina and city park and a 19th century contender for Canada's national capital. Many New York residents scoot across the St. Lawrence for a visit to Kingston, a distance of less than five miles. North of Kingston on the St. Lawrence is the 10,000 island area, a summer playground for Canadians and Americans.

CHAPTER 13

THE TRENT-SEVERN WATERWAY

They were celebrating Canada Day (July 1st) in Kingston while we were there, and there was a parade through town led by some of Canada's favorite sons—hockey players, actors and politicians. Dan Ackroid, the actor, led a Harley Davidson motorcade. It was fine assortment of throbbing, rattling and snarling Harleys in full dress. Each "Hell's Angel" had a honey on the back who didn't look anything like my wife, my sister or the girl next door. Ackroid wore a baseball cap backwards like a 14-year old and had his own buxom babe on the back of his bike.

Of course, the celebs gave speeches. The hockey player mumbled something about how he gave up his teeth for Canada and he hoped all the kids in the audience would find the same nobility of purpose to do the same. (Since Wayne Gretsky defected to Los Angeles, they consider hockey players their principal export.) Ackroid gave an imitation of former Prime Minister Trudeau, and then became as serious as a television preacher, calling for pride in Canada and love for the Francophones of Quebec who are always toying with the idea of a divorce from Canada. The audience sang the Canadian national anthem like a hymn while munching popcorn and looking around, and we all fell asleep standing up.

It was such a sharp contrast to **our** national anthem and the way we sing it, that I would say it's the principal difference between the two countries. The Canadians are soft and sensible, the Americans strident and vulgar. We sing our national anthem drinking beer and eating hot dogs. We crescendo to the jugular-bursting verses like..."the ROCKETS RED GLARE, THE BOMBS BURSTING IN AIR...OE'R THE RAMPARTS WE WATCHED WERE SO GALLANTLY STREAMING...FROM THE

LAND OF THE FREEEEE, AND THE HOME OF THE BRAVE. YAAAAYYY. PLAY BALL." Now, how can you sleep through that?

A three-day bass tournament was in full swing while we were in Kingston. One of the dock hands told me about it. He said some of the biggest names in sport fishing were going to be there. "*Really* big names!" he repeated.

"Who?" I felt compelled to ask, and he rattled off names I had never heard of. I muttered to myself, "Where have you been? You are soooo narrow."

The fishermen were all coming in from the first day's fishing on Lake Ontario. There must have been a hundred Ranger bass boats with engines big enough to push QE2. They brought their live fish in a large plastic bag full of water, then emptied the water and fish in a laundry basket and weighed the fish. After the weigh-in, the handlers placed the fish in a recovery tank and released them back in the lake. Whoever had the heaviest, biggest catch of six fish, or the heaviest single fish, won prizes. Small and large mouth bass were running to seven pounds. The purse was about $80,000. Professionals and amateurs were paired together with the purse going to the pro. The amateur learned from the pro. It was fascinating.

At 7 a.m. each morning, they assembled, signed in and were off, their boats throwing huge rooster tails as they scooted to their favorite fishing holes and reedy shores. They returned each afternoon around 4 p.m. for the weigh-in.

We left Kingston for the Lake Ontario run to Trenton and the beginning of our Trent-Severn Waterway tour. There are a number of large islands in Lake Ontario's Bay of Quinte and as we made our way westward, we ducked behind them for protection. It was a comfortable ride and by nightfall we reached a bay close to Belleville that was too pretty to pass so we dropped the hook. Eva made sole with a Béarnaise sauce over wild rice and we had another lovely moment on the water, eating on the aft deck in the twilight's last gleaming. I took my bride for a little dinghy ride during the afterglow and spent a peaceful night on the hook.

The next morning we rose late after nearly all the other boats had left and made the short run to Trenton where Laura and Tim were going to join us. It was a perfect day of warm temperatures, bright sky and gentle winds. We found Fraser Park Marina and I changed the oil on the diesels while Eva did a little house cleaning in preparation for our guests. We bought groceries, did laundry and were sitting on the back deck in the evening having a margarita when Laura and Tim arrived. We showed them through the boat, got their luggage aboard, ate out at Micky's and parked their car across the river.

The next day we passed through 17 locks, a good breaking-in exercise for our new crew. The Trent-Severn Waterway is a combination of lakes, marshes and rivers built between 1858 -1920 to open the interior of Ontario and provide a short cut between Lake Ontario and Lake Huron. Lumber was the chief export and cruising steamers brought cottagers to the interior. By the time it was finished, roads and railways usurped waterway travel and the Trent-Severn became another Canadian Parks Heritage Waterway; and so it remains, operating during the summer season and closing on their Thanksgiving Day, during the first week of October.

After completing the 45 locks of the Rideau River alone, Eva and I had a routine, but now we had help. Laura womanned the bow line and Tim manned the stern, while Eva caught the mid-ship's line and stopped and started the engines. I sat at the helm watching the crew and taking pictures. We were good. The lock masters, who are accustomed to inexperienced boaters who rent houseboats and cruisers on the Trent-Severn, remarked how cool we were and were pleased to see us staying out of the way while clumsy boats and excited captains bumped their borrowed boats against the doors and walls of the locks.

Originally there were 45 locks in the Trent-Severn Waterway; now there are 44, and 43 of those are on the direct route through the waterway from Trenton to Port Severn.

We traveled though Murray Marsh, an extensive wetlands downstream of Percy Reach. This protected marsh is one of the largest and most important estuaries for fish and migratory waterfowl in Canada. At Percy Reach we read about a parallel walking/bicycle trail north to the next lock so Laura and Tim took down the bikes and rode along the trail while we cruised and met them there and put the bikes back on the boat. I think that was enough of that.

As we progressed north through the Trent-Severn, we moved from the lowlands of mud, weed and glacial alluvia, to the clear waters of the Canadian Shield, the granite and limestone bedrock of Canada. The water is clear and ideal for swimming and recreation. Small drumlins dot the waterway, sometimes only big enough for a single cottage and a few trees. Some islands are barren, some large with pines and firs growing in the humus of depressions. Blueberries grow in bushy swales on the granite islands, and white cedars and pines thrive on the limestone outcroppings.

Laura and Tim were away from their two kids for the first time in five years and they were behaving like teenage lovers. Between line-tending at the locks, they would nuzzle and hang on each other in a state of oblivion. The amused lockmaster was afraid of a conjugal conflagration and announced over the loudspeaker, "Maybe we ought to turn a hose on that couple to cool them off." Dauntless and giggling, they continued unashamedly.

We approached the Peterborough hydraulic lift lock, the highest lock in the world when it was built in 1904. It carries boats in one of two tubs to the next level in the Otonabee River on the Trent-Severn Waterway. A lock worker was waiting for us and the chamber on the right was down and ready to be loaded, so we drove the boat into the chamber like we did at other locks, tied *Genie* to the bollards and a gate raised to make us a closed container. When everything was secure, our tub began to rise and the one on the left of equal size but with one more foot of water descended, driving us upward by way of a huge hydraulic ram. It was like a giant seesaw, the heavier one lifting the lighter one. It was marvelously scary. Thirteen tons of boat, four people and 3,400,000 pounds (425,000 gallons) went for a carnival ride.

When we reached the top, we overlooked the city of Peterborough. Behind us was 65 feet of free fall and ahead lay the continuation of the watercourse, as ordinary as any river shoreline. We made supper at the top of the Peterborough Lock, then walked the streets looking for ice cream, ending at a ball field where a softball game was in progress.

At the end of the next day we arrived at Lovesick Lock, one of the prettiest locks in the system. Boat campers were enjoying the hot summer weather along the lock and were swimming and preparing supper over smoky grills. We went through the lock, docked on the uphill side, got into our swimsuits and played like kids.

After supper we stoked the Wizard for a ride in the dinghy, plying the waters between small islands and reedy coves while the setting sun threw magenta rays across still water. We shut off the Wiz and listened. Bull frogs thrummed, fish jumped and a great blue heron stood as still as a lawn ornament. It was creation before the time of man and boats.

We started the air-cooled Wiz again and putted until it began to smell like a dirty oven. I thought the little guy was burning itself up pushing us four mammals around, so I shut it off (again) and paddled home for more ice cream and cookies on the aft deck.

The Gallery on the Lake, an art gallery near Buckhorn, is located along the watercourse and we stopped mid-morning to browse. We didn't trundle

At Buckhorn we stopped at the Gallery on the Lake for objects d'art.

off any art treasures but it gave us an opportunity to see the works of some of Canada's notable artists.

On the way toward Bobcaygeon, Tim helped me play with the trim tabs while Eva and Laura ran the boat. They called down to us that the boat had slowed down to 4 knots, but the engine speed was the same, so I went to the upper helm to see what was going on. I slowed the boat, put it in reverse and blew-off a tangle of weeds. Putting it back into forward gave us our usual speed of 7.5 knots.

We came into Bobcaygeon, one of the oldest locks in the system which was where Eva's dream began four year before. Summer boaters were everywhere and cookouts were in full gear. There are many boats tied up to the walls and near the locks in the Trent-Severn, and many folks boat camp. They drive their boats to small towns on the canal, stay overnight at the locks where they can swim and cookout, and walk the town for ice cream.

Every region of Canada and the U.S. has their own favorite ice cream, the dairy equivalent of brew pubs, and for Bobcaygeon it's the Kawartha Lakes Dairy. It's reassuring to see dairy stores where milk and ice cream are sold and the place has the musky odor of souring milk, an odor I find as intoxicating as mating pheromone. My mouth waters and I have a rutting experience similar to being near chocolate. We all bought small, which at Kawartha Lakes Creamery is family size, went outside in the hot summer sun and licked and swirled our cones in a frantic effort to keep the ice cream from running over the cone and through our fingers. Despite gallant efforts we were messy and sticky and had to go back inside for water to rinse.

We took Laura and Tim back to Trenton with a rental car that was delivered to us from the town of Lindsay, and they jumped in the Saab for the ride home to Chicago. When we got back to the boat we discovered we had head problems again. The electric head was inoperable and the forward, manual head had a broken spring on the foot pedal. I spent all day Saturday trying to find a suitable replacement spring for the forward head and a source for a new electric macerator for the aft head. I found a spring at a lawn mower shop, and ordered a new electric macerator at a nearby marina, to be delivered in a few days to a marina near Orillia, which was on our way.

After a hot day in the heads I decided to go for a swim. A group of teenagers across the canal were horsing around and they threw one of the girls, fully clothed, into the canal. I observed her swimming along the edge of the canal grasping for a handhold like a dog in a swimming pool. There were no ladders nearby and I wasn't sure she was strong enough to stay in the water until she found a ladder. Her friends, meanwhile, had walked away from the edge of the canal where they could no longer see or hear her. I swam toward her in the event she needed some assistance. The lockmaster saw the two of us swimming in the canal's shipping lane and ordered us out. I tried to explain the situation, whereby he chastised the kids and told them that throwing damsels into the canal during the summer months was forbidden. Fall and winter was fine.

Boat traffic ceased and three young boys from a nearby boat paddled in the canal near our boat. They wanted to know where I was from and how we had arrived from Philadelphia (the name of the hailing port on the transom of our boat) to Canada, so while I treaded water and they floated with their buoyant tubes, we talked about rivers and locks and the Intracoastal Waterway. They were fascinated with the notion of living on a boat for a year and I was entertained by their playful curiosity.

A thunderstorm approached and rain fell. Outdoor fires sizzled, kids ran to the security of their boats, families disappeared beneath roll-up canvas on convertible boats and the canal was transformed instantly from noisy summer fun to the quiet of fall. The rain continued until nightfall and cool weather came.

We walked to the neighborhood United Church of Canada in

Bobcaygeon on Sunday morning. Their circuit rider pastor strolled in mid-service as unobtrusively as he could, but a coal-black man in a white gown is hard not to notice. In his Jamaican accent the black shepherd led the white flock.

By the time we were ready to leave Bobcaygeon, a parade of bag pipers came through town in a salute to the veterans of Canada. It was a short ride to locks 33 and 34 at Fenelon Falls where Eva's sister, Cora, and friend, Eric, were to join us after a 1300 mile car ride from South Dakota. We tied below the lock where there was a fine park and great views of the falls. By nightfall we began to plant signs around the locks to direct them to our boat and at 10:30 p.m. they were knocking on our door.

The next day we quickly introduced our new crew to the task of boat handling as we went through the locks with an assortment of other boats. Later that day we approached the high point in the canal system, the 1907 Kirkfield lift lock. Like the Peterborough lift lock we entered a chamber, tied up, and (in this case) dropped 49 feet to the next river level.

Eric was a member of the CIA, the Culinary Institute of America, and lives to cook. He watched me prepare supper and under his tutelage we created Chicken Provencal served over rice accompanied by a good bottle of wine (Gallo Rhine, $7.99/gal.). In the days following, Eric turned the galley into a French kitchen, creating things most of us couldn't or wouldn't

Eric, Eva and Cora review the excitement of dropping 49-feet in the water-filled chambers at the Kirkfield Hydraulic Lift Lock.

do in our home kitchens. On the streets he was like Garfield the cat, sniffing and looking, and if, perchance, he found a fresh fish store, he lingered, with images of fish dishes dancing in his head. Inevitably he bought something that became "gourmet cuisine" for our table. If I could choose between a good deck hand and a skilled chef, I'd go for the chef. He turned our nights into gastronomic revelry and we couldn't wait to stop traveling when Eric was preparing the evening meal.

A troop of Boy Scouts joined us near the Gamebridge lock. They put in upstream and were taking out near the lock at a campsite. They stopped short of the lock and almost made it to shore, but the temptation to swim, horse around, sink fellow canoeists and commit aquatic mayhem overwhelmed them. Soon the water was thrashing with demonic scouts gone berserk on the intoxication of cool, clean water. We got out of there.

There's a wonderful romance to farmland in summer. The sweet perfume of hay and grass and the breath of living things is exhilarating.

At the breakwater near Lake Simcoe while Eric was sweating it out in the galley, Eva and I took a walk along the waterway. A boy named Matthew (another one of these kids—Canada has a raft of them) was jumping off the sides and swimming in the canal. We talked and I began coaching him on diving into the canal instead of jumping. "Get your suit on and show me," he said innocently.

So I said, "Well, okay, I guess I can do that."

The day was hot and since it would be a while before dinner was ready, we got our suits on, met *The Kid*, and began doing dives and flips off the side of the canal. We went from straight dives to jack knives, swan dives and forward and backward somersaults. Cora and Eva began to rate each dive on a scale of 1 to 10. 'Course they let the kid win. Then *Kid* and I swam across the canal several times until he said in the middle, "I'm really getting tired."

So was I, especially if I was going to have to save him, so we quit and *Kid* asked if he could see our boat. He poked in all the closets and opened the hatches, and then dispassionately said, "See ya," and joined his dad who was fishing and who was probably glad to loan out his son for an hour so he wouldn't have to answer all the questions an 8 year-old boy asks. I thought again of kidnapping a boy, but his father seemed to love him, so we let him go. Thanks to the *Kid*, I got a gimpy shoulder from doing all the athletic show-offy things, and neither heat nor cold nor aspirin would make it go away.

Eric's culinary talents were richly demonstrated that evening at dinner. He prepared consommé and an assortment of hors d'oeuvres which, in my faulty memory included such things as artichoke hearts, tiny sardines fried in batter, marinated mushrooms, baby calamari, small onions in a fresh tomato sauce and cold mussels. Then the main meal came—rosy slices of lamb cooked with whole cloves of garlic and a golden potato and onion galette. The finale was a puffy, light-as-a-cloud dessert soufflé topped with fresh berries. My interpretation may be a bit overstated, but I do recall vividly the galley being a mess because it was our turn to clean-up.

While we slept, we had a million visitors. Mayflies, who spend most of their life in water, save for a day or two when they mate and lay eggs, decided to spend their nuptial hours on our boat. Transparent winged creatures with long tail spikes clustered in the thousands, making *Genie* look pretty and lacy; but they defecated and died in place leaving the boat a nightmare of dead bodies and poop that didn't come off.

The passage through Lake Simcoe was uneventful with us each taking turns playing Captain. We stopped at the marina on the other side to pick up and install the new macerator kit in the aft head. Then we went on to the Port of Orillia town dock for the night. The galley needed to be restocked after Chef Eric's culinary delights and we heard that there were grocery stores within walking distance of the dock.

There was a blood-curdling cry as I was eating breakfast in Orillia. "Ron, there's no water!" I had just installed the new macerator in the aft head, and now there was another problem with the water pump. Eva was showering, and was fully lathered and ready to rinse. The dastardly little piston pump found another critical moment to default. Bolting from my place at the table with cereal and milk dribbling from my chin, I dropped into the engine room to take a look at the troublesome little wretch. Faulty pressure switch, I presumed. I gave Eva the analysis and encouraged her to finish her shower at the marina while I did some further testing.

We walked to town later that morning, and voila, a marina had a replacement switch for the Groco pump. Only $53. "I'll take it," I said. I used to think $53 for a little switch was robbery, here I was grateful. Figure it out. It was the first time in boating history that a boat part broke in front of a marina that had the part.

Three hours later we were on our way through Sparrow Lake and the deepest conventional lift lock in the system, 47 feet, at Swift Rapids. This area was a dreamland of vacation cottages, granite islands and woods. The river winds and twists with bays and narrows and fascinating views. I want to live here (but only in the summer).

"Fred, watch out! There are four boats crossing the road on some kind of weird contraption."

By 6 p.m. we arrived at the Big Chute Marine Railway. The carriage was making its last run of the day with boats shackled to the carriage and hung in slings like creatures going to the aquarium. The huge four-wheeled contraption drove over the hill to the other side where it rolled into the water and set all the little fishes free again.

The carriage is driven by cables and runs along rails that are offset to keep it level throughout the run across the hill and down the steep incline to the water. In the morning we took our turn. It is large enough to hold several small boats, but we had it all to ourselves because of our size and the weather.

The carriage rolled into the water, we slid into the harnesses, got lifted out of the water, drove past the observers deck where everyone saw our bottom—rudders like udders shamelessly exposed, our props dripping and still, the whole of us exposed to the comments of passersby who were eager to give us an account of our ship's derriere. It was the feeling you have when the nurse comes in and asks you to take your clothes off and don one of those "open to the public" hospital gowns.

After that there was only one more lock in the Trent-Severn Waterway, the lock at Port Severn, the 115th lock that we passed through since we left Florida in February. The security of an inland waterway system was giving way to the uncertainty of cruising the Great Lakes.

CHAPTER 14

GEORGIAN BAY TO DE TOUR VILLAGE

We left the Trent-Severn Waterway at Port Severn and entered Lake Huron's Georgian Bay, an inland "sea" of 30,000 islands. For the next five weeks we would be in the waters of the Great Lakes—deep, windswept and threatening, but immensely charming and scenic and some of the best fishing anywhere along our route. Not that we were fishermen, we weren't, but fresh fish and wild blueberries became staples of our diet.

Georgian Bay is a nursery of granite islands, some no bigger than a whale. We were uptight when entering large bodies of water, and even though the open water of Georgian Bay is broken by barrier islands, it is part of Lake Huron and we were apprehensive. From there until we entered the Chicago River at the end of Lake Michigan, we were in bodies of water the size of small oceans.

The day was calm, the sea molten, reflecting myriad humpback forms emerging through the surface. We peered through the mist to numerous buoys that outlined the course. The brown, rounded boulders protruded from the water like potatoes in a pot and were aptly named the Potato Islands. It was a poke of granite 'taters waiting to bend a prop. The markers were so numerous it was difficult to see a pathway through them. In one instance, the route turned sharply right, nearly turning back on itself. Eva was at the charts with her nails on the buoys and I was calling them out as we picked our way through the peck.

In our confusion, we missed a green marker and were off the route in weedy shallows when a local boater pulled alongside and volunteered to lead us through the maze. The water was crystal clear, the bottom hard as granite and the only thing greater than their beauty was the threat to our hull if we ran aground.

Beausoliel Island is one of the largest islands in the Georgian Bay National Park. We came in at the main dock (Parks Canada Dock) after most of the runabouts had settled in and were sending dinner smoke signals into the air. Seeing our approach, they dropped their tongs and grabbed our lines. Without complaint and with unexpected cheerfulness, the little-boat people made room for the cruiser that overwhelmed their view and disrupted their peace.

We hiked to the visitor's center, got educated about the natural features of Georgian Bay Islands and walked the Firetower Trail. The path led over open slopes, boggy bottom lands and through dark woods. Regular ferry service from Honey Harbor brings campers to the island, and the Cedar Springs Campground was a city of tents, kids, outdoor fires and leashed dogs.

The boaters were friendly and offered advice and warnings when we told them that we were headed toward Pointe Au Baril. "The cottagers don't like transients to muddy their waters," they said. One boater gave us a detailed chart of the Pointe Au Baril area, along with his address so we could mail it back to him when we were finished—an act of simple faith and unexpected kindness.

Returning to the boat we stoked the outboard and cruised in the dinghy to neighboring bays and glaciated shorelines. Lazy summer vacationers lounged, motionless in sculpted boulders that fit the contour of their resting bodies, soaking up the scenery and listening to the sounds of quietly lapping water. Summer is a wink of time in these parts of Canada; soon it returns to the ice age of winter months.

The next morning we left for Honey Harbor and had a dickens of a time docking at Admiral's Marina. The long dock parallel to the channel was anchored so loosely that waves created by passing boats set the thing in motion like a giant snake. I was not aware of this until we made our approach. The dock hands were ready to receive our lines but I could see from their faces that something wasn't right; then they were running toward the back of the boat. A backwards glance showed me that the snaking dock was about to whack us, and the dockhands were preparing to push us off. I was embarrassed and felt like a novice. The chained sections of the dock rattled and bucked and sent the whole dock whipping back and forth. Walking was uneasy and the evening was rough and noisy with the passing of boats who callously snubbed the *No Wake* zone. Even early morning boaters blasted through the channel with nary a thought about the boats tied to the dock at Honey Harbor.

The next morning we changed crew when Cora and Eric left us. Eva's sister, Lelia, volunteered to bring mother, Mary, age 85, and Aunt Audrey, 82, from South Dakota to be with us for a spell, and there they were at 9 a.m., smiling, eager and ready to go. They hung onto each other as the snaking dock gyrated and snapped.

These were not your average "ripe" ladies; these were late-life adventurers who drive the country like truckers. They were game for everything, which included running the boat and helping with the chores. When things got slow they'd sit on the aft deck and play cards. It was another portrait at sea, three of us at the upper helm reading the charts and pointing to scenic wonders while the two mellow mothers on the aft deck slouched in their chairs as they scanned their cards, barked out bids and swept their cards off the table. I thought about stringing lights across the roof and putting a faux paddle wheel on the back. *Dream O' Genie* had become a floating casino.

The following day at noon we searched for a place to have lunch. The charts showed a number of picnic islands in the provincial park islands of Georgian Bay so we ventured off the route and headed into a narrow channel to a small dock with on-shore picnic facilities. But these are popular stopping places for recreational boaters and the site was already occupied, so we sounded our way into a quiet cove, dropped the anchor and had a wonderful respite among the small granite islands.

Later in the day I was below deck doing something and Eva, Lelia and the two wintry widows were running the boat. Mary was at the wheel trying to stay within the buoys when several boaters went by and saw the four ladies from Philadelphia (our hailing port) running the boat. They thought that was great and said amongst themselves, "Look at that cruiser with four women on the bridge. The *captain* has to be the age of my *mother*!"

We met them later at Fryingpan Island. I was at the helm this time and as they took our lines they said to me, "Where did *you* come from? We saw your boat earlier in the day and there were four *women* on the bridge. We thought how neat it was that four women, a long way from home, were cruising Georgian Bay. But now we see that you're aboard."

World Famous Henry's Fish Restaurant on Fryingpan Island is considered one of the island hot spots in these parts. That's pure hyperbole, but for $15 we got docking, water, electricity and a continental breakfast. Of course, we also had the opportunity to eat from Henry's table, a pine board banquet in a screened cottage laden with the treasures of the deep. Henry Lepage is a commercial fisherman who serves fresh Lake Huron pickerel, whitefish and perch in his "World Famous" restaurant.

Henry's grandchildren run the docks and take the lines of boats coming in. His 12 year-old granddaughter, Juliann, was dockmaster and dictated to the boat captains where to dock and how to tie. There was no discussion, and if you tied the lines yourself, she'd come back and redo them, letting you know you were going to do it her way, or you don't stay. We heard Grandpa paid her $30/day for her dock work. When she becomes the dictator of a small maritime country, we'll remember her teenage years on Fryingpan Island. We suspect that their battered pickerel passes through her hands before it hits the pan.

Henry's stays open all year and in the winter visitors make the run across the ice using a Scoot, an air boat with pontoons designed for use on thin ice.

After dinner at Henry's, the platinum persons and I went for a walk in the blueberry patches behind Henry's and picked a few. The island has only had life on it for 10,000 years (since the last ice age) and there isn't much soil for the mosses, lichens and blueberries. The silver foxes showed more of that willingness to experience it all and had little trouble negotiating the terrain. Audrey picked a bouquet of wild flowers and a sprig of blueberries for the boat. Meanwhile, Eva and Lelia were in the thickets collecting blueberries by the bowls-full for our morning breakfast.

After a brief stop at Parry Sound, we arrived at the home of Harry and Margaret Marwood. We met them in Elizabeth City, North Carolina, several months before and traveled throughout the Chesapeake together, but they were anxious to get home so moved faster than we did. When we separated, they invited us to dock at their home which is off the small craft channel near Kilbear Provincial Park. *Phoebe*, the all steel trawler that Harry converted to pleasure craft, complete with wood burning stove, was at the dock. They expected us and were on the pier for their afternoon swim as we came into view. Harry got on his boat's radio and brought us in.

We walked the woods, bicycled through the nearby provincial park, and in the evening went for a ride on their boat with the two senior-itas sitting on the bow and the rest of us on pillows in front of the helm. Margaret prepared tea and a tin of homemade cookies and Harry gave us a tour of his neighborhood, plying the waters under a sherbet-colored sky. Harry knew the waters of Georgian Bay in the area of Parry Sound from his childhood and took great delight in scaring the pants off us by skimming rocks and getting off the course and beyond the buoys. We ventured into channels suitable only for canoes and kayaks; he skirted great boulders and left the helm to talk to us on the bow leaving the boat to figure out things for itself. He wormed his way through uncharted channels near Snug Harbor and showed us the family cottage. A full moon rose, daylight dimmed, and when we docked back at their home we were welcomed by a party of three million mosquitoes who made our steps light and quick. In no time at all we were in Harry and Margaret's kitchen having ice cream and blueberries.

At midnight we had a beautiful light display which quickly evolved into screaming winds and torrential rains. Harry looked from the distance of his home as the five of us sleeping on *Genie* caught the full impact of waves and winds. The trees leaned and groaned. Eva and I went out in our pajamas checking lines and making our position secure. Our two long-lived ladies were getting the ride of their lives and in the morning their hair was white as snow.

The following day Lelia and the two octogenarians made the cross-country trek back to "the little town on the prairie," De Smet, South Dakota. Eva and I were alone again. We said, "good-bye," to Harry and Margaret and headed westward through Georgian Bay.

The Ojibway Hotel is in the middle of cottage country. It's a grand old place built in 1906 for city folks who took the train from the big cities of Ohio and Michigan to Pointe Au Baril Station and then rode the launch to the hotel. Sepia photographs that decorate the walls of the hotel show women in long skirts and men in spats, awkwardly formal in this natural environment. In later years roads were built, automobiles came, individual cottages were built and the trains stopped. Eventually, the hotel was forgotten, and neglected, then closed in the 1960's.

The islanders, seeing their cultural center decaying and boarded up, bought it from the original owner, cherished it back to health, and made it again the center of their summer life. Cottage kids are now the staff, and most of the program revolves around them and their families. Every youngster has a title and a function—canoe trainer, assistant canoe trainer, helper canoe trainer, canoe student. For many teenagers, this is their first job, and with seniority they assume higher ranks, rising to ethereal heights such as general store clerk and gift shop attendant.

We were warned that cottagers around the Ojibway Hotel and Pointe Au Baril are clannish and hostile to transient boaters but we were curious and risked our alien status for a closer look

The dock was alive with runabouts bringing kids to programs, buying provisions, picking up mail, attending meetings and shuttling tennis players. We docked *Dream O' Genie* between the runabouts and capitalized most of the long finger pier, making our presence overwhelming and giving the cottagers rightful cause for intolerance. Instead, we found helpful folks willing to take our lines and move their boats. We walked the stairs to the porch of the hotel, licked ice cream cones, and observed the comings and goings of boats like bees working a hive.

The line of travel is extremely tight and treacherous through the islands of Georgian Bay. At Nares Inlet, we turned 90 degrees right to pick up a range, maneuvered through Shoal Narrows, then 90 degrees left through a maze of markers. At Hangdog Reef we turned 135 degrees with water lapping rocks close-by on either side to squeeze through Hangdog Channel.

The water is so clear that every rock can be seen. Islanders drink the water from the bay without processing and boaters are admonished to take great care with their waste. When we stopped behind a group of islands in an anchorage near Bayfield Inlet, "Mrs. Scrooge" stood on a prominent rock motioning with hand and arm signals un-befitting a lady, which we took to mean, "We don't want transient riffraff parking outside our cottage." We were warned about this and I wondered if we would receive a visit or a midnight buzzing from a high speed boat.

The weather was rotten and we had no home except for this sheltered cove, so despite the message, we stayed and spent the night and the next day, bobbing on waves and holing-up inside to write and pass a rainy summer day in July.

I was at the computer late in the afternoon when we heard an outboard motor next to our boat and a voice call out, "Hello. Anybody home?" Eva tentatively stuck her head outside, waiting to catch heck from somebody with a bad attitude, but a smiling voice called up, "You've been sitting out here all day, and we thought maybe you'd like to have tea with us." She stammered some kind of surprise response and we got ready to go ashore.

We had heard of unfriendly cottagers and experienced one of them first hand, but here was a couple going out of their way to welcome us. We donned our rain gear and dropped the dinghy for an afternoon on land in a house where everything was solid and stable and a real retreat from bad weather. Arnie and Marcie McCallum met us at the dock and led us over smooth granite boulders toward the cottage. They had brought in enough humus to create soil in the cracks of the sloping glacial granite where brown-eyed Susans, tiger lilies, phlox and ornamental grasses grew. Boardwalks spanned the chasms and led to an A-frame cottage with a large screened porch facing the water. Tea was served, the stories of our lives told and a new relationship established.

When the weather lifted we walked the island and met their neighbors and spent an aimless afternoon basking in the friendship of "the enemy." Eva and I separated ourselves from the incubation of land, homes and friends to make supper back on the boat in the cove.

"Why don't I make a pineapple upside-down cake?" Eva said, "We can invite the McCallums for dessert." I returned to McCallum's cottage with an invitation for dessert on *Dream O'Genie,* and with raised forks, we toasted our friendship, upside-down cake, clean water and peace between cottagers and cruising boaters.

In the Alexander Passage of Georgian Bay we were one of many boats traveling west toward the North Channel of Lake Huron. Part of the small craft channel took us beyond the barrier islands and exposed us to Georgian Bay's long fetch. Three foot seas were on the beam and against the transom. We either rolled right to left, or wallowed in a confusion of forces that left *Genie* adjusting constantly to the changing forces. The course varied from wide rivers to canals, wound among small islands, then went back out again to open water. We disliked the exposed sections but we realized that this is the way it was going to be until we got into the Chicago River at the southern end of Lake Michigan. After nearly six months on the water we thought our anxiety level would subside, but my basic insecurity and the imagination of things that could go wrong kept me uptight, while Eva became more relaxed. She had more confidence in my ability to handle the boat than I did. A near drowning experience when I was a 10 year-old was probably the skeleton in the closet that made me tight-lipped every time the surf was up and I couldn't see the shoreline.

Boaters, both power and sail, are brave and adventurous to be on the Great Lakes. We heard many stories of extreme weather, capsizings and death, yet many venture into the North Channel for the unexcelled experience of anchoring among islands in protected coves.

Fox and Puddick Islands stretch from north to south like long fingers, probably the result of glaciation. Winds were kicking up a chop on the bay so we debated going through open water to the Bustard Islands as planned or taking the more protected alternate route through Dores Run near the Eastern Outlet of the French River. This course required going through Parting Channel. The guidebooks suggested that only boats under 40-feet use this channel, and then only in calm weather. We were 40-feet and the weather was not stable. Eva was waffling. I said, "It sounds like a challenge, Toots. Let's go for it."

Parting Channel is the tightest, trickiest, most treacherous channel we ever encountered—even worse than Hangdog Channel. It was hidden by a bluff and wasn't in view until we turned the corner. A right turn took us into an extremely narrow channel bordered by stone cliffs. A huge boulder island stood smack in the middle. "Oh, Lord, send all the other boats another way," I muttered. "There is not room for two of us. There's hardly room for one."

A red buoy marked the safe water on one side and a green buoy marked the other side; they were spaced so closely together that I was sure our beam was too wide to fit between them. It seemed impossible to negotiate, but there was no turning around...or backing up. Mindful that only the V-shape of the hull was in the water, we sliced the buoys and slid *Genie*'s hull between the slot in the rocks. This required a hard left, inch forward a few feet, then a hard right turn, forward a few feet to pass the boulder, then a hard right followed by another hard left. Each turn demanded a turntable maneuver with no lateral movement. We made it, gave high-five's and slid into a lovely secluded anchorage where we dropped the hook with four other boats (who probably came by a different route, and had no fun at all). We were so intent in making safe passage, neither of us thought to grab a camera to record the moment.

At our anchorage near the Eastern Outlet of the French River my true love said to me, "Honey, let's get a sailboat." Yikes.

We lowered the dinghy and stoked the Wiz for a ride upstream to a small waterfall and wooden walkway that led to a home in the hills above. The walkway was in such good condition that we were convinced cottagers probably brought in provisions by boat and carried them up the hills with carts. Pulling the dinghy to shore and walking the rocks above the falls we clearly saw the cottage, or rather a village of frame houses. Some were in good condition and one of them was furnished with decaying furniture and signs of recent habitation. It looked like our son's room when he was living at home, but it was obviously used by hunters and fishermen. A note on the table welcomed anyone who wanted to stay for awhile. We walked the board walks that connected one cottage to the next. We guessed this was a logging camp when Canada cut its primary forests at the turn of the century.

There was still time to do some blueberry picking and we scrambled over rocks to thickets guarded by curtains of spider webs.

The next morning we left the isolated cove near the French River by way of an unobstructed route and made a run into the wide open waters of Georgian Bay. Stormy weather was again in the forecast but we thought we could make it to Killarney before the front approached. Purple-furrowed skies with hanging drapes of water were visible to the west. We watched it move toward us and we quickened our pace, which for a trawler used to 8 knots, was a gain of about two knots. As we approached Killarney we thought we had won the race, but the sky darkened and that beautiful veil of water reached us before we could make the mouth of the harbor. We hustled valuables downstairs, donned rain gear and caught the storm just as we neared the lighthouse. Our vision was reduced to fifty feet and winds swirled, carrying the rain against the boat. I slowed *Genie* to a stop, pointed her into the wind and used the lighthouse as our reference point. The radar helped us maintain a central position and see any other boats that might be on the water. Rain turned to hail until the foredeck was white and *Genie* got the cleaning of a lifetime. The canvas bimini sagged with the weight and we shivered with the expectation of a deluge if it should break. Eventually the storm passed and we made our way into town as people came off their boats and out of the shops to size up the weather.

It was just as well that we didn't reach Killarney. Many boats were milling about in the water before the storm, all vying for available marina slips. Normal boating courtesy takes a beating when safety from a storm is the overwhelming concern.

The tug at the fish market left for a short time and we tied at the wharf while we considered our next move. A cruiser at the public dock saw our dilemma and offered to let us raft to him, and later a sailboat rafted to us.

We bought provisions, filled the freezer with fresh fish, and headed for Covered Portage Cove, a lovely spot made unlovely by 38 other boats seeking paradise on the hook. The horseshoe-shaped bluffs gave the cove protection from all sides and everybody wanted to be there. Finding a place where each of us had swing room was a problem.

I was in bed and asleep when Eva did her final walk around the boat before retiring. She came to the bedside, "Ron, you've got to see this," she whispered excitedly. I stumbled out of bed and followed her to the foredeck. In the moonless dark were 39 boats in black space with anchor lights reflecting off the water like twinkling stars.

As it turned out, our rode was insufficient and our plow anchor was unable to fully penetrate the thick grassy bottom, but we held through the night. The next morning as we were preparing to leave, the wind came up and we drifted toward another boat before we were alerted.

We made our way into Baie Fine (pronounced Bay Fin), one of the few fjords in Canada, a narrow channel bounded by headlands. Our GPS indicated we were at 46 degrees latitude, the northernmost point on our odyssey. Okeechobee Lodge is at the mouth of the fjord and their sightseeing plane was getting ready to take patrons for an aerial view of the North Channel. I watched the plane as it preceded us into the fjord, then turn 180 degrees and head for us as it prepared for takeoff. I didn't cut the engines at first because I thought the pilot had the distance figured, but then became convinced he didn't. It roared toward us, a fearsome spectacle of grinding mouthparts and windsheared water. Pontoons danced nervously on the water and wings dipped from side to side as it struggled heavenward. In the time it takes to die of a head-on air crash, it lifted off, flashed its underbelly and furled our burgee.

At the end of Baie Fine there is a reflective pool, a perfect evening anchorage. A foot path on shore leads to Topaz Lake on top of a white marble mountain. Streams ran down the trail and we rock-jumped over rivulets and along a mountain trail to the lake in the woods. Campers had set up camp and smoke furled from the shore and over the water. From a ledge we saw *Genie* and other boats in the crook of the bay.

We reflected for a moment on the fun of boating. We were isolated from our land life, removed from the daily news of starving people and warring sects. Eva and I were having more time together in one year than some couples have in a marriage. Sure, there were times when she wanted to start the engines while I was in the water cleaning the props, and yes, there were times when I was tempted to troll her in a school of white sharks, but if it wasn't for her I'd be grounded in a minute or up some creek I thought was the main channel; and if she had to go it alone (without me) she'd know where she was going but she'd still be tied to a dock in Florida because she was too chicken to move. We needed each other and found a mutual dependence that deeply bonded us.

As we approached Little Current, the principal city of the island of Manitoulin, the 18-foot bridge (according to the chart) appeared to be too low for us to run under, so we hung out with a dozen other boats to wait the hour-on-the-hour opening. When the bridge was raised, the waiting boats made their way toward the docks which were full as overnighters had not left yet. We spotted an opening and I slowed so Eva could prepare our lines and fenders. We were close to the dock and treading water when a sailboat saw our situation and sped ahead to cut off our approach. Eva shouted and pointed to communicate our intentions while I interpreted this move as blatant opportunism. I made a decisive move to the dock, blocking his way. The sailboater cut his power and went into a tirade that included verbal denunciations and hand signals reserved for rush hour traffic motorists on Chicago's Dan Ryan Expressway. It was the first incident on our trip when boaters exhibited animosity and disregard for each other. Of course, we were innocent and the other guy was a bum. Years on the Dan Ryan taught me this.

It turned out that the dock we slid into was the fuel dock, so the cock fight was unnecessary. We were full of fuel, so we pumped out and headed back out to find another spot. A motoryacht offered to let us raft to him while we waited. We spent time in the town of Little Current and located a spot at the dock later in the afternoon. We shopped, did laundry, made phone calls and got ready for another extended stay away from land.

The following days were spent in and around Croker and Benjamin Islands. The North Channel is open and exposed along the northern coast of Manitoulin and bounded by the wilderness of Ontario's mainland. A few clusters of islands in this wide expanse are not only protection in stormy weather but are also a summer playground for the boaters of Michigan who get their summer fixes by laying at anchor in the protected coves. There are no marinas, docks or convenience stores. This is wilderness camping aboard a boat. Boaters pick a spot, drop anchor in 15 to 30 feet of water, back towards shore and tie to a tree or large rock with a line they carry ashore with a dinghy. The waters are uncharted and require visual inspection. A

We had never heard of boat camping, but many Michiganders get their summer camping fix on the Benjamin Islands in Canada's North Channel.

spotter on the bow hangs out and calls to the captain. No problem when the water is clear enough to drink.

When we arrived at South Benjamin Island, a dozen boats were anchored or tied to shore. Families clustered around smoky fires on shore and kids jumped off rocks into water in a scene right off the cover of a Canadian vacation brochure. We launched our dinghy and went ashore in swimsuits, picking blueberries until we were sweaty and strung with spider webs, then swam out to a huge rock a few inches below the surface. We watched sunsets from the aft deck, dinghied to neighboring islands and wiled away days of lazy living. The weather was warm and comfortable and we recuperated from days on the move when there were storms that frayed our nerves.

The big rock a few inches under water became a favorite swimming-to point for Eva, but one time she swam out to it and couldn't find it. I heard her call, "Ron, I can't find the rock. Where is it?"

I know that tone of voice. It's on the edge of hysteria and it drives me into action. I scanned the water from the shoreline. She was too far right, so I called back, "Go to your left, it's only a short ways off."

She swam as I watched, but still couldn't find it. "It's not here," she shouted, her anxiety level rising perceptibly.

By this time my adrenaline level was peaking and I dove in to help her find it, but I couldn't seem to find it either. In our excitement, closing in on panic, neither of us was able to locate it. "Take your time and swim slowly," I said. "We'll find it eventually."

But by this time she gave up and headed for shore like a retriever going for a duck. I followed a short distance behind hoping she would be all right, because in my exertion I was winded. She made it to shore fine, but the smooth, algae covered rocks prevented her from climbing ashore. The dinghy was tied to a rock on shore, so with a boost she reached the dinghy painter and scrambled like a crab onto the slick rock, then to dry ground and safety. We sat in the afternoon sun and breathed easy and drank the sweet rest of life on land safe from deep waters.

Eva had gone mad over blueberries and couldn't walk a foot on the granite islands before she was grazing. Purple knees, purple lips and purple fingers; she'd become a blueberry gourmand. She was getting her thrill on blueberry hill and often I wasn't even in sight.

On the last Sunday of July we were at the village of Kagawong on Manitoulin Island. We walked uphill from the dock past fields of Queen Anne's Lace and goldenrod to the United Church of Canada (circa 1881). The church was as pretty as country flowers, situated alone at the top of the hill. At 1:30 in the afternoon a circuit preacher visited Kagawong, the last church on her day's ride. An aged man sang a solo unaccompanied, the highlight of the service.

We took the village historic walk guided by a brochure which included the dates and trivia of everyone's home. To live there is to be part of the attraction. Many of these villages thrived when fishing was good and the climax forest was ripe for plundering. The lakes have been devastated by the lamprey eel which parasitized the lake trout, and all the trees are gone, so these shoreline villages of the north country survive on traveler's interests. Lake trout are still caught in limited numbers but Canadian and Michigan fisheries have transplanted rainbow trout, brown trout, large and small mouth bass and salmon. These fish populations are not self-perpetuating and it's an artificial system, but everyone is enjoying fish farming in a natural setting. The water is clear and clean, and sport fishers and cruising boaters love these waters and the charm of old towns along the shore.

The walk through Kagawong after church led us to the falls. Kids were swimming and standing under the waterfall, enjoying the skull-crushing force of water falling 40 feet. A walk into a cave behind the curtain of water is the bonus for those who get into the water, so we went back to the boat, got our swim suits and played like kids, trusting that logs or other objects wouldn't float down the river and make us numb-skulls.

Manitoulin Island is big enough to have its own inland lakes, streams and waterfalls; in fact, Manitoulin has more fresh water inland lakes than any other fresh water island in the world. Its only road connection to the mainland is the bridge at Little Current where the waters of the North Channel funnel through a restriction to Georgian Bay.

We heard the story of a family out cruising that ran aground and storms broke up their boat. The family donned life jackets, tied themselves together and waited to be rescued. The children died within hours from the chilling water, then the mother and another adult. Two persons survived and the boat was recovered a week later. The bow of the 26-foot Chris Craft is now a memorial pulpit in the tiny Anglican Church by the dock.

Gore Bay was one of the prettiest towns we visited on Manitoulin Island. We biked to the lighthouse at the end of the day and enjoyed the moody silence of this north woods cottage country. The morning brought northeast winds and half-meter waves in the channel according to Environment Canada, so we left the protection of the bay and quickly concluded that the forecast was not for this place. Three to five foot waves rolled in from the NE and hit us on the beam. *Genie* quickly became entrapped in a wave pattern that had us rolling from side to side. The aft deck furniture slid from one side to the other and we could hear the dishes in the galley cabinets shuffle and clank. While turning into the waves, we caught a giant wave that spun us towards shore. We had been hugging the shoreline, now we were headed right for it. Waves crashed on the rocks 400 feet ahead. I threw *Genie* into reverse and as soon as it was safe, turned her into the waves.

Eva shouted, "RON, THIS IS AWFUL. I CAN'T TAKE 32 MILES OF THIS. GO BACK!" I didn't need to be persuaded. But turning back to Gore Bay meant we had to run parallel to the incoming waves. We made it and got back to the protected water of the bay and our slip at the marina.

The rest of the day I sanded the teak rails with the palm sander and got them ready for successive coats of Cetol. This was a job I began in New York and continued whenever I could. The inverter which we added to the boat in Florida converted 12 volt DC to 110 AC allowing me to run electrical tools at anchorages or along the way when there were long stretches and Eva was running the boat.

At three o'clock in the afternoon, a boater came in and we asked how things were in the North Channel, expecting to hear them say that things were rough, but the captain said, "The channel is smooth as glass and the winds light and variable. The kids were even sitting on the bow for the last hour. But let me tell you, before that it was wild."

Within five minutes we untied our lines and made the run to Meldrum Bay, a pleasant trip that was a complete contrast to our tough morning start. We ran from point to point along Manitoulin Island leaving a long row of stern waves that made it to the shore and rolled beach stones. At 6:45 p.m. we passed the Vidal Wilderness Islands. Conifers created a steepled profile beyond a long exposed marsh. The long summer day gave us light until about 8:30 and we made it to Meldrum Bay before dark.

Meldrum Bay doesn't have much, and in the words of a young traveler making a telephone call home to her mother, "*There is nothing here!* Just one little store. Otherwise *there is nothing here.* It's advertised as having a bakery and grocery store, but *there is nothing here.* Oh, yeah, there is a hotel up the street, but other than that, Mom, *there is nothing here.*"

We sampled the fare at one of Meldrum Bay's restaurants, and had a poor meal that was *nothing.* We left *"nothing here"* and crossed Mississagi Straits which was choppy and unpleasant, passed Cockburn Island, and crossed False Detour Channel which we feared because of its southwesterly exposure, but it was a pussycat and we made it easily. Our fathometer registered water over 192 feet deep. From this point we headed south.

We were sensing the shortening days and the cooler than normal weather. We felt like migratory animals with the urge to move south. It was hard to believe it was the first of August.

At Drummond Island we reported to customs, paid our $25 re-entry fee and moved on to De Tour Village on Michigan's Upper Peninsula. We had been out of the U.S.A. for fifty days, the longest for either of us. We planned to leave DeTour Village and make the wide Lake Huron run to Alpena, Michigan, the next day; but the weather was foul again, and temperatures reached the lower 40's. It rained and blew all day, and we sulked and did inside chores.

The following day was supposed to be better, so we set the alarm for 5:30 a.m. to listen to the weather report. We were reluctant to leave our cocoon for the uncertainty of wet and cold.

De Tour Village, Michigan
to
Grand Rivers, Kentucky

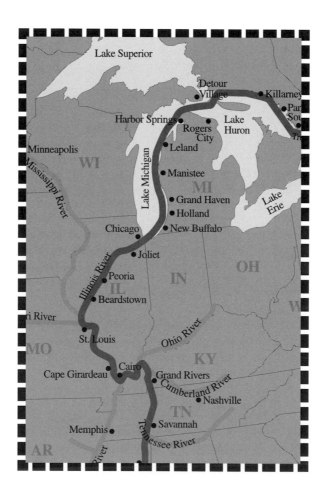

CHAPTER 15

THE BIG, BAD LAKES

I tumbled out of bed at 5:30 a.m. and walked across the cold hard-wood floors to the radio. The NOAA report crackled. I retreated back to bed, and listened. Eva stirred. To leave or not to leave, that was the question. Temperatures were in the 40's again, a record cold for the fifth day of August in Michigan's Upper Peninsula. Relatives in Alpena, Michigan, were waiting for us, but neither of us wanted to face a rough day crossing Lake Huron.

The forecast was good enough. Winds were supposed to be 5-15 mph from the NW, turning westerly. We were going SW across the lake from De Tour Village to the northern coast of Michigan. This would put the waves on our beam, always an uncomfortable and potentially dangerous position for our slow-moving trawler.

But this is sometimes as good as it gets in the upper peninsula of Michigan. As we left Detour Harbor in dawn's early light, all was calm and quiet for the first couple of hours, then the wind and waves began to increase. We turned toward Hammond Bay, then Forty-Mile Point, then Rogers City.

The sound of engines from the stern of the boat sent Eva to the aft deck to see what was happening. An F2 fighter was coming over the horizon and *Genie* was his target. He locked onto us until he was within striking distance, then screamed overhead and was lost like a comet.

The day wore on like a dull tooth ache. Waves built to 3-5 feet and were following, picking up *Genie*, then letting her rush until she had spent the downhill energy. She'd labor at the bottom of the hill until the next wave slid beneath her. We fought to keep her on track and not let her be bullied into a sidewise position in the troughs. Only the anxiety and the work kept me warm. Eva huddled in the hunkering position she assumes when she knows she simply has to tough it out.

Eva's sister, Patsy, was on her mind as we crossed the lake. Patsy died twenty-two years before at the age of 28, and now we were going to visit Patsy's daughter, Teresa. Patsy's husband, Dave, has since remarried and resides with his wife, Suzanne, and two daughters on an 80 acre farm on the outskirts of Alpena. Eva played scenes from the past, including the time of Patsy's original cancer diagnosis and her eventual death. With sister, Cora's illness on her mind, and the memories of Patsy, there was a feeling of melancholy.

Rogers City finally came to view. I argued to stop here instead of going on to Alpena or Presque Isle. The waves and the wind had fatigued us and made us agreeable for an early stop. Sailors who had come in from the North Channel were in full safety gear as they made their way into port, looking fatigued and exhausted from a day's sailing in winds and waves.

Teresa, with husband, Bruce, and son, Cameron, met us in Rogers City, and on the following day we had a pleasant visit with Dave and his family. We walked through farm fields, watched the cattle dogs bring the cows home and reminisced, capping the day with a bountiful farm meal of corn, tomatoes, zucchini and hamburgers. We invited everyone for a sunset cruise, so we packed up the dessert and cruised Lake Huron until darkness sent shivers through everyone and the appeal of home brought us off the water.

On Sunday we went to church with everyone, visited Patsy's grave, ate some more and accepted Dave's offer to go fishing. The day was too windy and stormy to go out, so we went back to the boat on Sunday evening and got ready for a run to Mackinac (pronounced Mackinaw) Island on Monday morning.

The weather had returned to being rotten, but was going to get even rougher on Tuesday and Wednesday. The wind was predicted to be 5-15 mph from the S-SW then would turn, becoming westerly late in the day. If we could get to Mackinac Island early enough, we might be in the harbor when this happened. As we left in the mist on Monday morning, we could see visible lightning strikes in the west. We were going into the face of the storm. By 9:15 a.m. we were in the thick of it. Rain fell, hard. Visibility was reduced to less than a half-mile. We were on instruments, trusting the radar that showed the shoreline and the bays, and the GPS that gave our latitude and longitude. Eva meticulously plotted our course with the help of the electronic equipment aboard.

The wind picked up and waves built. The thunder and lightning storm turned out to be miles deep. Water spilled around us. Fog followed rain. Eva popped an umbrella to keep herself and the charts dry. We dressed in full weather gear over layers of clothing. Still we were cold. The rain continued until 11 a.m., then stopped. I dried the isinglass and we slogged along in a heavy haze.

We heard a report of a MAYDAY call but could only hear the Coast Guard's side of the call. A boat had an engine fire so again we counted our blessings for our little seaworthy vessel.

By 1:00 p.m. the wind and rain began again and the lake developed a heavy chop. Strong nor'westerlies whipped up the lake until *Genie* was rising and falling. The canvas bimini flapped the sound of trouble and woe. We were grateful for our GPS and radar as visibility became a few hundred feet, but we could see a sail boat moving with us off our port beam. Within a few miles of Mackinac I questioned Eva repeatedly about the certainty of her calculations. She kept her markers on the chart and tried to reassure me that we were on the right track. I was completely disoriented and confused. The radar showed the shoreline of Round Island at the end of Bois Blanco Island but nothing was visible.

As we made the turn toward the harbor we caught sight of the lighthouse at about the same time a high speed ferry boat coming from St. Ignace roared toward us with its rooster tail high in the air. It approached audaciously, riding the waves and sliding into the curve. It was no race between the lubberly *Genie* and the wave runner. We gave way, catching the brunt of her wake which rocked us and sent the contents of the galley cabinets into a clamor.

We called the Marina and learned they had no room for us. "We suggest you tie up at the coal dock," they said.

"Mackinaw Island Marina, this is *Dream O' Genie*, over."

"Go ahead, *Dream O' Genie*."

"Can you tell me what the coal dock is and where we can find it, over?"

After nebulous directions from a college student whom I suspect had questionable nautical credentials and probably had never approached the harbor in a boat, we made our way to the Arnold Transit Docks (which was not even close to a coal dock in appearance or name) and resorted to standing on the bow and looking pathetic, which was not hard under the circumstances. With a hang-dog expression, we whined, *"We don't have a home and nobody loves us and we're crabby and wet and lonely and we don't have a place to dock. Won't you help us?"*

It worked. A dock worker stopped shoveling manure and gave us directions. "Tie up along here," he shouted. "They'll take your slip fee at the hardware store at the front of the dock."

Belgian draft horses were working the dock, pulling skids and shuttling wagons of hay and building materials like a scene from the 1890s. It was a working dock from the past, the perfect introduction to Mackinac Island which has lived without motorized transportation since 1901. Besides horses, bicycles and feet are the modes of transportation of goods or people on the island. Taxis are horse drawn carriages, busses are larger horse drawn carriages, the cops are on bicycles and everyone pedals to the store and around town or walks.

No one received our lines so Eva got up on the dock and muscled a few thousand pounds of horse flesh around. "Pardon me, horses, but I've got to tie up this boat. Move, please. C'mon you guys, give me a little room, will you?? Move, you muscle heads or YOU'LL REALLY GET HURT!!" They did, and she did (get us tied up) while I looked on. The sweet smell of manure was in the air and the clopping of feathered hooves on a working dock was our neighborhood. We never did find the coal dock.

We got back on the VHF and informed the marina that we were tied up at the Arnold Transit Dock, that we never did find the coal dock, and that we really liked the horses and the manure and urine running in the gutters, but, *IF*, in the morning they had a spot for us beneath the smiling face of 19th century summer homes lining the bay, where the sound of morning and evening bugle calls from the Fort announce the beginning and end of the day, and lovers stroll and bicyclists roll and summer folks lick ice cream cones or wander in sweet oblivion, then it would be okay if they called us and we would consider leaving the "coal dock" where the sweet smell of manure....

In the morning we got an early morning roll call from the marina. "Is *Dream O' Genie* still in the harbor wishing for a berth at the marina?"

"Yes, she is." In about the time it takes to drop a hot cup of coffee and abandon two sunnyside-ups, we were goosing the Volvos for a spot among the elite in the elegant harbor of the privileged. Ah snobbery, how we love it when we are included. On the aft deck of our YACHT we sipped cool ones in the afternoon and walked in the gardens of the Grande Hotel while beautiful people kissed bocci balls with mallets on the green and laughed the carefree laugh of summertime.

The weather turned pleasant. We had dinner on the aft deck with Teresa and Bruce who drove from Alpena to spend another afternoon with us, and Teresa revisited haunts from her college years when she worked on the island for a summer. We were like Brown-Eyed Susans after a rain...and we were away from those smelly horses on the working docks.

Mackinac Island was designated a national park in 1875 but turned over to the state of Michigan for a state park in 1895. Before that, Mackinac was the headquarters of John Jacob Astor's American Fur Company. From 1780-1835 Indians, trappers and traders bought and sold furs. As much as three million dollars went through the market street in 1822, the heyday of the fur trade. After 1835 the trade went west.

Going back even further, Mackinac was a possession of England. They built a fort on the island in 1780, relinquished it to the American Revolutionaries in 1796, repossessed it during the war of 1812, gave it up for the last time in 1815 and went home for good. United States troops were garrisoned there until 1895 when the island became a national park. Every evening a trumpeter from the fort plays the Star Spangled Banner and the island stands still in salute to its military past.

Tours of the island are conducted using open-air coaches pulled by teams of horses. Some of the grades are steep, requiring three or four teams. There is so much horse flesh in front of you grinding and rolling around as you ride the carriages that it's hard to concentrate on the scenery or the

The Grand Hotel on Mackinac Island overlooks the Straits of Mackinac.

narration. The size, symmetry and power of working horses is the post card image of the island. Few islands measure their commerce in horse power; Mackinac does.

In one of the longest, wordiest, most rambling and redundant petitions ever penned, Thomas Chambers, Anthony Corrigan, J. N. Chambers and Joe Leggett petitioned the city council at the turn-of-the century (we trust with tongue in cheek):

"We the undersigned, being engaged in the carriage business in this village would earnestly protest against the granting of a license to any person for the purpose of operating or running any vehicle known as a *horseless carriage* and we would respectfully request that your honorable body take such actions as may be necessary to prevent the operating of any vehicle known as a *horseless carriage* on the streets or roads of this village, as the running of such a vehicle on the streets or roads of the village is dangerous to the lives and property of your petitioners and their patrons and to all others who use the streets and roads of the village as such vehicles known as the *horseless carriages* when operating and running will frighten even a quiet horse and will cause any timid or spirited animal to run away to the danger of both lives and property, as there is such a vehicle operating and running on the streets and roads of the village at the present time we would respectfully request that you take immediate action to stop the running of such a vehicle until you decide on the course you will pursue." Whew.

Apparently the honorable body found this a convincing, if not excessively wordy, argument and did in fact ban all motor vehicles. To this day.

Mackinac has 3 veterinarians for 600 horses and one doctor for the human population that numbers in the thousands during the summer. During the winter, most of the horses are removed from the island and maintained in pastures and stables until the next spring. The human population dwindles during the winter months and when the last ferry runs from the mainland, the islanders are island-bound until the ice freezes (sometime in January). Our guide said that they make a tree-lined roadway across the straits with their Christmas trees, using the oldest man in the village to test the ice and place the trees. If he comes back, the path of human commerce continues to St. Ignace and Mackinaw City until the thin ice of spring isolates them again. The last one across the ice the past winter was a fellow driving a tractor with a load of hay. He and his load fell through the ice into 100 feet of water and were never seen again.

The Grande Hotel was built by two railroad companies in 1887. In her early years the rich and privileged strolled her 660-foot porch facing the straits and enjoyed the respite from hot summer days in the big cities.

She is an elegant cream puff with long staircases and panoramic porches. No bridge was ever built to the island and its isolation and remoteness is part of its appeal.

When we went strolling by the hotel one evening, we were stopped and advised that at the dinner hour jackets and ties were required of men, and dresses for the ladies. Would we please come back in proper attire? And, if we wished to tour the hotel, and were not registered as guests, there was a $5 charge.

The next day we went for lunch at the hotel, and didn't pay the $5, nor did I wear a suit and a tie. It was the informal noon hour. The hotel had a lavish buffet, 100 feet long and heavy with the bounty of the land and water, salmon in a horseradish whipped cream dressing with capers and chopped red onion, roast sirloin, shrimp, oysters, fresh asparagus, salads and for dessert—cream puffs, chocolate-raspberry mousse trifles topped with fresh blueberries and strawberries, and a hundred other fattening delectables.

After two hours, we wobbled down the front staircase, past the waiting carriages under the canopy and into the gardens where patrons were lawn bowling and playing croquet. The gardens are planted in large forms, with phlox, delphinium and ornamental grasses arranged in artful curves around grassy lawns and stone benches arched with roses. It's a stunning setting. A matched team of dappled grays pulled a classic carriage up the road toward the hotel. All the imagery of the past was captured in a few breathtaking moments.

We burned off our lunch by biking around the perimeter of the island, a total of 8 miles; not

The bridge over the Straits of Mackinac is a five-mile span between Mackinaw City and St. Ignace.

a good idea following such indulgence. It's a pleasant ride on a paved road and shared by many other bikers. The entire circumference can be covered in a few hours with breaks at scenic spots.

We left Mackinac when the weather was pleasant and mild, and assured of a trouble free run to Beaver Island. Beaver Island is situated in the middle of the upper end of Lake Michigan, half-way between the Michigan and Wisconsin coast lines. We arrived at 4:15 p.m., had a quick supper and brought the bikes down for a ride around the old fishing village.

Beaver Island was a Mormon community from 1847-56, when King James Jesse Strang broke with Brigham Young and formed his own kingdom. Other men got jealous (the unofficial record) and assassinated him. Mainlanders flooded the island following his assassination and persecuted the remaining Mormon members until in disarray they left the island.

There was an influx of Irish immigrants who became the fishermen of the next century. In the 1880's Beaver Island was an active fishing village bringing in tons of whitefish and lake trout. Over 30 fishing boats operated from St. James, the port city. They took a million pounds of fish in peak years. Many of the net sheds, company houses and stores are still there. In 1910 the population of Beaver Island was 1,095. In 1964 it fell to 175, then rebounded to the present population of 350.

Now it's a back roads community of beat-up pickups and country people, a contrast to the trendy boutiques and specialty shops of Mackinac Island. Old Jeeps are available for touring the island's back roads and a few enterprises, such as the Shamrock Restaurant and their "Ribs on Saturday Night", satisfy the needs of summer visitors and the resident islanders.

They were celebrating a ten-year interval since the last time an islander was lost at "sea." A plaque at the foot of the flag pole down by the water had the names of those lost in storms on Lake Michigan. Entire families were listed in some years.

At 3 a.m. Eva woke me and said she heard voices on the dock. She thought someone was in trouble. As democratic as we are in our relationship, I'm the person who is expected to get up in the middle of the night and uncover the source of strange sounds.

When I got off the boat onto the dock, I saw a man and woman leaning over a man. He was trying to get up, but the couple were keeping him down. And for good reason. He was fallin'-down drunk. He had been walking the dock looking for his boat when he lost his balance and ended up in the water. With not much more than slippery boat hulls to hang onto, he was thrashing around like a dog in a swimming pool. Fortunate for him, he found a boat's line and held onto it. Some good sailors in the boat next to us, heard his cries for help, got out of bed and threw him ropes and a ladder. The drunk's friends appeared and took him away, and we all went back to our boats for another attempt at being unconscious.

The weather forecast was for more nasty weather, but the predicted high winds and rain weren't supposed to start until the afternoon, so we left Beaver Island for Harbor Springs, Michigan, in 10 mph southerly winds and had a rocking horse ride across the lake. By 11:15 a.m. we arrived in the lee of Big Rock Point that sticks out from Little Traverse Bay protecting us from the long, southern fetch of the lake.

The waters quieted and became a marble sea once we were within Little Traverse Bay. Eva took over the boat and I went down to the galley to get coffee and rolls.

The weather turned foul after we settled in at Harbor Springs. The harbor was full, and boaters came in throughout the day, weary and worn. Six-to-eight-foot-waves kept everybody in port for the next few days, but Harbor Springs is not a bad place to be in good or bad weather. The snail-shaped harbor protects the city from every direction.

Harbor Springs is the ultimate boutique city, with specialty shops and restaurants. The "cuisine" is gourmet. Everything is homemade, custom made, imported or one-of-a-kind and, "too cute, I must have one," like the teddy bears we saw in a store window dressed in paw-length flower-patterned skirts and Laura Ashley bonnets. Art galleries are more common than convenience stores. You can't find a "Twinkie" within 20 miles of Harbor Springs.

One-hundred-foot Browards, the stretch limos of the boating world, clogged the dock and made *Genie* look like a tender. Private cottage associations were fiefdoms with fences and guarded gates, cutting up the hillsides into quarantined compounds. Mansions on the hills look like institutes, and clusters of tennis courts were alive with pros teaching the upcoming generation. Chicago and Detroit corporate executives use Harbor Springs as their summer rutting grounds and the place has the air of "Wall Street on the Lake."

We played tennis with Larry and Felicity one afternoon and were badly beaten. Next day we played with William and Mary, fellow boaters from Terre Haute, Indiana, and had a good match, with Eva making some outstanding shots to bring us the victory. William and Mary were 70 years old. William recently had surgery and fell down while playing, and Mary had severe pain in her shoulders. We take our victories however we can.

On a cold Sunday morning we walked through town to the Presbyterian Church. It was a warm and welcoming little church. The walk back to the boat was beneath the bluff where stately homes with big lawns and sunbathed porches line the harbor. Harbor Springs looked particularly cozy on that quiet Sunday morning, but then, I think most places look idyllic on Sunday morning.

After three days in port, boaters were getting eager to move on Monday morning and many left, only to return a half-hour later. The lake was too rough even for very big boats. One boater returned saying, "I bought a boat to have fun, but that's not fun."

Later in the day we made the run across Little Traverse Bay to the town of Petoskey. From there we thought we could better gauge the lake, so we tied-up for a few hours and did our laundry at the Petoskey Marina. Sailors were coming in and we asked them as they approached the dock how things were on the lake. Some said that the waves and winds were okay, but there was a woman among them that retorted, "It was fun. Hey, waves and wind are what boating's all about." Sailors.

So we went for it and arrived in Charlevoix's protected harbor in Round Lake around 7 p.m. We launched the dinghy and made our way to shore; but as I approached the dock I discovered my wallet was still back on the boat, so Eva jumped off to reconnoiter the waterfront while I went back to the boat. When I returned she had the place cased—supper at a Tex-Mex joint and a late night movie at the adjoining theater. *A Clear And Present Danger* was playing.

It was midnight when we left the theater, taking with us some of the shivers and fright we had collected watching the film. We made our way to the waterfront, found the dink, wet and cold, and moved out onto black water. Nothing moved. *Genie* was invisible in the dark. We moved instinctually in her direction, still not seeing her. Another small boat rowed across the lake like a ghost, leaving small ripples. Finally *Genie*'s anchor light stood apart from the backdrop of city lights. We approached, I swung the dink next to the swim platform, slid myself off, fastened the davits and helped Eva on board. We still had not spoken. We left the dinghy in the water and went inside, lighting our way and feeling safe again.

Round Lake is a beautiful refuge from the big lake and a water playground in its own right. Cottages line the shore, and it's a busy vacationer's haven in the summer. In the winter it falls asleep and there is hardly anyone around.

By 10:30 a.m. the next morning we were racing for the open bridge, out of Round Lake and back into the big, bad lake. Two to four foot waves smacked us on the nose as we left the breakwater and we resumed that nearly continuous feeling we've had since we entered Lake Huron and Lake Michigan, a mix of depression, anxiety and fear. We longed for the rivers and canals again, but we were not going to see those until we entered the Chicago River.

The way across Grand Traverse Bay was through totally confused waters, choppy and with occasional swells. Waves seemed to hit us from all directions. Some waves were on the bow, some on the beam, making for an insulting slap and roll effect. *Genie* torqued in the waves but managed it gracefully. Boats are marvelous things, threading through chaos and creating direction in a schizophrenic world.

Every 10-20 miles there is a designated harbor of refuge on the Michigan state coasts so boaters are never far from a safe place. Northport was difficult to find. Our waypoint on the GPS showed it a half mile ahead, but we saw the shoreline only on the radar. Finally the faint image of land and cottage doors became visible, and then the breakwater. Northport is a charming old steamer port with square front buildings and tall trees that run up the main street from the dock. Canada geese honked over the water as we pulled in, and the overall impression was pleasant and welcoming.

The Grand Traverse Lighthouse on the point is easily reached by bicycle, so we spun out there, rolling past rustic farms and burnished barns and fruit orchards ready for harvest. Long horned grasshoppers sung in the grass and crickets chirped.

The lighthouse is at the end of the Lelanau Peninsula. It was built in 1858 by the U.S. Lighthouse Service and is the oldest lighthouse on the Great Lakes. It was fully furnished and looked just like the last family left it—dirty dishes in the sink, the laundry stacked in the corner of the room and a mouse brought in by the cat near the kitchen table. (Of course not.) Museum recreations are always artificially orderly.

When we returned to town we decided to buy provisions so Eva perched herself on a bench while I went to the boat for money. There was only a little tequila left in the bottle so I took it with me to drink on the city bench with my girl. We swigged alternately, emptying the bottle and looking like lushes. 'My kind of woman, a biker, a boater and a drinker. From there it was a relaxed ride to the liquor store and grocery store to re-provision, backing the bikes near the checkout conveyor so the groceries could go right into the saddlebags of the bikes.

The next day we took the ride to Leland, another bumpy ride on the big lake. The towns along the shores are charming, picturesquely tucked into coves along the water's edge. It was only a four-hour ride, but we had to get up at 6 a.m. and leave by 7 a.m. to beat the lake at the game of "Let's terrorize a trawler."

The coastline from Northport to Leland, and in fact most of Lake Michigan's eastern shore, is dunes with high eroding bluffs. Leland lies at the base of the bluffs with summer cottages teetering on eroding slopes. In town, the Victorian homes and cottages have been converted to banks, bird stores, pottery emporia and boutiques. There's hardly a serious store in town. It's a long way from the earthy fishing village of the past and seems to be the outpost for eclectic Americana artifacts or things hand-made in Milan or Barcelona. Oshkosh? Too pedestrian.

A pair of swans with their cygnets were in the marina, the kids as big as the adults but without primary (flight) feathers. They were kinder and nicer than the adults, who were obnoxiously parental, hissing at anyone who came close. I thought they were looking for a handout, but it turns out they were eager to eat the hand that fed them.

Leland thrived as a fishing village in the early 1900's and used the Carp River to tie up their sailboats and primitive gasoline powered boats. Ice and smoke houses and fishing shanties lined the river, and many of these still exist. Carlson's Smoke House and Fish Store carry on the tradition of smoking whitefish, salmon and lake trout. The whole town smokes when Carlson's is cooking. Their smoked fish sausage is particularly good and is great with crackers and a glass of chilled chardonnay. It might even be good with Thunderbird. We bought enough to last for weeks to come and were grateful to have a large freezer on board.

The smoking process includes soaking the fish in a brine for 15 hours, then smoking for six hours at 225 degrees. When the inside flesh reaches 180 degrees for a half-hour, the process is stopped. The rack full of bronzed fish is cooled and displayed for sale. Kissing a person who has just munched on smoked whitefish is like getting to know a fire fighter.

It was amazing the number of boaters within ear shot and sight of Carlson's Fish House, the town and the surrounding dunes, who were busy washing and waxing boats as if there wasn't anything interesting to do. I made the mistake of asking someone about his boat, and had one boring time of it, listening to a guy extol the beauty and virtue of his boat as if he engineered, designed and built it himself. He went on with the boat's pedigree, its custom features and how this boat saved his life, brought his marriage together, made life bearable after his hair loss...ad nauseam.

Then there are people like us who treat their boats like farm trucks. They're fly specked and webbed from a million happy spiders who cruise the U.S. for nothing. The hull wears a mustache like one of the Marx Brothers and people look away when they walk past.

The coastline of Michigan reminded us of the California coastal mountains. Mist-shrouded headlands rise like an escarpment and creeks and rivers tear through the wall forming river-cut canyons. Big Bear Dunes National Park was set apart for the public, and Big, South and North Manitou Islands are part of this national preserve. Scheduled excursions are made to the islands, which have no docking facilities for pleasure craft.

As we left Leland we caught a NOAA weather report from some guy who had not taken the federal exam for official humorless, bureaucratic, dull and lifeless speaking. This guy was a little like George Carlin, the hippy-dippy weather man, and obviously his immediate superior was not listening, "We've got some thunder boomers over that big, bad lake today. Those nasty clouds are going to hang over LOOOOOwer Michigan, so you boaters out there, take care, and we'll see if we can't talk the Big Guy up there to hold off until you're in port."

At Manistee, an old industrial lake town that bills itself as having the largest number of historic buildings (factories?) of any town in western Michigan, we tied up to the city docks and rented a car for a weekend trip to Grand Rapids and an engagement party for my nephew and his bride-to-be. When we returned, we spent a night in the back waters of Lake Manistee, on the hook and in the neighborhood of white swans. They were gorgeous, and far more interesting than Manistee, although the town has a new boardwalk along the river that extends out to the breakwater.

What we didn't know until early (very early) in the morning, was that our anchorage was in the middle of the channel for fisherman leaving from a nearby marina. With only fish on their mind, they raced past us, oblivious to the rocking and rolling they were creating.

The big lake was the texture of hot fudge when we left later in the morning for the run to Pentwater. It was strange to see it so quiet. Numerous fishing boats were out and we could hear them on the radio complain to each other that nothing was biting. These were the same hot dogs that tore past our boat on their way out in the wee hours of the morning so we knew God was punishing them.

We rounded Sable Point near Ludington where fishermen were trolling between the center depths of 950 foot and the ledge of 40-100 feet.

Pentwater, like Charlevoix, lies hidden behind dunes. A breakwater and canal form a magic tunnel that leads to inland lakes and cottage communities. We anchored in quiet waters under a bright moon. Eva went to the bow of the boat to check our position before we went to bed and I heard her excitedly call out, "Ron, there's a light moving across the water." Then there was silence. I waited. She came inside with the light of surprise on her face. "I just saw something that really had me baffled." She told of a light that came across the surface of the water, hit our boat, moved away, and disappeared. The mystery light was the result of moonbeams reflected off a small wave produced by a boat in the distance. The surfing moonbeam hit the boat then rode the reflected wave back out again.

November 11, 1940, was a bad day in Pentwater. Seventy mile per hour winds whipped the lake into 25 foot waves. Two freighters and a tug went down that day between Little and North Sable Points where the lake has a long fetch to the west, south and north. Seventeen men were rescued from one of the freighters; all the others lost their lives.

Near Pentwater is the Dunes Recreation Area. Sections of the dunes are open to off-road vehicles and the hills are barren from the action of paddle-wheeled dune buggies and ATVs. It's a striking contrast to the natural dunes with its slopes of dune grass and ravines of woods.

The next day we rode into White Lake, traveling the length of the lake for an anchorage near the towns of Montague and Whitehall. Peter Ostroushko, bluegrass songwriter and performer, and his side kick, Dean McGraw, were giving an evening concert in the Montague open air pavilion, so we jumped in the dinghy. Actually we slide into this dinghy because it is very tender, not as in loving and kind, but as in tipsy and undependable, so if we jump into it, we may find ourselves in the lake. At any rate, we putted the Wizard to the town dock and sat on damp grass for several hours of totally enjoyable summer music in a town on the lake. Our ride back was another one of those spooky rides with Eva holding our little flashlight in case any other nuts were out at that time of night.

The wind began to pick up after midnight and by morning it was wild. On the big lake waves had built to 7 feet with winds to 25 knots, so we stayed put on White Lake, finding it even too rough to drop our tender dinghy for a ride to town. We wrote, read, ate and consumed the day profitably.

The following day Lake Michigan had a new face, the appearance of an ocean, large swells instead of its regular chop. The vestiges of yesterday's storm were transformed into swells, like sighs following heavy exercise. Our way to Grand Haven was bobbing and weaving with waves on our beam, but in three hours we were in the protection of the Grand River.

Niece Tammy and spouse, John, were our official town greeters and we had dinner with the them the first night. We sat on the aft deck of *Genie* at the municipal docks to watch Grand Haven's celebrated musical fountain, a 1940's style presentation of spouting water, dramatic music and narration conceived by a local dentist. Computer operated and billed as the world's largest, automated water display, this fountain brings many local and traveling boaters into the river to watch. The narration is corny, and Tammy and I snickered; but we heard from boaters in days following how wonderful the show was. Some boaters stayed several nights to hear the various narrations and themes. I think Tammy called it: *Squirts and Notes*, or *Lawrence Welk Welcomes the New Age of Plumbing.*

Days following brought my brother and sister to the boat with their families. Sister, Joyce, spouse, Don, and daughter, Megan, stayed overnight on the boat, and went from Grand Haven to Holland with us. The sky was blue, the clouds were white and Don was green. Poor guy. He turned sour and spent considerable alone time in the downstairs salon looking like he was meditating. Gagging and meditating. The lake was a little rough for a guy who had been hardened (theoretically) by four years in the navy.

A small warbler hitched a ride with us from Grand Haven to Holland. The little bird flew for a while, glanced toward land and opted to perch on the rail again, feathers furled by the wind. He'd fly off again, dipping and grinning and land back on the boat. Megan, eight, thought this was wonderland—boat spiders, yellow warblers hitching a ride, wind and water, big white boat cutting through the waves, dad in the salon turning green. She loved it and decided she was born to boat. Joyce looked at her like mothers do when kids say something stupid, but Megan believed this with all her heart... until the next day when Tammy and John came to Holland with their new Four Winns *speed* boat, then she thought she was born to water ski and look cool on Lake Macatawa in a speed boat (not some old cow of a trawler) with her hair flowing back and a brilliant scarf flying in the wind. The kid has class.

The next day we were off to New Buffalo where the weather turned horrible again and we waited for good weather to make the run across the bottom part of Lake Michigan to Chicago. It was here that we met Roger and Lea who were also from California and were doing the Great Loop.

Roger and Lea invited us aboard *Knight-N-Gail* for cocktails before dinner. I was returning to our boat carrying glasses and dishes and descended the steps into our galley with wet sneakers when I slipped and fell backwards, cracking some ribs. For over three weeks I was little more than a plaything. By the time I was well, Eva had taken over the boat.

From a board walk on the sand bluffs north of town we looked across the lake and saw Sears Towers, the John Hancock Insurance and the Standard Oil buildings. The days were clear but high winds out of the Northwest made the lake troublesome and rough.

After several days we left, taking on fuel first at Michigan City. The 32 mile crossing was uneventful and I recalled my college days driving the rim of the lake from Chicago to Grand Rapids, Michigan. The steel mills at Gary, Indiana, are still spewing out tons of highly visible smoke that covers the south end of the lake. At the half-way point we viewed the entire south Lake Michigan coastline, from the industrial strength cities of Indiana to the downtown hi-rise centers of Chicago. We programmed our GPS to the designated waypoint but as we mugged the Chicago skyline there wasn't a clue where to go ashore. We had the name of the marina and we knew that it was near Meigs Field, Chicago's waterfront airport. Following the dotted line on the GPS, we unerringly slid behind Meigs Field and into Burnham Park Harbor.

I called my daughter Laura's home on Friday and thought I was talking to the baby sitter. It was a voice that was very familiar to me and I wondered why a baby sitter would be there in the middle of the day when the kids were in school. She said her name was Amy and she had just arrived in town. Still no connections, but finally bells clanged and lights blinked and I realized I was talking to Eva's daughter Amy who flew in to cruise with us for a few days. Son-in-law Tim came out to pick us up from the boat and we spent the night in Glendale Heights with the family, then we all went back to the boat on Saturday night for a sunset cruise of the shoreline.

This was the Labor Day weekend and though we were on schedule for the whole trip thus far, we were eager to keep going.

We listened to NOAA who had a terrible forecast for Monday. There was a window of decent weather on Sunday, so we advised everyone to be on the boat by 9 a.m., ready to go. If we could safely make the open lake run into the Chicago River we'd be protected by inland waters for days to come.

We took down the anchor light and radar dome again to ensure clearance under the fixed bridges on the next stretch of waterway in downtown Chicago and waited for dawn.

CHAPTER 16

DAT OL' MAN RIVER

Eight adults and six kids surfed for the Chicago River. The wind on Lake Michigan was out of the southeast when we left Burnham Park Harbor and three to four foot waves sloshed against the breakwater as we made our way out. A number of boats milled about near the entrance adding obstacles to the confusion. I wasn't comfortable with this situation. We had children and grandchildren, nieces, nephews and cousins on board and the lake was unsettled and potentially dangerous. The forecast was for worsening weather in the days ahead so we decided to go for it.

All the kids got PFDs (Personal Flotation Devices) and the parents were given strict orders to keep the kids in their seats at the upper helm. We rehearsed emergency actions. I didn't want to terrorize everyone, but my parental mind played a quick scenario of a capsized boat with kids in the water, mayhem and woe—the kind of nightmare that makes the sphincters tight and the face thin-lipped and grim.

I kept *Genie* on a course straight into the waves to avoid the inevitable rolling that would occur when we swung north and took the swells abeam. Someone asked anxiously why we weren't turning toward the breakwater and I explained that I was looking for the right waves, or the absence thereof, to make the turn. In an effort to get the feel of the crashing waves and the pitching boat, I was getting farther away from the Chicago River inlet.

Grandson Dillon was sitting nearby and was not enjoying this. He had that down-in-the-mouth look. "Keep your head up, Dillon," I called out. "Look out on the horizon and watch some of the other boats."

But the other boats were in that same rocking and rolling position, which was little consolation for a nine-year old about to lose his breakfast.

Tim watched Dillon as I negotiated our turn, then grabbed him and headed for a corner of the aft deck where they hunkered together and got in a position where Dillon could lean overboard and feed the fishes. The rest of the kids on the flybridge kept their places and their breakfasts, but *Genie* did not look like a cruise ship that morning.

Daughter Laura and Cousin Jane were sitting on loose chairs at the table on the back deck when *Genie* began to roll. They let go their nonchalance and assumed the appropriate uptight look the rest of us already wore. Our trawler, always more sure of where she was going than I, plodded ahead steadily. As we made the corner around the Chicago River breakwater and the lock was in view, the waters calmed, the motley crew relaxed, kids regained their color, adults let go their molar-grinding tasks of supervising and *Genie* became a party boat.

The lock was open so we entered; the gates closed and we moved to the wall to tie-up. Almost before we were secure, the forward gates opened and we dropped four feet into the Chicago River. It was the quickest lock passage of the 117 locks we had done since we left Florida.

Ahead lay the city, quiet on a Sunday morning, a granite canyon spanned with pewter bridges. Walkways paralleled the river. Pinnacles of concrete left trails for people and cars. The river, being the lowest of all, looked up at everything.

Some bridges were classic with Gothic watch towers. The Chicago Tribune building stood on the north side, a monument of white in a gray world of weathered stone and winter-hardened metal. Marina Towers Apartments rose like a bakery concoction, balconies in curved layers aspiring to views of the city. It was a girlie-looking edifice in a brotherhood of business buildings.

There were many fixed bridges to pass under but our 15.5 foot height (with anchor light and radar dome down) was low enough to get under all except the Amtrak lift bridge which raised to let us through. If boats can't clear heights of 17 feet, they have to enter the Illinois River by way of the Calumet-Sag Channel near East Chicago and Whiting, Indiana.

In a few miles office-space high-rises yielded to industry—Union Station Railroad Depot, warehouses, gravel yards and tank farms. In a twinkling, administration and marketing bowed to manufacturing. Barges replaced city tour boats. The Chicago River became the Chicago Sanitary and Ship Canal, an avenue that carries the burdens of the city to the Gulf of Mexico.

The historic Illinois and Michigan Canal was the first attempt to tie the Illinois River with Lake Michigan. Now the Des Plaines, the "plain river", is conveyor and barge canal. The river is the workhorse of the city as well as the shipping lane to the Gulf. Pleasure boats look prissy and super-fluous in this blue jeans world.

The Des Plaines left the city and the landscape became bucolic. Cliffs of limestone lined the canal and trees grew naturally along the shoreline.

The barge traffic became serious. Tows pushing 15 barges negotiated tight river bends in the Des Plaines with only inches to spare. We got out of the way and wiggled into corners to let them pass. We had a long wait at the first lock and kids jumped onto canal walls to stretch and burn-up energy.

We had a long wait at the Lockport Lock where a tow split his load of 18 barges (three wide, six deep) and sent half through the locks, then the second half with the tug behind. We tied to a wall on the west side and dads took restless kids for a romp on the land while the rest of us waited. We dropped 40 feet in elevation when it was finally our turn to lock through.

At Joliet we spotted the city's riverside park and tied to the wall oppo-site Harrah's floating casino. The river boats are warehouses of gambling machines that escape municipal law, leaving the docks regularly to trans-gress without penalty.

Randy appeared with his family and *Genie* sunk into the water with the addition of five more kin. Laura and Jane shoveled vittles out of the galley like school cafeteria mommas. Food was consumed and converted into more body heat and noise.

At about 8 p.m. the dads left with Randy and his family to bring cars from Wheaton. I went to Harrah's and bought four giant ice cream sundaes for us kids. The sundaes were piled high with whipped cream, nuts and a mix of flavors and colors. We passed them around in a circle as if they were on a carousel, each person spooning into the gooey mess until the kids were sugar-high and walking on water. Why did I do that? When the dads came back with the cars all the children and mommas left. Eva and Amy and I were the only ones aboard. It felt like the quiet after a tornado.

In the morning I did the guy things on the boat—checking engine fluid levels, cleaning, and replacing the anchor light and radar dome that I had removed so we could clear the fixed bridges through Chicago. As Eva handed me the fastening bolts, I didn't hear her comment about two long bolts and two short bolts. I screwed one of the long bolts into a short hole, piercing the bottom of the radar and the circuit board, which of course disabled it. When the dome didn't sit level, I realized I had done one of those really *stupid* guy things that was going to set us back a few more dollars to undo. Oh, well, it's only money. Some morning or evening along the Mississippi or Tombigbee Rivers we might need this electronic eye to pierce the fog and keep us in visual contact with other boats and the shoreline.

While I was sabotaging the radar, Amy and Eva were walking along the sandstone bluffs of Joliet's waterfront where the first merchants set up shop—Herschberger (1860-1900) who made carriages and wagons, Fred Beuttenmuller, the gunsmith, and Frank Kramer who ran a saloon. Dr. Adams had Golden's Mortar Apothecary and John D. Paige (1837) bottled flavored water under pressure, creating soda pop. And of course, there is mention of Louis Joliet and Father Marquette who passed here in 1673 when the river was known as the *River Plain*. The weather on Noah (NOAA) reported winds of 25-30 on Lake Michigan with waves 5-7 feet, but we were cozy on an inland river, and the weather was mild and maudlin. Cruising on rivers is possible in just about any weather, in contrast to large bodies of water. We were happy to be on protected water from here to Mobile, Alabama.

At the Brandon Road Lock we stepped downward 34 feet. Chicago is about 660 feet above sea level so all the locks from here to the Gulf on the Mississippi River step down.

Below the lock and dam was the Empress dock where tour buses take people aboard another gambling river boat. It seemed strange; there wasn't a town around, just a dock for a floating casino.

Despite the obvious industrial nature of this river and its reputation as an open sewer, Great Blue Herons and common egrets fished along the shore. "Maybe there's more life in these waters than we think," I said.

In another ten miles the river looked natural and inviting. Homes appeared along the banks. At mile 273 the Kankakee River came in from the east and the "plain river" and the Fox River from the north became the Illinois River.

We arrived at Seneca late in the day. Nobody answered the VHF so we eased in and caught the attention of local boaters who found an open slip for us. This marina is a Mecca for Chicagoans who use the Illinois as a recreational cruising river. One of these friendly folks took us into town in the morning to stock up on food.

At the Dresden Lock (drop 35 feet) we met a Canadian couple also going to Florida. They were aboard a Trojan cruiser aptly named *Play'n Safe* and their dinghy was *Pin Hole*. We had time to get to know them while sitting on top of a cell, the large cement bumpers used by tows to guide their barges. When tows with a line of barges go through the locks, it's not unusual to spend an hour or two waiting for them to lock through. They have first priority on all the waterways, so often pleasure boats cluster together in restless pods waiting to lock through.

The Illinois River is beautiful near Starved Rock State Park. Limestone bluffs and wooded canyons line the river. At the Starved Rock Lock, a tow with 15 barges (three wide, five long) locked through. Splitting his load, he sent the first nine barges up on their own while he stayed below with the remaining six. The nine barges rode up and were taken out of the lock by cables affixed to the top rail of the lock. The lock went back down, and the tow and his remaining six barges entered. Then they rode up. The tow pushed the six barges to the nine, all were tied together and he was on his way upstream, a veritable train threaded together by steel cable.

It was awesome to meet them on the waterway. There was usually time to call the tow captain on the VHF to find out how we should pass him, one whistle (to the right) or two whistles (to the left). The problem was that these tow boat captains, though well schooled and qualified in technical aspects of boating, speak a dialect spoken only in certain isolated "Loosiana" bayous.

I got on the radio, "This is the southbound pleasure craft on the Illinois River at mile 219 approaching the tow going north. Captain, shall I pass you one whistle or two?"

He came back: "Yaaaahcruisahcomin'upheah, 'boutgivinmealittle moroomderindemiddle, thenI'llgetyaondaonewhistle."

Astonishing fact: Just one of those barges is equal to the cargo transported by 16 eighteen wheelers or 15 jumbo hopper train cars. An eight barge tow moving cargo one tenth of a mile is equivalent to a string of truck traffic 19.2 miles long (assuming 150 feet between trucks).

We anchored on the Illinois River in an uninterrupted slack water anchorage off the channel behind an island and below the bluff town of Hennepin, safe from the night traffic of tows. We dinghied to the town park on the river and walked the town—a grocery store, credit union and hardware store.

Amy proved to be very adept at handling the boat and reading the charts. In fact, she was the only person deemed worthy enough to assume Eva's navigating chores. Eva would never allow me to do it. My mind is like a wad of yarn—soft, fuzzy and confused. Hers is like a circuit board. Amy was obviously a chip off the old board.

The river wound plaintively along wooded shores. Beyond the woods lay corn fields. At Peoria we docked at the Illinois Valley Yacht Club. Amy helped me change the oil on the three diesel engines. This was a task I loathed, inasmuch as the oil pump connections came apart, and the runaway hoses twisted and jerked like a water hose under high pressure. By the time I caught the squirting lines, the engines were splattered, the ceiling in the engine room was freckled with oil and I looked like I had lost a battle with a giant squid.

When I finished, I was insane, unrecognizable and totally contemptible. Eva was doing the wash and insisted that I drop my oily drawers and all the accompanying oil-soaked underclothes. She carried them to the washer like you carry a dirty diaper...to be washed alone. From that point forward it became a dedicated set of oil-changing clothes (which was now the fourth set of clothing set aside for this purpose. By the time we finished the trip, that's all I had). Some guys on boats look toned and sporty with designer shirts and white shorts. Others look like junk yard dogs.

I thought of marketing a set of oil change clothes for boaters. It would be a pre-stained, Rorscharchian spotted bodice with a splat in the crotch, an artistic spray of dribble down the arms, and rivulets of black on white socks. The face mask would have a mixture of blood, oil, pain and suffering, and as soon as you donned it you would be in the right (more like inevitable) mood. The nifty thing about this outfit is that boaters could be total slobs before the job begins, thus freeing themselves of the growing feelings of disgust, hate and revulsion that accompanies this task.

Peoria is the brunt of many jokes and the theoretical test city for any new ideas, but Peoria from the river side looks ambitious and prosperous. Caterpillar has many industrial plants here and a myriad of materials handling yards.

We took Amy back to Chicago from Peoria. We rented a car, drove to O'Hare International Airport and returned later in the day. Our favorite means of connecting with guests aboard was to rent a car from a port city and pick-up or deliver them to nearby airports. Our guests and family were usually generous enough to pay for this expense.

In 1993 and again in 1995, the Illinois River was in flood stage along with the Mississippi, but in September of '94 the water was below average and below pool. In the spring these commercial rivers run, but in late summer, with declining rainfall, the rivers are little more than pools impounded by successive dams.

There were very few places to stay along the Illinois River. When we arrived at Beardstown, we looked for the barge that the guidebook said the

Above: A staircase of eight locks lifts boats from the Ottawa River to the city of Ottawa and the beginning of the Rideau Canal.

Below: The Dream O'Genie rests along the lock wall at Chaffeys Lock in the Rideau Canal as the crew dine at the historic Opinicon Lodge nearby.

Left:
Laura Uselton
enjoys a moment
of reverie at
Healey Falls near
the site of locks
16 & 17 on the
Trent-Severn
Waterway.

Below:
The canals of the
Trent-Severn
Waterway are
popular during
the summer with
boaters cruising
and stopping at
the small towns
and alfresco
canal restau-
rants.

The Dream O'Genie stopped at Fryingpan Island in Lake Huron's Georgian Bay for a platter of fried fish served at World Famous Henry's Fish Restaurant. We also discovered fresh wild blueberries, just ripe for picking.

Left:
Mother at the Helm.
Mary, age 85, proved
she could drive any-
thing. Here she pilots
Dream O'Genie through
traffic in the small craft
channel in Georgian
Bay's 30,000 islands
near Parry Sound.

Below:
Baie Fine fjord, near
Killarney, Ontario, ends
in a quiet pool where
cruisers spend a
peaceful night at
anchor. From here it's a
short dinghy ride to the
trail head for a hike to
Topaz Lake, a beautiful
high mountain lake.

The Strawberry Island Lighthouse, near Little Current, is one of many picturesque lights guarding the rocky coastline of Lake Huron's Georgian Bay.

Horse drawn carriages pull up to the Grande Hotel on Mackinac Island, which has virtually banned the use of motorized vehicles for nearly all of its civilized life.

Left:
Carlin Rykse stands on the bow of Dream O'Genie as we make passage through the lock from Lake Michigan into the Chicago River which passes through the windy city.

Right:
When you see the beauty of the fall colors along the Tennessee River, you wonder why you don't live there. We stopped wondering and a few years later bought property along the shores of the Little Tennessee River near the head waters of the big Tennessee River.

Above:
Mist sets on the water
in the Blue Bluff
Lagoon as Dream
O'Genie lies at anchor.
The ante-bellum town
of Aberdeen, Missis-
sippi, is a short bike
ride away.

Right:
As far as you can see,
boats line up for the
Blessing of the Fleet at
the Florida Seafood
Festival, held each year
in November at
Apalachicola, Florida.

Above: Eva walks along Sandy Beach on Peck Lake looking for shells. Near Stuart, Florida, this was the final stretch of our Great Loop Cruise.

Below: Fort Lauderdale, aptly called the Venice of America, has numerous canals. The city has a municipal marina downtown on the New River. Las Olas Boulevard and its sidewalk cafes are favorites with boaters.

city provided as dockage for transient boaters. The boating guide also mentioned a marina. We drifted in the river, seeking help from a workman shuttling in a jon boat between barges. I leaned from the upper helm and hollered, "Where can we stay the night? Does the city have a barge that we can tie to?"

"A tow with barges smashed it last year. It's not here anymore," he called back.

"And what about the marina?" I asked. "Is it still open for business?"

"Not for a boat your size. Since last year's flood the entrance is so silted in you couldn't get in there."

"Got any suggestions where we can stay? It's late and we need a place to get off the river."

"You can tie to one of our barges."

"Do you charge?"

"Fifteen bucks."

I turned away from him and muttered to Eva, "He's gotta be kidding. Why would anyone want to pay $15 to tie up to his crummy barge."

She shrugged, "Honey, we don't have a choice. It's too late to go anywhere else."

. She was right. This was the only gig in town. I called back to the guy in the jon boat with a radically changed attitude, "Good idea. Where do you want us?"

At Beardstown on the Illinois River we were part of the working riverfront.

I brought *Genie* next to a supply barge loaded with cables, oil drums, ties, and miscellaneous junk. All it needed was a Doberman. But we were secure.

A path on the barge went through the equipment and debris to a metal walkway and ladder (with some broken welds), that ascended the flood walls of the city and down the other side to an older neighborhood where small frame homes with narrow faces lined the streets like thugs in a lineup. We walked the town, seeking to discover the magic of this river town (it had none) and went back to the boat.

We celebrated our evening in *Junk Yard City* on the aft deck with margaritas and Skin-So-Soft (you drink one and apply the other). It was a beautiful evening—the sight of hundreds of yards of rusting cable, the smell of diesel fumes from working tugs, the sound of straining engines, the threat of runaway barges in swift current and jillions of biting insects—all of it was reason to drink.

Eva applied too much SSS on her legs and offered to share some with me. Rather than making our drinking hands greasy, she slid her legs around mine and mine around hers in an elaborate ritual that makes grasshoppers look unimaginative, all the while balancing our margaritas. This writhing, wrapping, ritual required a fair amount of coordination and control (which was quickly declining). The longshoremen of Logsdon Tug Service observed us beneath their peaked caps with a mixture of disgust and amusement.

I tried to repair the troublesome water pump which was again defaulting and vowed to replace it as soon as possible. No more will this little squirt stop whenever it feels like it, (which is usually when you're finishing a shower and you're all lathered up).

The following night, we anchored in the lee of Twin Islands, a slack water spur where the water rested. The afternoon was young, and there was time for tea and cookies on the aft deck. Eva got into a lounging mood and with dreamy and mischievous eyes, invited me to slow "dance", and so we did, leaving murmurs on the water.

Tugs occasionally traveled by, and in the night scanned the shores for obstacles and day marks with their cyclopean eye. The beam caught us like a death ray, then swung around to other objects. It was a new moon night as black as velvet and one of the most peaceful places we had visited, despite the intrusive lights of the tugs.

In the morning, we raised the anchors, including the Danforth which we had dropped from the stern. Because of my painful cracked ribs Eva, the capable farm girl from South Dakota (still with long red nails), took on the task, hauling the 35-pound anchor up and over the rail.

Canada geese were pouring down the river, validating our southern migration. Fall was in the air and many of God's creatures heeded the urge to move.

The Illinois River became more scenic as we traveled south, with sandstone bluffs on one side and flood plains on the other. Near Pere Marquette State Park the river was broad and adjacent sloughs entered the river. Herons and egrets stood as numerous as pickets near the entrance to Swan Lake. In three miles we were in the Mississippi River. The exhilaration of discovery and the fear of entering the fast current and heavy commercial traffic on the river was delicious.

At the confluence of the two rivers, the water was choppy and confused. Small islands, barely visible, were recreational islands for hundreds of boaters. The water boiled with their wakes, and their darting action across our bow with skiers in tow made us particularly aware and cautious. If skiers fell, they'd be salsa.

But it was really the tows that own the river. Some are 36 barges big, six across and six deep, pushed by tugs of 10,000 horsepower. They're like city blocks in motion. They have little maneuverability, and with skipping speedboats and fluttering sailboats, they simply maintain their course and hope everyone gets out of the way. We did.

The Mississippi is broad and wide and images of Tom Sawyer and Huck Finn and catfish fries on hot summer days ran through our heads. It looked more like a lake than a river, except for the current. Sailboats made points on the water. We hadn't seen them since Lake Michigan. The southern and northern fetch on the Mississippi is long enough to build wind and waves.

Like the Illinois this area was badly flooded in recent years. Homes on stilts bear water marks to their second story windows. Many were abandoned. The river towns of Grafton and West Dalton were devastated, and may never recover. We called Venetian Harbor Marina, but they never responded. Nearby Palisades Yacht Club answered and offered us a covered slip.

The Venetian Harbor Marina ship's store was open, however, so we walked up the road and replaced our troublesome water pump and got the name of an electronics repair shop that came out and repaired our radar. Bless those repairmen who repair instead of replace. This guy had the ingenuity to re-solder broken circuits and replace resistors and capacitors instead of ordering a new circuit board. New parts would have taken weeks and by that time we'd be hundreds of miles away.

We rejoined three boats we had traveled with earlier in the cruise and caravaned down the Mississippi together. We'd get together in the evening for cocktails and hors d'oeuvres and play games after dinner. The men and Eva would get out the charts and guidebooks and plan the next day's travel while the women and I talked about recipes and books. Decisions were jointly made and a strong bond of friendship developed

Our four boats eventually made it to Florida, but there was a lot of water that slipped beneath us before that happened. The relationships that we established while boating were wonderful, and the constant stimulation of a new destination each day was exciting. There were times, however, when I wished for the permanency of a real home, where the bed is attached to the floor, and the floor rooted to the earth. Eva didn't feel that way. She could easily become a permanent boater. We may have to buy a riverside cabin where I live on land and visit Eva who will be rocking on the boat. I love the idea of going home each night to the solidity of the known. We both cherish small things like a grocery store close-by, a newspaper delivered each night and radio and television reception that doesn't waver and flutter. Some of our friends live full-time on a boat; others have homes up north and cruise Florida during the winter or have homes both in the north and in Florida.

We approached the confluence of the Mississippi and the Missouri Rivers six miles downstream. The run-off and sediments of the Bitterroot Mountains of Montana made their introduction to the Mississippi. The two rivers ran together like a team of horses, snorting and tumbling across a section of rapids opposite the Chain of Rocks shipping canal.

This area was the push-off point for the Lewis and Clark Expedition of 1804. The French and Spanish owned this territory at the time of their exploration, but following the expedition, settlers streamed in and the American footprint ensured ownership.

The river is heavily industrialized and it is difficult to imagine the wilderness that stood before the explorers. The highway along the bank parallels the river northward to Minneapolis, and south to New Orleans.

Our four boats had to wait an hour and a half at Lock #27 while commercial traffic came through, then we proceeded downstream to St. Louis. The Gateway to the West Arch in St. Louis came into view and we pulled the boats out of gear and drifted by, photographing as we went. At that time the city provided no docking facilities for pleasure craft, so there was no

The Lewis and Clark Arch in St. Louis commemorates the expedition that set out from there in 1804.

opportunity to go ashore. (Since then, the city built a new pleasure craft dock and we understand access to downtown St. Louis is now available.)

Wing dams channel the river's waters into the center of the channel, automatically deepening it and keeping the current running. With water current speeds of 2-3 knots we boosted our overall speed to 10 & 11 knots. At sharp bends in the river there were boils and eddies, and the boats assumed crabbing positions as they were caught in the currents. Captains sweated and wrestled their boats back into downstream positions. The Mississippi River is a strange mix of quiet pools and races. You can see these areas from a distance, and it's fascinatingly scary to enter them and feel the raw power of the current on the hull, but even the single-screw trawler amongst us had little trouble. We reached our highest current, a four-knot raceway that registered our speed over ground as 12.5 knots on the GPS.

In the evening we docked at Hoppie's Marina, 23 miles downstream from St. Louis, a wide spot in the river with a long barge-dock. The river traffic flows by and it's strictly a wayside station, but the nearby town of Kimmswick provided us a chance to take the bikes down and ride the streets of this second-oldest town in Missouri. Log cabins line the streets and flat-front business buildings stand behind covered walkways. The Old House Restaurant is a 1770 building moved in from the village of Beck. Ulysses S. Grant visited this building frequently in his travels through these parts during Civil War days.

The tow boat operators chatter to other tows on the Mississippi, whiling away their monotonous days while creeping up the river at speeds of four knots or less. They talk about other tows, currents, objects in the river, weather and idiot pleasure boaters. One tow operator was relating how tight it was up on the Illinois River meeting other river traffic. "It was really taht in der, I'll tell ya. It was so taht, I was jus a pointin' and a strokin' to get 'roun em. Day ain't no water up dere in dat Illinois."

The Mississippi is forested on both sides, with frequent sandy shoals and beaches. Boaters use many of the beaches during the summer months when water levels are low.

We conferred with our traveling companions and learned that we could tie-up overnight below the Kaskaskia Lock & Dam, a short detour off the main channel.

The last time we called South Dakota, Eva's 46 year-old sister, Cora, was failing fast and it sounded as though she was in her last days. We searched for a place where we could leave the boat and motor back to South Dakota, but no place existed in this stretch of the Mississippi near the Ohio River.

We received notice on our VHF that the tow Zeus was grounded with three petroleum barges. The US Coast Guard asked him many questions because of his volatile and environmentally toxic load and requested he do soundings to determine if his barges were leaking. He was trying to make the upstream curve and was pushed into the southern bank. Often tows will ground their cargo on purpose to allow downstream tows to pass. When the way is clear, they back off their temporary moorings and go on.

We met canoeists going down the Mississippi river one morning. Two brown-roasted fellows from Minneapolis had tied their canoes together and erected a mast with sail. They were drifting in the river waiting for the strong southerly winds to die down so they could make some way. We pulled alongside and talked with them for a while, offering assistance. They were both keeping journals, and on this 15th day of September, I imagine it was nearly a blank page.

At Cape Girardeau, Missouri, near the southern tip of Illinois, we tied to Kidd's Fuel Service barge on the river. This dock (no longer in existence, but they have relocated and fuel only is available) was right in the current, on an outside sweep. A new casino will replace a perfectly useful fuel depot and dock. Pleasure boaters are going to find it harder than ever to locate a place to tie-up while navigating the Mississippi.

A walkway ascended the river bank to a high flood wall where a steel staircase rose up and over, then descended to the other side. Friends, Erwin and Ann, from Carbondale had received our mail and planned to meet us, but we weren't sure they could find us. From the vantage point of ordinary earth creatures, scaling a river wall to find us in 3 knots of current along the river didn't seem easy; but near the appointed time, they climbed over the wall following a search along the railroad tracks and the shady part of town.

Coming back to the boat after dinner in real darkness with the current streaming by was another one of those occasions that made us wonder why we were doing this, but the fatigued body dragged the recalcitrant consciousness into the world of sleep. Many tugs visited during the night and I faintly remember *Genie* tugging at her lines like a dog aware of strangers. In the morning we dropped the lines, turned the bow into the current, and continued southward.

On the 16th day of September we approached the Ohio River and turned upstream, trading our following current of three knots for a bucking current of about the same speed. Immediately our progress became a crawl of six knots. After a night at an inoperable dam on the Ohio, we left early for a 12-hour day to the Tennessee and Cumberland Rivers.

We heard the Kentucky Lock and Dam, which impounds the Tennessee River, takes a lot of commercial traffic and we may have to wait two to six hours, so we went beyond the Tennessee River near Paducah, to the Cumberland River and the Barkley Dam and Lock which impounds the Cumberland River. The Barkley Canal connects Kentucky Lake and Barkley Lake.

The Cumberland is rural and beautiful. Wooded hills and limestone bluffs line the river. The river is narrow and we were surprised to find short tows negotiating such a tight channel. This is the way to Nashville and other places of intrigue, but we'll have to wait to do that trip when we buy *Genie II*. Or will this trip mark the end of our boating days? We have that Tom Sawyer wanderlust and we're already talking about the next boat.

We arrived at Barkley Dam & Lock and had a long wait as they were locking through a tow with several barges. We pulled into Green Turtle Bay Marina near the town of Grand Rivers, Kentucky, late in the afternoon and decided, after further calls to family in South Dakota, that this is where *Genie* would rest awhile. We tied her up under a covered canopy, said "adieu" to our friends and took a rental car 950 miles into the desolation of the Dakota plains.

Cora passed away on September 29 after we had been with her for a week. She died in her sleep with all of us around her in mother's home in the "Little Town on the Prairie". We stayed for the memorial services and arrived back on the boat on the 7th of October.

Dream O' Genie was at a covered dock and the resident spiders had flourished in our absence. They were living in the creases of canvas and the nooks behind rails and poles, venturing out under cover of night and snaring innocent creatures who were fatally drawn to the lights. After sucking their victims dry, the spiders left behind monuments to the dead, a veritable polka dot field of desiccated fecal pocks which permanently scarred the white fiberglass, even after thorough cleaning.

We checked the engines, the bilge, the raw water strainers to the engines, generator and refrigerator, wiped the spiders away and got *Dream O' Genie* ready for the next leg of the trip. The Tennessee and the Tombigbee Rivers were out there to be explored so we got ready to drop the lines and begin the southward journey through Mississippi and Alabama to the port cities of Mobile and Pensacola.

Grand Rivers, Kentucky
to
Key West, Florida

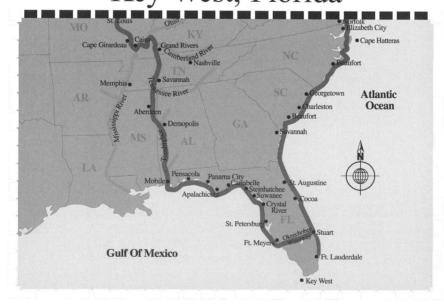

CHAPTER 17

THE TENN-TOM WATERWAY

Getting back at the helm after we had been in South Dakota for nearly three weeks reminded me of my feelings of inadequacy at the beginning of the trip. I felt like a new boater again.

We fired *Genie* up, checked the winds, looked into the water for currents, and released the lines. I had that old full-bladder feeling. We slid out of the slip, turned 90 degrees left and began the glide out of Green Turtle Bay and into Barkley Lake. After a few miles, it all came back as naturally as riding a bicycle or kissing. The trip was back on.

Barkley Lake is the impounded Cumberland River. If we continued on the Cumberland we would travel to Nashville, but that would be another year on another boat. In a quarter-mile we took the cut over to Kentucky Lake, the impounded Tennessee River that lies next to Barkley Lake. The Land Between the Lakes is an unspoiled recreational land with campgrounds and day use areas and the home of a herd of elk. There is a lifetime of boating experiences on the Cumberland and the Tennessee Rivers and we felt reluctant to move on.

The land is rolling and wooded and Kentucky Lake has numerous coves. The lakes are deep from one side to the other, but along the shoreline drowned trees provide bass habitat and a reminder that once these were wooded ravines with streams.

Late in the afternoon we dropped the anchor in a cove near Fort Heiman far removed from the traffic on the lake. Shimmering waves of small fish flashed across the water as bigger fish chased and devoured them. Evening set softly and the woods fell silent and cool. The fall colors of sweetgum were a deep burgundy and dogwood a bloody crimson. The woods were both peaceful and ominous as we lay quietly on the water. Suddenly the sacred silence was broken by an alarm that went off in the forest nearby. Something triggered the sensor and a loud recorded voice called out repeatedly, "Burglary, burglary, burglary. You have entered an area protected by a security system. Please leave immediately. Burglary, burglary, burglary."

One man's security is another man's pollution.

We left our sanctuary in the morning, catching the full glare of the open lake and 15-20 knot winds. There are few homes along Kentucky Lake and no evidence of cities or towns. Nearby, a small open boat flying the diver down flag sat unattended, a chugging compressor providing air to a diver on the bottom of the lake. The diver was probably collecting mussels. The Japanese use the shells of these mussels for seeding oysters. Because the oyster pearl closely resembles its nucleus in texture and appearance, this seed must be perfect. The Japanese have tried pellets of marble, silver, ceramic and even fish eyes, but none compare to the quality of "seeds" made from the Kentucky pigtoe mussel.

North of Savannah, Tennessee, the land rolls into rock canyons. The shoreline is terraced limestone with cedar, hickory and oaks. Eva had picked out Marsh Creek as a favorable overnight spot, but as we approached this obscure overgrown dribble I wasn't sure she had figured this one out right. Two fishermen were angling nearby and we slowed to a drift, hanging over the upper flybridge to talk with them. "Have you fellas been up this creek? We were hoping to anchor here tonight, but it looks awfully small for a boat of our size."

"No, we haven't been up there but if you'd like we'd be glad to run up and take a look." And so they did, coming back with the report that depths were nearly 10 feet shore to shore and that the creek widened out around the bend. Their boat had a depth sounder and with the knowledge they provided, we edged *Genie* into the veil of foliage that covered the opening and entered a still, inner sanctum. Behind us, in the bright light of the main channel, other cruising boats went by without the slightest inclination to stop. We marveled that they hadn't discovered these places that could go on a list of exotic and private hideaways. We dropped the bow anchor and sat as still as a bobber, a purple and cream colored sky covered us.

We wondered what happens to the current when the lock at Pickwick lets water out. Eva dropped a leaf in the water and it floated slowly upstream toward the marsh. Ah-ha, the downstream current backs up to this point and there is a temporary flooding when the lock opens. When the

The coves and gunkholes along the Tenn-Tom Waterway are quiet and secluded. This one on Marsh Creek was one our favorite.

lock closes there is a temporary decline in water level. We set the Danforth anchor off the stern because pool level was likely to ebb and flow throughout the night. If anyone wanted to get by, they were out of luck. We owned the creek.

We dropped the dinghy for a ride through the wooded creek to the marsh where we sat and observed the waterfowl. I ran the dink onto a sandbar and we sat as quietly as decoys while life on the marsh went on. Killdeer called and flashed across the flats. A Great Blue Heron gwalked its ruptured call. There was a cacophony of bird melodies. We rowed the dink to shore and walked the shoreline, observing the shaggy bark of hickory, the silver hide of beech, and the red berries of sumac.

Back on the boat, Eva brought out the fishing rod and reel and tried her hand at angling for supper. "If you don't catch anything, it's Spam again," I warned. She didn't. The sun set and a great horned owl hooted. *"And God saw everything that he had made, and behold, it was very good."*

The morning was dark and dreary. Rain fell gently. It was the kind of morning that suggests, "Stay in bed where it's warm and dry, read a book, make Cream O'Wheat and hot coffee." We did. When I couldn't sleep any longer I listened on the VHF to the river traffic. By noon we left the cold woods dripping and dark, and entered the brighter world beyond the veil that disguised Marsh Creek.

Mist hung in the valleys and made halos around the top of hills. White plumes moved across a mosaic of cinnamon browns and forest greens of the distant wooded slopes. Each tree species possesses its own profile, texture, and color. Lime green was at the riverside, burnished forms on the upland slopes, and gray limbs seared by early frost toward the top of the hill.

Near Savannah, the Tennessee River is broad with small houses on the shore and a number of fish camps and campgrounds. Before the Highway 64 bridge we caught sight of the ante-bellum home where General Grant spent time during the battle of Shiloh, a few miles downstream. South of the bridge is Pittsburgh Landing and the Shiloh battlefield. We could see a part of the battleground from the water's edge.

Pickwick Dam was a few miles farther south and we locked through, stopping for a weekend stay at the marina at Pickwick Landing State Park, one of the prettiest areas we had seen. Towering hills create a protected cove and the state park lodge and their smorgasbord of catfish, hushpuppies and regional dishes (for $8) made it one of the best food buys along the trip.

Connie and Ted caught up with us in their 50-foot Ocean Alexander, *Jubilee*. The last time we saw them was in the Trent-Severn Waterway of Ontario, Canada. We rented a car and invited them to come along with us for a tour of the 1862 Civil War battlefield at Shiloh.

Shiloh National Military Park is a cemetery with interpretive talks and literature of the battle sites. It was a bloody and a decisive battle for the Confederacy. Though neither side won decisively, it became clear that the South was not going to be able to dominate the federal troops and guarantee their sovereignty. They threw everything at the Union troops at Shiloh, and lost. It was the beginning of the end which came three years later, in 1865.

The day of the battle was hot, and with death came decomposition and disease. General Grant made quick work of burying the dead in mass graves. The Union soldiers who fought to preserve the nation were later exhumed and given separate grave stones with names.

The Confederate fallen, though their cause was noble in their view, were not entitled to national recognition. Their bodies lie in mass graves. In one grave, 700 Confederate soldiers are stacked in layers 7 deep. Ted and Connie, from Richmond, Virginia, the Confederate capital, were puzzled by the disrespect and failure to decorate the Confederate dead, but the message was clear. Those who sought to destroy the United States were the enemy and did not merit honor and recognition.

Captain Theodore O'Hara served as a Confederate officer and wrote poetically of the carnage at Shiloh:

On fames eternal camping ground
their silent tents are spread
glowy guards with solemn round
the bivouac of the dead

No rumor of the foes advance
now sweeps upon the wind
no troubled thought at midnight haunts
of loved ones left behind

The neighing troops
the flashing blade
the bugles stirring blast
the charger, the dreadful cannonade
the din and shout are past.

On Sunday the dockmaster took us to the local Methodist Church where we were befriended by a couple who took us to lunch and then gave us an extensive tour of the area. We were smitten with the beauty of the place. The southern part of Tennessee that touches Mississippi and Alabama is rolling countryside of woods and lakes.

Yellow Creek comes off the Tennessee River south of Pickwick in the northeast corner of Mississippi. Leaving the Tennessee was another time when we wistfully looked upstream and thought about all the good things we were missing—Chattanooga, Oak Ridge, Knoxville and the headwaters of the Tennessee River in the Appalachian Mountains. We looked at each other and said, "We have to come back here again."

At the southern end of Yellow Creek the man-made cut of the Tenn-Tom Waterway begins, a straight-as-an-incision cut that is as predictable as an engineer's rule. It runs for 24 miles with spoil banks on either side. The Tenn-Tom, begun in 1972, was completed in 1985, and since then sycamores and willows have established themselves in the chunk rock berms, providing some relief from the angularity of machine-graded contours. Nature dominates, and in another 10 years the straight edges will yield to the variety and spontaneity of an unmanaged area.

The Tenn-Tom Waterway is the biggest civil works project ever undertaken by the U.S. Army Corps of Engineers. Over 150 million cubic yards of rock were removed for the divide cut, more than was excavated for the Suez Canal. At least 350 million cubic yards were removed from the entire waterway which was twice the earth moved during construction of the Panama Canal.

There are two man-made projects which are discernible from space. One is the Tenn-Tom Waterway, the other is the Great Wall of China.

It's a 341-foot drop from Yellow Creek, near Pickwick Lake, to Mobile, Alabama, a distance of about 453 miles with 10 locks. Most dams lower the water level about 30 feet, but the first one near Bay Springs dropped us 84 feet, the deepest lock of our entire trip. Before we negotiated the Bay Springs Lock (now called the Jamie Whitten Lock), we spent some time in their resource center which shows the details of the Tenn-Tom, then it was off to anchor in Coot Cove a short distance away. It was a cozy gunkhole with wild turkeys in the woods and families of water otters along the river banks.

We were reluctant to leave our cozy anchorage so we lounged over a leisure breakfast. When we were ready to leave, we called the lock and they could take us. We locked down with Barney and Madelyn from Tobermory, Ontario, Canada, in *Pilothouse* whom we met the night before when we were looking for a place to spend the night. We traveled together through two more locks and stopped at Midway Marina where we provisioned and did chores.

Early the next morning we were told that if we wanted to go through Lock "C" (now called Fulton Lock) that day we should do so immediately as they were going to shut it down for repairs until later in the day. Eva was still in bed so she jumped up, got dressed and we left. No shower, no makeup, no breakfast. She got her shower indirectly as it rained a misty rain most of the day.

The water course through northern Mississippi is rugged and wild, a Jurassic jungle of heavy vegetation, vines and strange animal sounds. The river was full of logs, some partially submerged like alligators. Water hyacinths clogged the channels, their dark green trumpet shaped leaves and pastel purple flowers adding an exotic note to the river. They are the dandelions of the Tombigbee and boats plowed through mats of plants leaving a furrow for those coming behind.

North of Aberdeen, Mississippi, we watched logging operations along the shore. Logging trucks tumbled in from the hills in an endless line as giant cranes picked up their entire load in one bite. Extended arms stacked the logs into mounds to await shipment by barge to log heaven where they will metamorphose into the daily news. Nearby chip mills were steaming in the cool autumn air, looking like giant breakfast cereal bins.

The approach into our overnight anchorage near Aberdeen was behind a wooded hill in the Blue Bluff Recreation Area. Floating debris covered the water and we slowed to one knot as *Genie* nudged through the stuff until we were in the middle of the lagoon. We were alone again. Most of the other boaters had gone on to the marinas and left us in this misty pond of flotsam surrounded by sleepy hills. One last bass fisherman raced in, backed his truck down the ramp, loaded the boat and was gone.

The nearby dock was suitable only for small boats so we dropped the hook and settled in. Rain had fallen throughout the day and continued as we lowered the anchor; but late in the afternoon it began to clear and we decided to explore the ante-bellum town of Aberdeen.

The distance to town was a few miles away so we chose to take our bikes. We had never floated our bikes to shore in the dinghy before. Carrying them off the back of *Dream O' Genie's* matronly rear sundeck was like carrying bicycles down a fire escape. I slung them from one hand and with the other hand clutching the hand rail, lowered them down the ladder into

The coves along the Tombigbee are wild and scenic. We give this anchorage near the Blue Bluff Recreation Area five stars for beauty.

the nine-foot dinghy. The bike's frames and wheels took up the entire dinghy, partly hanging over the edge. The trick was then to get Eva in, or on the pile, while I steadied the chine-less dinghy, which under the best of circumstances, had the stability of a rolling log. Eva climbed on top in the slow motion of a chameleon featured in National Geographic—prehensile hands, prehensile toes, a dirge of sliding, grasping appendages.

Thinking we might need some dependable flotsam to cling to if we tipped, I threw in a couple of oars, then squeezed between bike wheels at the stern to operate the outboard.

Cranking the engine made the top-heavy dink wallow threateningly. A couple of pulls on the line, and BAM, we were gone. The throttle of this quirky outboard had to be in the *Start* position, which is a neighbor to *Fast*, so when Wiz started it was like firing-up a hot rod with ether. We made an instant wake, then slowed to a crawl and made a gliding drift into the dock.

The landing at the boat dock had to be done with great care. Eva climbed off the pile repeating the *chameleon-in-slow-motion* drama while I held the boat, then I slipped out of my cubby and grabbed the dock with one hand, single-handedly lifting the bikes onto the dock with the other.

The reward was a ride along a country road to a town of historic homes and wide rolling streets canopied with century-old trees. We crossed Mattubby Creek which was steaming in the cool fall air, then went on into town. Some of the grand old homes have died and are in hopeless decay. Curved drives led to stairs and phantom homes that have left only a trace of their prominence. But most of them have been restored by folks who know the value of 19th century craftsmanship and architecture.

Eva sat on the porch of the Magnolia house, circa 1850, and pretended she was the mistress of the house. She rocked and admired her domain and hummed an old folk melody, wondering aloud what the cook was making for supper. So did I, because I was the cook.

Holiday Haven, also built in 1850, is filled with rare documents, collections and family antiques. Cedar Grove, circa 1844, Sunset Hill, circa 1847, and numerous other plantation-era homes grace the city and are available for tour. Winding streets and hill top homes create an ambiance as elegant and seductive as the genteel south at the time of the Civil War.

Aberdeen flourished as a river town before 1850 when cotton was king and the economy ran on the backs of slaves. Planters built expensive homes so their families could enjoy the culture and stimulation of city life. Steamers were able to make it this far upstream from Mobile, although currents were swift and shoaling was common. Steamboat traffic brought exotic world goods to the interior—tea from England, imported European furniture, ice from the north, and salt. On the downstream run, the steamers shipped 30,000 bales of cotton each year to the warehouses in Mobile.

To be competitive steamboat companies lavished service on their passengers, serving gourmet meals and hard-to-find foods. Passenger cabins were beautifully appointed and ornately carved woodwork and heavy draperies decorated the recreational parlors and salons. Wild duck, turkey, sea food, melons, oranges and pineapples were served.

But steamboat travel also had its perils. Boilers ruptured; heavy rains produced swift currents. Shoals developed overnight. There was no maintenance of the waterways and each steamboat captain had to be dexterous, brave, and a little foolish to make his run, given the uncertainties.

When railroads arrived around 1850, most of the farm produce and cotton was shipped by rail. The farmers thought the railroads were gouging them on rates and called for a congressional survey to study the feasibility of improving the waterway and expanding river traffic so steamboat transportation would be a competitive way to ship goods. Congress ordered the survey in 1871, and concluded it was not feasible to improve and maintain the navigability of the Tombigbee. Aberdeen lost its status as the last great river city reached on the Tombigbee.

More than 22 presidents and 55 terms of office later, the Tenn-Tom Waterway became a reality and Aberdeen again became a river town. The ten dams have created depths sufficient for commercial traffic all the way from Mobile to the Tennessee River, and not only is Aberdeen on the path of commerce, but nearby Aberdeen Dam creates a recreational lake. Coves and backwater sloughs provide some of the best bass fishing in the state.

The benefit of tow and barge traffic is the extraordinary capacity of the river to move raw materials. One barge holds as much as 15 jumbo hopper railroad cars, or 16 eighteen wheelers. An eight barge tow, not uncommon on the lower stretches, is the equivalent of 120 railroad cars.

We rode the country roads back to the boat. A heavy fog lay on the water. *Genie* sat quietly in a peanut brittle surface of limbs and logs, seemingly strangled by debris. It was getting dark. Doing our circus act with the bicycles at eventide was even more exciting than when we had full light. We rehearsed our boarding (or is it piling?). Bikes on first, then Eva, splayed on the stack, me squirming behind the wheels to the outboard motor. Several cranks and we were off and still afloat. I calculated the distance to the boat, cut the engine and glided toward the swim platform. Not too fast or we'd upset things. I grabbed the edge of the platform and steadied the dink while Eva slid off as easy as a spider. Man, I'm glad she's not a klutz. She fastened the right davit; I got off, fastened the left davit and took the bikes off, walking the vertical ladder with the bikes hanging from me until I reached the platform of the sundeck where Eva grabbed them and tied them up.

By the time we were ready to retire a full moon shone through the trees. Frogs croaked and fish splashed, and the world seemed full of wonder.

Radiation fog enshrouded us like a cocoon in the morning. The sun was a faint halo through the mist and everything was motionless. We rowed the dinghy to the dock on the opposite side of the lagoon and walked the trail up Blue Bluff, a clay and limestone cliff 80-feet above Aberdeen Lake and Blue Bluff Lagoon. Fall was in the air and summer crowds were gone. We had the hills and trees to ourselves. I didn't think there were cliffs and hardwood forests in Mississippi, but it was like a scene in Kentucky, a diverse woodland of hickory, cedar, oak, and long leaf pine.

Spiders had been busy during the night making newly-born lace for us to admire. A soft breeze brought down the first leaves of fall, and we walked the trails congratulating ourselves for staying in the Blue Bluff Lagoon instead of choosing the predictability of life on the docks at a marina. The Blue Bluff Campground and Recreation Area is a Class A facility open to campers year-round, and one of the most picturesque recreation areas on the Tombigbee.

Before leaving the lagoon we radioed the lock to alert them that we wanted to lock through and were told to come on down, so we threaded our way through the labyrinth of half-submerged logs and flotsam back to the main channel. At the junction we became confused by the buoys and started down the channel that led to a marina. The sharp-eyed lockmaster watched us and called out on the radio to see if we were the cruiser that wanted to lock through. We flipped a quick U-turn and headed for the lock.

At mile 366 the Tombigbee River becomes incorporated into the contrived Tenn-Tom Waterway, but the Tombigbee is still young and too rambunctious at this early stage to be a real navigable course, so it wanders across the engineered route like a ditzy teenager. In many cases the loops (oxbows) of the Tombigbee are dammed so that the water course follows a straight line rather than wandering aimlessly. Up to this time the Tombigbee had been a canoe and fishing trail, but finally it got serious about being a river.

Eva was an excellent navigator and I love her dearly for her careful attention to matters I treat nonchalantly, but sometimes her anxiety level can be like being in a wind storm at the glass factory. She got her comeuppance as we approached the Columbus Lock (now called the John C. Stennis Lock). I radioed ahead, "Columbus Lock, this is the pleasure craft, *Dream O'Genie*, approaching from the north." Misunderstanding the name of our boat the lockmaster came back in his southern drawl, "*Screamin' Genie,* we'll have the lock ready for you when you get here." I wonder how he knew.

Jets flew overhead. We were nearing Columbus and West Point, major military posts. West Point was the site of a civil war battle. Several Union officers found the area so attractive, they came back to establish a town.

After the Columbus Dam we were in the Tom Bevill pool, a mere 136 feet above sea level but more than 300 miles from Mobile and the Gulf. I wondered aloud if a huge tidal wave could wipe out half of Mississippi and Alabama.

Water hyacinths became even more populous downstream, and mats of plants made islands to support wading birds. Water lilies also grew luxuriously, and the two plants covered the river so that boats had to virtually screw their way through.

Tom Bevill, senator from Alabama, did a lot for the region by pushing the development of the Tenn-Tom Waterway, and though he is called a public servant, he is treated like a king. A monument is erected to him and a lock named after him.

The Tom Bevill Visitor Center above the dam is a 3.2 million dollar white elephant that looks like an ante-bellum mansion dropped from the sky. The design is a composite of Waverly, Rosemont, and Kirkwood mansions nearby in the Mississippi countryside. Inside there is a grand curved staircase, tiered crystal chandeliers, intricate woodwork, period furniture, DeHaviland China, and reproduction paintings. Upstairs are historical exhibits and a large relief map of the entire Tenn-Tom Waterway.

Parked on the waterfront is the steamboat *Montgomery*, a snag boat paddlewheeler that was used earlier in this century for removing downed trees and debris from the navigational channels on seven major rivers, including the Tombigbee and the Black Warrior. The boat, fully restored as a working river steamboat, is on the National Registry of Historic Places.

We anchored for the night at the Sumter Recreation Area near Gainesville. It was a stormy night with thunder, lightning and rain. The morning was still soggy and we thought about spending the day ensconced in this protected cove, but we raised the anchor, and as we approached the lock, the sun broke through and we had a pleasant day dodging the predicted showers.

After the Gainesville Lock (renamed the Howell Heflin Lock) we were in the Demopolis Lake pool, elevation 73 feet above sea level, and still 254 more miles to sea level at Mobile. Demopolis is a fine old town with several plantation mansions open to the public. On Sunday morning we went to the Presbyterian Church and were received like friends of the Confederacy. They said that they were blessed by our presence. How's that for generosity and southern hospitality? In the afternoon we worked on a newsletter and walked into town at night to see the movie, "Forest Gump" at the local theater.

The Black Warrior River comes into the Tombigbee at Demopolis and the commerce of Tuscaloosa significantly adds to the barge traffic. The Tombigbee still has tight loops, and when tows meet the upstream tow gives way to the downstream tow by pushing his load into a bank. We came up on the tow Chippewa that was pushing nine barges of wood chips. I asked permission to pass, "One whistle or two, captain?" "Ah see ya, *Genie*. Take me on a one." These guys know the river and if there are any obstacles or trouble spots coming up, they advise you.

At Demopolis we met two other trawlers going toward Mobile, so we left together and made plans to anchor at the end of the day in Bashi Creek. There are few marinas along this stretch toward Mobile, so everyone was anchoring. At the Demopolis Lock, a third trawler sped ahead and we were now a four boat parade. Frequent radio conversations were transmitted and received, but none were acknowledged by the strangers in our midst. When we concluded that only three boats could fit in Bashi Creek, we called *Good News*, the non-communicative strangers, and learned that they too were planning to anchor in Bashi Creek. *Jubilee*, our friends from Virginia, decided to stop short of Bashi Creek and drop the hook near a designated anchorage by a highway bridge.

The fog was as thick as a wet blanket in the morning, and all the boats stayed on their anchors hoping the fog would lift. Listening on the VHF we heard *Jubilee* coming downstream. She was negotiating a meeting with a tow and was going to pass our creek in about 15 minutes. We couldn't imagine how they were doing this in dense fog, so we got them on the radio and asked how the visibility was. They said there was no fog where they were; but as they approached us, they found out what life in whipping cream is like and slowed to a crawl. We started the engines, lifted the anchor, and slowly followed them. Our radar was not working again so we ventured out with our eyeballs extended off the bow like the protruding eyes of a praying mantis. In a few minutes we were in the clear and had a pleasant run.

The area south of Demopolis is rich in Choctaw Indian history. At our anchorage in Bashi Creek there was a bloody Indian massacre. Nearby was the Choctaw village of Oka Loosa or "black water", which was the home base of notorious gangs of thieves who preyed on pioneer settlers. Other Indian villages included Faulukabunna (English interpretation = Big Bunny). Pushmataha, chief of the Choctaw, signed a treaty in 1816 with the U.S. government near Tuscahoma Landing.

Cotton used to be king in the lowlands of Alabama. Today it's recreation and lumbering. A long growing season, heavy rainfall, and now good transportation on the Tombigbee, make trees a principal crop.

After the Coffeeville Lock and Dam there weren't many places to stay on the Tombigbee. Lady's Landing was our goal, but it was booked solid, and when we passed, we could see why. There was room for only three boats on their dock along the banks, so we traveled for two hours more to an anchorage at Three Rivers Lake where *Jubilee* and *Good News* had already planted themselves.

The lowlands of Alabama are beautiful. The forests are tall, many of the trees support mistletoe, the understory is thick, and it has a wild and untouched look about it. It's a bird watcher's paradise with orioles, belted kingfishers, osprey and swallows seen frequently. The US Army Corps of Engineers has done an excellent job in preserving the natural beauty of the waterway. Dredge spoil areas are hidden behind natural landscapes, and forest operations transpire behind a facade of natural growth.

At mile 45 (from Mobile) the Alabama river flows in from the northeast carrying traffic from Selma, Montgomery, and Birmingham. From this point south, the river is renamed the Mobile River. It's still the same pretty river, but there is an increase in tow traffic. We spent the night in Big Bayou Canot with the lights of Mobile in the distance.

As we entered Mobile Harbor in the morning, the waterway was choked with barges tied up in fleets to anchor pilings. Tows scurried about pushing and realigning barges, similar to a railroad switch yard. Grain elevators, coal chutes, ocean going vessels, booms and hoists, the US Navy fleet and container ships made it certain that the South has risen again. A monstrous ocean liner came into the bay from the Gulf of Mexico, scattering smaller boats in front as if they were coots.

Mobile has a surprisingly low city profile but a very busy waterfront.

We ogled and watched as we slowly moved through the harbor to the big bay. Shrimp boats were a comin', their outriggers spread so they looked like giant water striders. *Miss Lorraine* passed us, a veritable ornamented shrimp boat with a menagerie of gulls and pelicans adorning her decks, rails and booms.

Along the western edge of Mobile Bay were the markers designating the way to Dog River and Dog River Marina where we planned to stay the weekend and meet son, Phil from California.

The Gulf crossing was something in our near future, and we thought about it a lot like the apprehension you have about upcoming surgery. Unpredictable weather, shallow water, and a sea of crab pots makes the crossing perilous. Many slow boaters like us opt to do it at night, leaving in the afternoon, cruising all night, and arriving at the other side the next morning, or by making short day runs from the panhandle to the small towns along the nature coast until they are in Tarpon Springs. The sight of the open bay and the Gulf of Mexico beyond made us pensive and thoughtful. We heard too many horror stories of boaters who got into trouble on the Gulf.

CHAPTER 18

FLORIDA'S NATURE COAST

Gale warnings were in NOAA's forecast. We eyed Mobile Bay, which at the moment looked fairly calm, and wondered whether we should set out. We dawdled indecisively. Phil was in Tennessee on business and drove his rental car to Mobile to spend the weekend with us before flying home. If we didn't move toward Pensacola on this Saturday morning, we'd just have to poke around town with his rental car. We really wanted a day of cruising with him.

Maybe the couple on *Good News*, the Hatteras that had traveled with us, would like to use Phil's rental car on Saturday, and on Sunday drive around Mobile Bay to Oyster Bar Marina along the ICW where we planned to be the next day. I went to talk to Don and Wanda, and they said, "Sure, we'd be willing to do that."

Resident boaters and the dock master were on the dock at the time and I asked them for their opinion on the state of the bay, and they said, "No problem. It should be fine."

So I went back to our boat and told Eva and Phil the plan and that the wisdom of the locals was "GO".

The decision made, we tossed off our lines and picked our way out of Dog River Marina, through the narrow channel marked with buoys and into the shallow bay. In the southeast corner of Mobile Bay the ICW ducks behind barrier islands and we continued eastward, through lagoons, estuaries, wandering rivers and an assortment of linear puddles that comprise the waterway off the southern shores of Alabama and Florida.

Eva had picked out a popular anchorage at Ingram Bayou (bayou: any of various marshy or sluggish bodies of water) where ospreys hunt and call. Phil was engrossed and whipped out the field glasses in wide-eyed amazement. They wheeled; he panned. We had seen so many that we went about our business disinterestedly. Friends of ours in Florida who live along the water with their sailboat tied to the dock were beyond familiar and bored with ospreys. They complained that their resident osprey eats its fish from their mast, and after it eats, it discharges the remains of yesterday's catch, which one might call ash. Then again, one might call it by its real name, which stains the deck and makes it look like you're in the guano business. Slippery in wet weather too, they said.

Exploring with the dinghy was delayed as Phil put his mechanical ability to work fixing the "play" in the wheel at the upper helm. Our sons are very helpful and love to tinker when they come aboard. We thought of ways to extend their visits with us.

We slept quietly in that pretty cove where ospreys hunt. In the morning we awoke, had breakfast and headed east on the ICW, reaching Oyster Bay Marina where Don and Wanda met us with Phil's rental car. They left; we threw off the lines again and passed beautiful white sand beaches before entering Pensacola harbor later in the day. We had trouble finding the entrance to Harbor Village at Pitt Slip but were soon settled in.

I thought Pensacola was a big city, but it is modest in its profile and sleepy in its tempo. The downtown struggles for survival, but is quaint and intact, not showing the deserted character of other downtowns we've seen. The marina was near the Seville District, a fine collection of 1800's buildings including the 1832 Episcopal Church, the oldest in Florida standing on its original site. It was used by Federal forces as barracks and a hospital during the Civil War. Many of the two-story buildings had long windows, tin roofs and siding the color of tropical fruit. Military installations are close by, but recent closings have brought hardships and a shrinking economy to Pensacola.

The wind picked up while we were there and blew across Pensacola Bay, carrying one of our white plastic chairs into the water. We were using the chair as a step stool because Eva couldn't get onto the boat from the low floating docks. The water was 10 feet deep and the chair was invisible as it lay on the bottom. I threw in another chair, tethered to the dock, to see if I could spot it lying on the bottom. Only then did we catch a faint image of the first one. With a swim mask on my face, I leaned over the dock with my face in the water and groped with an eight foot boat hook until I snagged something. I pulled tentatively and inched the pole through my hands until I caught sight of the prodigal chair and brought it to the surface where it resumed its place with the other three around the table on the aft deck.

The ICW runs inside white sand barrier islands eastward toward Fort Walton Beach. This is a very attractive area with numerous islands, but does not have the tropical flavor of southern Florida, nor does it have the great confederation of people and high rise buildings. The woods are diverse, with oaks and pines and scrubby palmetto palm.

While crossing the Choctawhatchee Bay we had a conversation with a tow operator who was interested in our boat. He saw our "For Sale" sign and relieved his boredom with VHF chatter. He was pushing a fuel barge against the wind and waves, and we talked about his cargo and how much fuel he was using per hour to maintain his six-knot speed. He was using 35 gallons an hour, in comparison to our 2.5 gallons per hour (to maintain speeds of eight knots). We discovered that many planing boats use more than 35 gallons per hour to get their boats out of the water and on plane (fuel consumption of about one mile per gallon at speeds of 35 knots), and some fifty-foot sport fishing boats consume over 50 gallons per hour (fuel consumption of about 0.6 miles per gallon, 30 knots). Our lubberly trawler averaged about three miles per gallon.

We spent the night anchored on the east end of the bay along with another boat, *Roemer*, that we first met at Green Turtle Bay, then again at Pensacola. It was fun to see familar boats at various places along the route— kinda like meeting old friends. We invited them over for cocktails and had a great time exchanging cruising stories. That night fifteen mile per hour winds lapped against the bow and kept Eva awake all night.

Dolphins played in our wake as we moved toward Panama City. The coastal community of pine and palmetto palm is little disturbed and human development is sparse giving the landscape an open, pleasant look, although it is flat and without much relief. The marsh grass and upland woods make idyllic home sites.

There is a section the tow operators call the grand canyon. Bluffs of sandstone and chunks of rock give it a rocky road ice cream look. It's on both sides of the ICW and is an outstanding feature in a landscape of flat plains. I was interested to learn that Tallahassee, the state capital, a short way northeast of Panama City, is wooded and rolling, unlike the interior of Florida.

The white sand beaches of Shell Island, opposite Panama City, were inviting so we anchored *Genie* and dinghied to a dock where tour boats and runabouts tie up. Sea oats occupy the fore dunes and the scene of blue water, white sand and red tourists made it postcard quality.

The Gulf of Mexico is warm and rich and full of life. Fishing is excellent, sponges are still collected, and in many places windrows of bivalve and univalve shells color the beaches and turn morning walks into collecting expeditions.

A little sand crab as white as the sand scurried across the beach in that inimitable side-wise crab run that looks as if he has no idea where he's going. But he found his burrow in the nick of time as a size five female foot approached and a petite giant stood over his burrow peering in. "Anybody home in there?" He looked out shyly, then disappeared again, until the trampling feet were gone and he heard only the endless song of the surf.

We needed to put a few more miles under our keel that day and reluctantly left Shell Island. Near Panama City a pulp mill's smoke stack smudged the skyline with soft plumes that reflected the rays of the setting sun, and the bay took on a surrealistic warm glow like viewing through rose-colored glasses. We anchored in Pearl Bayou, south of Panama City, which was alive with diving pelicans and feeding fish.

Many boaters had cellular phones aboard, but we thought we couldn't afford that so we bought a beeper and got an 800 number when we were in Pensacola. We notified family and friends of our new method of communication and listed it in our ads to sell the boat. While anchored in Pearl Bayou, our beeper went off and startled us. Thinking there might be an emergency, we contacted the ship-to-coast marine operator by way of our VHF radio and picked up our message. We felt very secure in our new-found connection even when isolated in a secluded anchorage. Then we worried that the phone bill would be equal to a month's cruising costs, but we never got a bill.

We headed for Apalachicola, the western edge of the big bend area of Florida. Tyndale Air Force Base sent delta-winged craft darting overhead, cracking the silence. Cypress swamps, small canals, and wooded home sites make living here idyllic. We read in a local paper about a seafood festival in Apalachicola; and as we cruised the ICW southward, we encountered many planing boats that were passing us at 20-30 knots.

We caught one of them on the radio and asked where everyone was going. "To the seafood festival at Apalachicola," was the reply. "Unless you have reservations, you're not going to find a place to stay when you get there. We reserved our spot several months ago, and I know they are all booked."

We were bummed. "Can we anchor nearby?" we asked. "Yes," they said, "but we'd be glad to see if there are any cancellations when you get there, and save a place for you if we can."

With that they were gone, and later in the day we heard faintly through the long distance that now separated us, that they had tried and were unsuccessful. Once again, we were impressed with the generosity of the boating community. People who knew us only from a radio conversation were willing to help us in any way they could.

When we arrived at Apalachicola there was, in fact, no room for us anywhere except in the river across from town. We anchored, dinghied to shore and had a wonderful time in this old town which was a cotton exporting port in the 1800's, a lumber port at the turn-of-the-century when the last of the cypress swamps were decimated, and now a laid back fishing village with the Florida Seafood Festival the first week of November. We pigged-out on oysters on the half-shell, crab cakes, gumbo, and deep fried mullet. The fishermen were out in force opposing the proposition in the upcoming election that would outlaw gill nets.

The blessing of the fleet took place toward sunset. Every imaginable kind of boat queued up for a quasi-sacred procession. Cruise boats, working shrimp boats, sailboats and yachts streamed along the river and under the highway bridge to a point where a priest gave his blessing; then the entourage circled back making a great spectacle.

Between festivals, Apalachicola drones somnambulistically, cherishing its historic homes and taking life easy. There is a construction formula for a historic Florida home: build a single story home with long windows that reach the floor; cover it with a low-pitched hip roof of tin; paint the siding the colors of melon or hibiscus and wrap the house with porches; establish it with palms and in the understories have plants with large leaves and colorful flowers that drink the rains and drench the atmosphere with erotic scents; put rocking chairs along the verandah for long, warm evenings when the crickets sing and the atmosphere is "close"; invite frogs and salamanders all around for a cacophony of wild creatures who call in the night; then sit back and enjoy.

We turned eastward and north along the ICW to Carrabelle, our jump-off port for the run across the Gulf of Mexico. We feared this crossing and contemplated seriously how we might go.

Most make the crossing at night, leaving Apalachicola or Carrabelle late in the afternoon, cruising all night and arriving at the Clearwater area after daylight the next day. We were terrified to travel at night with just the two of us and no autopilot. Besides, we would miss portions of Florida's Nature Coast that we were eager to explore. We decided to hop across to

Steinhatchee, a run of about 10-12 hours that with our boat could be accomplished in daylight.

The weather report at Carrabelle called for 3-5 foot waves in the Gulf five miles out and winds from the northeast. We waited a day and learned that the Gulf had been quiet and easy. We should have gone. Other boaters waited with us. We listened to the weather reports and compared notes. One sailor had ventured out three times and three times returned. He was thinking of spending the winter at Pensacola or Panama City.

The next day the forecast was also for 3-5 foot waves and winds to 20 knots. We got groceries and hung around. Late in the day Barney and Madelyn called us from their 36-foot Albin, *Pilothouse*. They were going to anchor off Dog Island for the night and "go for it" in the morning. We discussed the weather and decided to join them. The next day did not sound any worse than today, and today would have been a good day to go, but again we were intimidated by NOAA's forecast. We heard that NOAA had been sued by boaters when they predicted fair weather and light seas, then conditions were worse than anticipated. Now they give worst case scenarios, so we learned to paint their sordid forecasts a shade lighter.

We motored across St. George Sound to Dog Island then into Tyson's Harbor where we dropped our anchor near *Pilothouse*. Eva and I had time to go ashore with the dinghy and walk the beach of this Nature Conservancy Island. There were a few homes, an air strip and a surprising number of running automobile wrecks corroded by salty sea winds gathered at the beach like bums at a Salvation Army soup kitchen. They were obviously used by the islanders to transport themselves and goods to the beach where a landing craft ran ashore to taxi them to the mainland. Dirt roads ran the length of the island to homes on stilts. We walked the width of the island to the Gulf, past yellow flowering shrubs growing in the dunes. Dog Island's high sand dune ridges include some of the oldest sand pines in Florida, and the island is an important barrier for the eastern Apalachicola River estuary.

We got back in the dinghy, started the outboard in shallow water and broke the shear pin, so we rowed out to *Pilothouse* where we sipped cocktails and had a strategy session. We would leave at dawn's first light and make the run to Steinhatchee River, 70 miles across the Gulf.

The afternoon was gentle and warm, but toward evening the wind came up and *Genie* tugged at her lines and felt restless and disturbed. We were in the lee of the island but the winds were sufficiently strong to make even our protected anchorage rough. Waves slapped the hull giving us a wet feeling even though we were secure and dry. Eva slept with one eye open, tossing and fretting over the fearful crossing. The alarm went off at 5:15 a.m. It was dark as midnight. *Pilothouse* wasn't showing a light yet. We showered, had breakfast, and got the instruments to the upper helm. The winds were sharp from the east and we groaned with disappointment.

We thought the day would start calm with winds picking up later, but the Gulf had at least eight hours of wind to whip it up and we were starting off in blustery seas. Barney and Madelyn woke later, but in a very short time raised the anchor, and in the half light of dawn picked their way through the buoys to the open water of the Gulf beyond the point of Dog Island. We hurried, finished our last preparations, weighed anchor and followed.

It was rough. Three to four foot waves and occasional fives rocked us. With waves on the her bow, *Genie* lurched and plunged through them like a sporting dog. I let her go and sat firm. We decided to give it an hour before turning back. Barney and Madelyn, life-long sailors and now powerboaters, were even less stable in their Albin, but they said that if conditions didn't get much worse, we would be okay. We lost two good days when NOAA predicted five foot waves and the seas ran to two feet. Now we are finally under way and we were getting what was predicted. As we traveled along, our full-bladder fear downgraded to merely uptight and tense. The sea punched and rolled, and lifted the boat high enough to compress water beneath the hull which made thudding percussion sounds and vibrations.

Pilothouse could only do about 7 knots so we opted to pass them, lead the way, and get off the water as quickly as possible. Eva set the GPS for a straight course across to the red buoy "18" at Deadman Bay. Much to our relief, the winds began to die down after a few hours and the trip became ordinary and dull. Our minds slumped and visions and sounds occupied our brains like apparitions.

I heard a cry and asked Eva if she heard something. "Are you going crazy?" she replied.

"No, I thought I heard a voice."

"Out here?" She said, "There's no one around but us."

From the Gulf waters came another cry. "It sounds like a loon," I said. "How can loons be here?"

We listened as *Genie* droned on. I peered through the haze and focused on a black water bird that dove and then reappeared, and called again. "It is a loon."

I called Barney and Madelyn on the radio and asked, "Have you been hearing loons? I think I'm hearing loons, but Eva thinks I'm looney."

They said they had heard and seen them too. They should know, I figure. Their home is Tobermory, Ontario, the summer breeding ground for loons. I checked the bird book and learned that loons join all the other Canadians to winter along the coast of Florida. Both the common and red throated loons are fish eaters, and catching fish under three feet of ice in Canada is impossible, so they migrate to Florida.

The day wore on and the weather improved with decreasing fetch and soon our GPS guided us right up to the red buoy near the entrance to Deadman Bay and the Steinhatchee River.

The coastal areas along Florida's nature coast are extremely shallow so our approach to Steinhatchee was a long ride through a dredged channel clearly marked with red and green buoys. Finally, marsh grasses came into view, then hammocks of pines and the channel of Steinhatchee River with its modest homes, docks and fishing sheds. Eva stood watch on the bow searching for shoals and dead heads (partially submerged logs). By 4 p.m. we approached the docks of the marina.

We had planned to splurge and eat out, but the one restaurant in town was closed on Tuesday nights. The obliging dockmaster lent me his truck to make a run into town to the fish market, which allowed me a roadside view of things. Steinhatchee is a little fishing village of RV parks, disheveled country homes on stilts and fish camps. Clapboard fishing sheds were falling into the water and many of the buildings look tired and worn. We bought our own fresh fish and invited Barney and Madelyn to join us for dinner.

We were warned that getting through the channel back to the Gulf was unsafe at low tide, and high tide was at 6:49 a.m. so we had to be gone early in the morning or risk running aground. By 8 a.m. we were ready to go, but there was fog, so we waited while the tide ran out and the channel became more shallow. Near the new bridge there was an abutment left from the old bridge which has less than four feet of water above it at low tide. With our four foot draft, we had to be out before that. By 8:45 a.m. we were over the abutment. The depth sounder screamed as we came across the shallow area. We put the props in neutral and glided over the hot spot, then continued out of Steinhatchee to a point in the Gulf where we picked up our waypoint to Suwannee, the next overnight port.

When we started the long approach to Suwannee from the Gulf, we were again near low tide. The flood stage had just begun so we anchored in eight feet of water near the green entrance buoy "1", three miles out in the

Gulf, to wait until the channel was deep enough for us to continue. We dropped the hook, took a nap, and did some writing while the water rose.

Except for large homes lining the river, the appearance of Suwannee River and the surrounding landscape is of a time before civilization. Thick wooded jungles and tangles of growth cover everything, and homes with clearings struggle against the invasion of vines and tropical plants. By the time we cut through the weedy channel to the docks at Miller's Marina, it was nearly 6 p.m. with only a few minutes of remaining light.

The docks were dilapidated and rickety. Water hyacinth grew luxuriously around the docked boats which made them look like they were parked in a farm field. The dockmaster coaxed us in assuring us that the docks and the water were safe. *Genie* and *Pilothouse* nosed into their stalls and sat there with their chins in a salad bowl. The dock master was ready to go home, so he quickly gave us instructions for the morning, "Leave by 7 a.m. or you won't have enough water between the daymarks going back to the Gulf."

Suwannee and nearby Manatee State Park are special places. Fresh water springs bubble to the surface forming fresh water streams. The area is profuse with tropical plants and has a splendid wildness about it. We got there in waning light and now we had to be gone at the break of day. We felt cheated.

The daymarks along the coastline of the Gulf of Mexico are roosting posts for diving cormorants.

The four of us went to the local fish restaurant and Madelyn and I had the all-you-can-eat-shrimp and Eva and Barney had the fresh catch of the day. The frogs croaked, the alligators splashed and it was evening of our only day in one of the wildest places along the Florida nature coast.

Soon after 7 a.m. we were passing the daymarks that line the channel back out to the Gulf. The red and green markers are mounted on steel posts at close intervals like street lights to an endless highway. Each is occupied by resident cormorants and pelicans who lounge around like drunks at light poles.

We didn't get caught by low water, and at 8 a.m. we were in eight foot deep water of the Gulf again, heading out five miles or more to catch our waypoints to Crystal River farther south along the nature coast. The weather forecast was warning of unstable conditions so we decided to skip Cedar Keys and Yankeetown on the Withlacoochee River and go directly to Crystal River.

Our depth sounder was set to alarm at six feet and crossing Seahorse Reef, south of Cedar Keys, it screamed at us. The chart indicated depths of five and six feet at mean lower-low tide, and we were at mid-tide. We radioed ahead to our friends on *Pilothouse* and they were experiencing the same thing. They assured us that we were okay and soon passed over into deeper water again.

The approach to Crystal River was like Suwannee, an interminably long and scenic approach through shoal water and marsh grass, and finally into the channel created by Crystal River. Fresh water springs in the interior create the river and make an ideal habitat for the manatees. They love the warm waters of the springs and can usually be found there. Speeds along the river were very slow because the manatees are slow moving and many have been hit by boat props. No one argues with the restrictions, and there seems to be a healthy regard for these lovely, ugly sea cows.

A large nuclear power plant at the mouth of the river offends the natural beauty of Crystal River but it is a favorite area of the manatees who like the warm water discharge. Air boats buzzed around...unbridled nature, visual pollution, noise pollution; this is the southern frontier where anything goes.

Near the marina were a number of boils where manatees were known to gather, but it was late in the day and we didn't have time to investigate. Millions of gallons a day spill into the river and run to the Gulf.

We wanted to stay here an extra day and explore the incredibly clear water with the dinghy, but the weather prediction was that the next day was going to be the best day of the next several for going on to Tarpon Springs. Tropical storm Gordon was down in Jamaica and conditions were expected to worsen. Also, we had a friend waiting for us in Tampa Bay so we chose to keep moving.

A fellow boater, a local with a vehicle, took us to a shopping center where there was a laundromat and grocery store and picked us up again after we finished.

As we left Crystal River early the next morning, we were flanked with dolphins, three on each side. They swam in front of the bow wave and seemed to be hardly moving. They were of all sizes and some of the biggest we had seen. We imagined it was a family troupe with members of all ages.

The humidity was 101% and the moisture coalesced, droplet on droplet until drizzle formed. Purple bags hung from the sky. Water birds were everywhere, diving pelicans, crying gulls, following in our wake, hoping to see small fishes washed to the surface from prop turbulence. The Gulf and the nature coast of Florida seemed to be on the verge of climax.

It took over an hour to ride through the daymarks to the open R "2" buoy marking the entrance (or exit) of Crystal River. The coastline is cut into numerous keys, islands and shoal water of one to five feet. In this area the depth increases by one foot each mile distant from shore. We had to continue westward for several more miles before picking up our waypoint to Tarpon Springs.

In the afternoon the breeze changed from a balmy southeastly direction to northeast. The temperature dropped and the wind picked up. Small white caps formed.

We navigated through fields of crab pots, many of which we were not readily visible. The rays of the sun were in my eyes and the floats on the crab pots were dark green from algae, making them hard to see. Eva kept an eye out also as I maneuvered around and through them. We were shoreward of the sea buoys so there was no designated channel and fishermen are not bound to place their pots in any order. As a result, their random placement requires constant attention. I saw one on the starboard side that I didn't detect until I was nearly on top of it, and I watched it pass alongside us. One I missed seeing was already snagged on the starboard side. Eva saw it first and cried out, "Ron, you caught a crab pot."

She saw the float burst on the water and the crabpot come to the surface about thirty feet behind the boat. It skipped and danced on the ship's wake for a few seconds, then broke off. Now just the line trailed behind the boat. I continued forward, dumb struck and wondering what to do, because the line did not seem to shorten, nor was the starboard engine laboring under the strain of the nylon line that should have been tightening like a noose around its shaft.

"Ron, stop!" Eva shouted. I pulled off the power and put the transmissions in neutral. Small white caps lapped against the stern of the boat and *Genie* slumped into a sidewise drift. Our minds raced toward solutions. The weather was building, six to eight foot waves were predicted for late in the day and we were anxious to be off the water. We had an hour and a half to go to the protection of Tarpon Springs, but here we were with a line snagged on a prop or rudder.

"I've got to get in the water and take off that line," I said to Eva.

"No, you're not! I don't want you in the water and me left on the boat. What if something happens to you and we drift away?"

She was seeing herself as a widow at sea commandeering a 13-ton boat into port with her husband drowned at sea. Our dinghy was on the swim platform and would have to be lowered if I was going to get in the water. Because there is no swim ladder into the water, a swimmer has to launch himself onto the platform like a penguin jumping onto an ice flow. I thought I could do it, but my first mate was vehement about me not going overboard. She had a point. Swimming around a boat in rough seas makes your position as a buoyant body uncertain at best, and banging into the boat while below the hull made it look like a spooky enterprise.

She suggested we drop the anchor to stabilize us, but I was eager to get the line off and keep going. I walked to the edge of the boat and with a boat hook retrieved the nylon line, holding it in my hand and tugging it. It was not going to come off simply by pulling it.

"Eva, go to the upper helm and put the starboard transmission in forward. Just touch it." She did and the rope wound quickly.

"Stop," I called back. "Now put the transmission in reverse. Just touch it."

To make certain I wouldn't lose the line because it was now considerably shorter, I ran it over the rail and tied it to the cleat on the sun deck. When she put the transmission in reverse, I expected the line to reverse its direction so I was pulling on it; but it wound the line further and cinched my fingers down on the hand rail. Three fingers escaped but the index finger was caught and the tip nearly severed. I removed the shredded finger which was bleeding profusely and torn to the bone by the filthy quarter-inch line. Eva ran inside the boat for a roll of gauze and we wrapped the finger to stop the bleeding, then discovered that the line had come uncleated and was back in the water. I tried to retrieve it again, but it was too short to bring on board so it stayed overboard.

Now we had a very short line in the water (but not so short it couldn't get caught in the other prop), a bloody finger that looked like salsa, Eva and me in a state of shock - confusion - consternation - anxiety, winds picking up, waves increasing and one engine disabled. We cut the starboard engine and continue on our way on the port engine alone. Barney and Madelyn caught up with us by this time so we followed them.

We called the Coast Guard and asked about a marina close to a hospital in Tarpon Springs. Of course, they suspected the worst and were asking questions like, "Is the patient conscious?", "Have you applied a tourniquet?" Eva responded, "We're okay and don't require any emergency services. All we need is the location of the nearest hospital to get a few stitches."

Barney and Madelyn anchored their Albin inside a cove by the power plant and we came in on one engine and rafted to them. Barney got *Pilothouse* situated while I circled with *Genie*, bringing her alongside when they were ready to receive our lines. I told Barney I was going to get in the water and get that line off because in a docking maneuver we had a good chance of entangling and disabling the other prop. He would have none of it and volunteered to get in the water and untangle the line. What a brother.

We were very close to a county park full of people and fishermen, so we dropped the dinghy and went ashore hoping to find someone who could take us to the hospital. The county park ranger was sympathetic but said he could not leave his post, but maybe the resident sheriff could help. But the sheriff said he couldn't leave his post either. At this point, two Good Samaritans from New Jersey came along and offered to drive us.

We passed the municipal marina where we planned to dock and where friend, Karin, from California was going to meet us. We talked our new found friends into stopping, and there she was just as we had planned. I waved a bloody finger in her direction and asked her to follow us to the hospital. Six stitches and two x-rays later I was put back together and we were on our way to the boat by 8:00 p.m. No torn tendons, no broken bones, a lot of masticated tissue, nerve damage that may or may not mend, but still a fingertip.

Barney and Madelyn had drinks and supper ready for us on their boat. The events of the day were reviewed and discussed until we were exhausted and ready to begin a new day after a long night's sleep. The potential for really serious injury was averted, albeit I had a finger in stitches and would never point the same way again. At any rate, we were grateful for friends,

This is the place for sponges and good Greek food.

guardian angels, good Samaritans and the chance to survive without severe penalty.

The wind blew that night, but we were in a protected cove. We spent the next day in Tarpon Springs, a fascinating sea port with a history of sponging. Greek immigrants came in the late 1800's, following the lead of John Cheyney who launched the first sponge fishing boat, collecting sponges in the shallow Gulf by grasping them with a long handled hook. The collector looked through a glass-bottomed barrel and pulled the sponge into the boat.

Diving for sponges began with the Greek fisherman, John Corcoris, who fitted himself with lead weighted boots, a diving suit and air supply tethered to a support boat on the surface. By 1908 Tarpon Springs had a Sponge Exchange which stored, distributed and sold sponges. Sponges are still collected from the Gulf despite the popularity of artificial sponges, and the inlet is lined with sponge boats that are cleaning and drying sponges. The cleaned sponges are strung along the ship's lines to dry in the sun, then collected for grading and sale. A number of shops sell the popular wool sponges, yellow sponges and many artistic forms that have little practical utility but are great in dried marine "floral" arrangements.

Greek restaurants and festivals give Tarpon Springs an old world atmosphere. To further our experience among Greek Americans we went to the Greek Orthodox Church on Sunday. There was no doubt we were among Greeks. It was like a heavy diet of lamb, grape leaves and feta cheese. The service was mostly in English, but there were ponderous overtones of Greek custom and dialect. Incantations, rituals, recitals and choral responses made it feel like the other side, and we pink-skinned western Europeans felt out of place among the sun drenched olive-toned people. Inasmuch as it was standing room only, we exited halfway through the service and found a milk and bread diet among the Presbyterians, a mile away.

We moved the boats to Poppa's Restaurant Dock and dined on Greek food that evening. The weather report in the morning didn't sound good but we decided to go anyway, so we left Tarpon Springs. Barney and Madelyn were going only as far as Clearwater where they were meeting friends from Canada. They were staying a while before flying back to Tobermory, Ontario for Christmas.

We made the open water run from Tarpon Springs into the ICW despite the small craft advisory that was in effect. We didn't feel it was sufficient to stop us. Tropical Storm Gordon was dancing around, through the Straits of Florida, and turning northward into the Gulf...where we were!

The winds were northeast at 20-25 knots but we figured that inside the ICW, the effect would be considerably less. Karin was with us and we wanted to give her a taste of cruising before it got too bad. It was rough, but not threatening and we were surprised to find white caps on the ICW all the way to Clearwater. The wind was sharp and making surprisingly big waves in the broad sections of the channel. There was no one on the water except us and *Pilothouse*, an indication that the advisory was being taken seriously. We cruised along undaunted. The sun shone brightly and we were having an easy time of it in spite of the stiff breeze.

The wind continued to build as the afternoon wore on. We were in the vicinity of St. Pete's Beach when I began to worry that the increasing winds could tear off the bimini. We began calling nearby marinas, but discovered all of them were full. Everybody was ducking into hurricane holes. Some of the marinas were fully exposed to the winds and boats were bobbing around wildly. We didn't want to stop at them because we'd be in for a very rough night. One marina suggested another, which suggested another.

We were approaching Tampa Bay, a large expanse of water open to the ascending winds, when the Great American Boat Yard in Gulfport responded to our pleas on the radio. They were a working marina that did not cater to transient boaters, but Eva pleaded with them to take us in. She sounded desperate, and we were. They told us to come in, directing us through a labyrinth passageway to their protected marina, and helped us tie up.

It was a working yard, but we were grateful for the accommodations. If a hurricane came through here, we were in an excellent spot with land on all sides, high rises nearby and many small islands of mangrove to dampen swells and surges. Nearby was shopping and public transportation. We were set for a few days. This was no way to show Karin the sights of Florida, but she understood and was a good sport, helping us ready the boat for high winds. We lowered the canvas bimini and secured it, reducing the drag of the upper helm and its cover. We doubled all our lines and walked the dock nervously checking to be certain that we had secured *Genie* for hurricane force winds.

The dockmaster also walked the docks, checking to see if all the boats were secured. A free roaming boat in a storm is as threatening to other boats as the storm itself.

The last indication was that Tropical Storm Gordon was heading north up the Gulf toward us. A local bus driver heightened our fear with the prediction that Gordon would cross the west coast of Florida and come into Tampa Bay like most other storms of the past. Karin left us there and returned to California, anxious about our safety. We had only to wait and see.

CHAPTER 19

TAMPA BAY TO FORT LAUDERDALE

Tropical Storm Gordon moped along the west coast of Florida, turned eastward across the state at Fort Myers (which was south of us) and exited again on the east coast where he graduated from Tropical Storm Gordon to Hurricane Gordon. He got mean and nasty and went up the east coast blowing and hissing.

We didn't know at that time that Gordie would go north, wreak havoc, and then return to Florida, but we were not waiting so we left the Great American Boat Yard Hurricane Hole and set out across Boca Ciega Bay alongside the Sunshine Skyway Bridge toward the mouth of Tampa Bay.

The waterway here is a plethora of chalk block houses and xeric landscaping. The domicile impact on the environment is overwhelming. We ruefully regretted the small amount of time spent in Crystal River and Suwannee.

It took us only an hour to cross the bay and be in the canals behind Jack and Teasley's condo. We met these fine people crossing Lake Michigan to Chicago and traveled with them along the Mississippi, Ohio and Tennessee Rivers. Teasley was the sweetest little thing and was fond of saying to her mate, "Jack, we're getting too old to do these things." We heard her whimper after we had put in a long day, or when turbulence in the locks was moving them around and they were hanging on. At their age (70-something) they think there's only a few more years of this, but they were planning to make the open water run to the Bahamas in the winter. All this in *Watermark*, single screw Manatee, a lubberly boat with a broad bow. We wondered how they would do in the Gulf Stream.

The last time we had seen them was at Green Turtle Bay on Barkley

Lake. They got ahead of us when we took time to go to South Dakota in September. They invited us to spend the night when we came through, so we pulled into an open slip and were treated to the country club lifestyle in Bradenton and Cortez.

The coastline southward is a relief from the sand box homes of Tampa Bay. There are many small islands and beautiful homes along the ICW southward. The skyline of Sarasota appeared like a fruit basket array of colors and shapes. Ringling Brothers Circus has their winter headquarters and camp here, as do the Chicago White Sox and Baltimore Orioles.

North of Venice the scenery improved again. Mangrove islands gave sanctuary and privacy to homes tucked away on hammocks only a few feet above sea level. The ICW worms its way through lagoons, small lakes and swamps. Most of these water courses are natural but some are engineered channels. All of it is maintained to comprise the west coast of the Florida ICW. We did not have to go "outside" in the ocean since Tarpon Springs.

South of Venice and Englewood are sections as wild as the nature coast of Florida in the northern part of the state. There were stretches when we lost all contact with landmarks and felt as if we were in early Florida before the deluge of humans and homes.

Palm and Knight Islands have ferry service to the mainland; otherwise they're isolated. All the homes are built on stilts because they are exposed to the brunt of storms and surges on the Gulf of Mexico.

We anchored for the evening in a picturesque pond at Stump Pass near Thornton Key, and in the morning moved toward Sanibel Island. Cool winds blew out of the north giving us a welcome change from the rank, dog's breath balm of the last few days.

Cabbage Key was on the way so we got off the main channel and followed the markers to this classic, rambling frame estate where meals are a happenin'. The food is mainstream (I had a hamburger and a beer), the service hurried and the decor neglected, but the romance is heavy. We sat on the back porch where the decor was dollar bills. There's $35,000 tacked to the walls and ceilings. Not a space is left uncovered. New layers of bills with messages and greetings from people around the world cover the old until there is a literal tapestry of money. It was hard to eat without stealing.

The porch slides decrepitly away from the house and toward the ages-old Zulu Fig tree that covers it like a cloud. Support roots drop from the branches to the ground and vines scramble up and across its buttressed trunk. Air plants nestle in the crook of its branches and the sun hardly shines under the fig tree on Cabbage Key.

The house was built in 1929 by Allan and Grace Houghton Rinehart on a 38 foot high (above sea level) Indian shell mound, one of the highest points in southern Florida. The old house is now the restaurant and inn. It was constructed with a solar system, 25,000 gallon water storage system and a concrete reinforced storm shelter. Visiting Cabbage Key is a look at Florida when paradise was unspoiled. Cottages with wide screen porches line a trail that wanders in and around the shell mounds and through black mangrove swamps. Live oak trees are draped in moss and covered with bromeliads. Strangler figs girdle and choke Sabal palms and any tree that will lift them into the light.

We made it to Sanibel later that afternoon and picked up our mail that was forwarded there. That was the good news. The bad news was that the rate at the Sanibel Marina was $1.50/foot (40' x $1.50 = $60, plus $5 for electricity and $2.10 for tax, Total = $67.10), the highest we paid all year for a one night stay. Obviously we saved the best, or highest, for last, but Sanibel was worth seeing. It's an environmentally aware island where strict codes and planning have created a civilized jungle. Bike paths and pedestrian walkways are hidden from roadways; businesses are tucked behind walls of vegetation. The entire aspect of the island is natural. The supermart, which was hard to find because there were no signs, had a courtyard with parrots.

A large portion of the island is the Ding Darling Refuge, a reserve of grasses, trees, marshes, lakes, waterfowl and recreational land. Many visitors come during the winter to stay at the hotels hidden in the forest and near the white beaches edged with sea grapes.

The Intracoastal Waterway turns inland from Sanibel into the Caloosahatchee River and is the beginning of the Okeechobee Waterway. We stopped for the night at Fort Myers and met up with Lou and Sarah on *Dunflyn*, more of our traveling companions on the midland rivers. They were situated for the winter here and were going back to their Maryland home in the spring.

The downtown area of Fort Myers had seen better times. Outlying shopping malls have stolen the commerce and it looked forgotten. Seniors gathered at a shuffle board park for some serious puck-smacking. There was a tournament underway; people had packed their lunch in little coolers, and they were there for the day.

That night at Fort Myers I watched a trawler come into port like a ghost ship with red and green beacons arriving from another planet. Its diesel engines growled like woofers, the deck crew prepared lines and the dockmaster extended his arms like a mother welcomes a child, taking their lines and tying them down. I wondered where they had been. Ships bring messages of far away places and of private hideaways. I longed to have it tell me its secrets.

Our travel up the Caloosahatchee on the Okeechobee Waterway was into the interior of Florida. After the Franklin Lock we were in fresh water. Palms and giant oaks lined the banks. Water hyacinths, pretty but as virulent as a pest, clogged the waterways just like in the Tombigbee River north of Mobile, Alabama.

The farther east we moved the more wild and pristine became the river banks. A few homes sat on the shore nearly hidden from view, a comforting quietness compared to the business of Tampa Bay. This is old Florida, plain and natural.

Citrus groves appeared along the shores after a number of miles. We came to the frontier town of La Belle. They had a free city dock but three sailboats were tied and there wasn't room for a fourth large boat. A motel/ marina on the other side of the river called out that they had room. We hesitated, then called out, "What are your rates?"

"Twenty five cents a foot," they called back. "Can you afford that?" It was like there was a tag to their question.

"Yes, we can afford ten bucks," we said to ourselves. The question is whether we want to spend $10 with them or hang on the hook like a couple of sailboats had chosen to do.

"Okay, catch our lines, will you?" We tied the boat and walked over the bridge into La Belle, a Florida frontier town without restrictions or plan. We needed an ATM machine so we hit the three local banks, but after hoofing for an hour to all the banks, we concluded that they all had the same ATM network, none of which worked for us.

We had five dollars between the two of us and had left our check book back at the boat, a half-mile away. Exhausted, we stopped at McDonald's and spent every cent we had.

The next morning, with checkbook in hand, we grocery shopped and went into one of the specialty honey shops. Honey is the item of fame in La Belle, all kinds of honey, honey from orange blossoms, from clover, from strawberries. We thought an assortment of different kinds of honey would be great Christmas gifts for our kids so we ordered up batches to be sent with greetings. Our Christmas shopping was done in one fell swoop. How sweet it was.

North of La Belle we entered the Ortona Lock and rose eight feet up the Caloosahatchee River. This was the 142nd lock on our trip and we experienced something different from the rest of the 141. No sooner were we tied to the wall then the front doors were cracked open and water began to pour in. *Genie* moved around like a cow that's been spooked in her stall. We managed okay, but we didn't think they would raise or lower water levels by simply opening the door; but that's the way the Army Corps of Engineers does it on this run to and from Lake Okeechobee. Most locks control the water through baffles so disturbance within the lock is minimal. We imagined this system catches some boaters unaware and sends them ricocheting throughout the lock.

Some of the Caloosahatchee is diked with high walls. Often sugar cane fields, cattle ranches with Brahma cattle, or citrus groves were on the other side of the levee. The sweet smell of burning sugar cane-chaff was in the air. The sugar is in the stalks, the rest of the plant is left on the field. Nearby Moore Haven has a long history in sugar cane.

We went through the Moore Haven Lock, (more of the..."once you're in, we're going to open the forward gate, so WATCH OOOOOOUT!") and entered Lake Okeechobee.

The gate opened to an environment different from anything we had seen. The channel cut through thick woods of Australian Pine on the levee side and Casorina and Bald Cypress at the marshy rim of the lake. The levee was built in the thirties when there was great flooding in southern Florida, giving Lake Okeechobee a tilted saucer configuration with the water pooling at the southern end. Diversion canals and sluice gates theoretically send the water where it's needed most, which usually means the Everglades ecosystem is last. There's a call for a discontinuation of tight water management and a return to the natural cycles of drought and deluge. Air boats were working in and out of the swamp like dragonflies, spraying the bases of the trees, for what reason we were not able to learn.

The Waterway makes a straight cut across the lake, but we chose to follow the dredged shoreline route from Clewiston to Port Mayaca, the longer way around (11 miles) because there was more to see. The winds were high and the lake was rough. It's the second largest fresh water lake in the United States (Lake Michigan is the first) and has considerable fetch when the winds are up. The lake is very shallow (deepest in the center is 14 feet) and carefully buoyed, but getting out in the middle of it can be trouble in high winds. That day we were having 15- 20 knot winds out of the north.

Bass boats were running about sampling the fishing holes. The lake has numerous fish camps, and many of the camps provide guides, boats, bait, and lodging. It's the wild side of Florida and a favorite for fishers looking to get away from civilization. We were just touching an area that many have spent a lifetime knowing.

We anchored in a surprisingly deep, secluded, Y-shaped basin off the channel along the shore of the lake in marshy grass where flocks of small birds called from the thickets and buzzards circled endlessly until the last light. They then congregated like a great family in a towering tree. We were treated to a spectacular sunset of streaked water colors and wondered if this would be our last night to anchor. We were hoping to see an alligator or a manatee, but alas, did not.

The last human habitation before leaving the sheltered shoreline of Lake Okeechobee was a fish camp with covered slips for bass boats. It was a one-story outpost that implied, *for men only*. We imagined guys away from their families, wives and work, coming up here to fish, play cards, smoke cigars and do guy stuff.

There was a road bridge across the waterway near the fish camp and we tried to raise someone by blowing our horn. Finally someone responded and we were on our way again. The tree protected channel abruptly ended and we were in a sea of grass with open water. We spotted a pair of Everglade Kites, a South American species that is common in the Everglades.

Sharp winds from the north created small white caps. It was a clear day but we could not see to the other side of the lake. Arrhythmic waves did not get *Genie* into any kind of pattern of pendulous swings, and she cut through the water without a shiver even though the waves were on our beam for the first few miles.

The lock's entrance at Port Mayaca was exposed to the north and waves washed into the open lock, creating a disturbing tub of churning water. As soon as we received lines from the lockmaster, they closed the aft gates and opened the forward gates. *Genie* bolted for the open door and we hung onto her lines, until, with a little rope burn and persistence, we got her under control and exited eastward, the last leg of the great loop.

We were nearly finished traversing locks. We both agreed that these locks require more attention and have the greatest potential for peril of all the locks we have been through. Their unbaffled waters create strong flows and there are only hand-held lines.

It felt good to put the last big body of water behind us. If we never see a big lake or threatening ocean again, it'll be all right with us.

St. Lucie River from Port Mayaca to the next lock is straight and engineered, but the borders are wild and charming. An alligator with snow tread hide pattern lolled along the edge of the canal, his expressionless face and unblinking eyes giving him the innocence of a stuffed animal; but we knew that we were looking into the soul of a mindless eating machine. Eva spotted him while she was at the helm. We backed up and watched him as he slipped away like a bandit, dragging his nefarious reputation to the bottom.

It was my birthday when we stopped for the night at the St. Lucie Lock and Recreation Area and went to the kiosk to register and pay our $16 docking fee. The lady behind the glass apologized for asking if I was old enough to have a Golden Age Pass. Eva asked, "How old do you have to be?"

"Sixty-two," she said.

"He's 62 today and I'm not lying!" Eva replied gleefully.

It was a pleasant surprise mixed with soulful recognition that I qualified and was entitled to the senior discount of dockage at half price. Other "seniors" (I hate that word) have discovered this and come with their camping trailers to stay in Florida's warmth all winter, using up their 14 day allotment, then moving on to the next Corps of Engineers recreation area, rotating until it's time to go back to Michigan or Virginia or wherever. We stayed a few days and did some work on the boat since the dockage was so reasonable.

We spent Thanksgiving eating the evening meal in a marina's restaurant with Roger and Lea (whom we met in Lake Michigan and traveled with down the rivers). They ended their great loop tour in Stuart where they had begun. It was the first time we had Thanksgiving outside the usual family realm, and eating blackened fish with a fresh salad was almost sacrilege. The next day we invited them aboard our boat for a real Thanksgiving dinner, complete with an oven-roasted turkey, mashed potatoes, stuffing and the works. We laid out a smorgasbord on the chart table with drinks set out on the converted helm seat.

Friends, Marci and Dave, came from Satellite Beach for a day and we had lunch on the aft deck after traveling through the St. Lucie Lock for a run on the lower St. Lucie River. We made the return trip back up river, through the lock again and reclaimed our spot at the park dock. Eva took sick for 24 hours following their leave and we spent a few days gathering up our resolve to continue, and end the trip.

We went through the St. Lucie Lock for the third time and into the St. Lucie River to Stuart. This is a very pretty section of river with a pleasant mix of river homes and wild mangrove.

We considered selling the boat in Stuart so we stopped and talked to brokers, but the consensus all along was that Fort Lauderdale was the best place to resell the boat. Back in the Intracoastal Waterway we passed through the Stuart Inlet and high-fived as we *closed the loop.* We had passed this point earlier in the year before our depressing and costly stay at Cocoa, Florida. As we moved toward Ft. Lauderdale, we remarked that it looked new to us. We decided we needed to do the trip in reverse to give us a fresh perspective and excuse to do it all over again.

We anchored in Peck Lake and dinghied over to Jupiter Island Refuge Area to walk to the ocean. We were savoring these last anchorages not wanting the trip to end. At North Palm Beach we identified the marina where we spent our first night. Feelings of terror and excitement returned as if it was yesterday. What an adventure this trip was, and so much of it done on the edge (of skill, knowledge, experience). The coast line along Jupiter Inlet to Palm Beach is splendid. We didn't notice the first time. Million dollar homes line the waterway, and some on the strand between the waterway and the ocean command views from either side.

We anchored overnight at Lantana, south of West Palm Beach. We dinghied to an open air restaurant where patrons and waiters toss left-over fries and food into the water and a school of conditioned catfish fight for the restaurant chum. At night, they hang around the bottom, playing cards and shootin' craps, but at mealtimes they're close to the surface lickin' their chops and vying for position. They have absolutely no manners. This could be efficient fish farming, but we understand these fish never make it to the kitchen.

In another day we were back "home." What a homecoming. We stopped at Bahia Mar where *Genie* was docked before we began the trip and learned that the rate would be $1.65/foot, which came to $66/night, so we drifted back into the ICW where we pondered our next move. We were told that the municipal docks were full, but we headed up the New River to check out the marinas upstream anyway. The Jungle Queen, a local tour boat, just about ran us down. Her captain came up behind us and sat on our transom, making us nervous and uptight. She's so big, she takes up the whole river. We scooted over as far as possible and let her by. We spotted an open space on the wall at the downtown Municipal Marina and asked the dockmaster on channel 16 if we could have it. A megayacht had gone into the yards for a few days and 100 feet of dock was open. We got the go-ahead and spent a few pleasant days in the downtown River Walk area of Ft. Lauderdale. The river is narrow and when the current is ebbing or flooding, the river runs. It is used by a large assortment of commercial cruise boats, water taxis, and megayachts. We later saw the Jungle Queen decked out with Santa and his reindeer, blasting Christmas music from her oversized stereo system.

Our cruise of America's Great Loop was over. We had maintained our schedule and arrived on December 1st, the day we had predicted. We were close to budget which was a surprise considering our rough start. What we overspent in one area (additions and repairs), was balanced by being under budget in other areas (docking, dining and fuel). We had cruised 900 hours, covered nearly 6,300 miles, traversed 147 lockages, and had not damaged a prop or run hard aground. While our goal had been accomplished, there was a feeling of sadness. We had completed the cruise and the last page in our deck log was filled. There was not going to be a tomorrow of new places to go and things to see. Of course, this wasn't the end of life's adventures, but forward thinking and planning met a void without a boat. If the boat sold quickly, we could begin thinking about the next excursion, but her sale was dampening the sweet sense of completion.

We decided we would both go home for the Holidays, then I would come back to Florida while Eva stayed in California. She hated to think of going to work, and I hated the prospect of coming back to the boat alone.

From our place on the New River we sought a semi-permanent place for the boat. We found one on Isle of Venice, a canal with condos, villas and apartment buildings. Behind the buildings are docks with live-aboard boaters and boats visited only occasionally by their owners.

Fort Lauderdale was the place where we began and ended our cruise.

We had our last great moment in boating when we left the New River dock. There was a strong ebb flow and *Genie* was pointed upstream. I started the engines and got back off the boat to release the lines and hand them to Eva. But as soon as I untied the bow line, the boat began to swing into the current. Eva yelled, I jumped aboard and got to the helm to bring her back into the dock, but the current was too strong. We still had the stern line attached and I was unable to bring *Genie* back to port. We were midstream, fighting the fast current with the stern line tethering us. Francois, our neighbor, left his boat and came to our rescue,

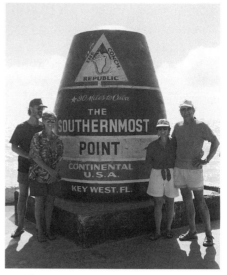

The United States dips deep into the Caribbean at Key West, Florida.

loosening the line and tossing it to Eva. We turned with the current like a fly on a trout line, and headed downstream.

By dusk we were on the Isle of Venice and behind the Bay Palms Villa where *Genie* joined a city of sail and power boats. We had a little time before we went back to California so we called Bill and Lynne in Key West and asked them if we could come down to see them on their sailboat. We rented a car and drove the only road which bridges the islands to the southernmost point of the United States.

When we arrived, Lynne was swaying in the ship's hammock, looking the part of a Key West free spirit. We walked the streets, past the Casa Maria Resort, a turn-of-the-century hotel that served the Flagler Railroad when it ran to the Keys. The 1830 Geiger House stands as a tribute to a modern day pirate. With lanterns luring boats into shoals, the nefarious Geiger became a millionaire salvager as ships went aground and their cargo and their ships became his opportunity. Audubon came to Key West in 1832 and his home is a designated national historic site.

Probably the most celebrated place in Key West is Mallory Square. Every evening a lot of craziness goes on. Tourists discover that watching weird people do strange and amazing things is as interesting as another sunset. A Frenchman with two house cats screamed and sweated and ran around while his pussy cats sat disinterestedly on stools licking their paws;

but through some kind of miracle, he got those little felines to jump over people and through flaming hoops.

It was a dramatic moment to look across the water toward Cuba and see the Western Union Telegraph cable enter the water. Castro severed it in 1962. At the nearby immigration service were rafts, tubes and miscellaneous flotsam that Cubans have used to float to our shores.

We went back to the boat at Fort Lauderdale and the following weekend Bill and Lynne came to stay with us and see the Fort Lauderdale Christmas boat parade.

We arrived early on the Intracoastal Waterway for a place to see the parade, swinging on one anchor with the changing tide; but as the evening wore on, other boats using two anchors squeezed between. Just as we were sitting down to dinner, a neighboring boat loaded to the gunwales with people drifted too close for comfort. We all tried to stay civil, after all this was the season to be jolly, but I was losing my cool. Eventually, after the food was stone-cold and holiday cheer had degenerated into scrooge-like behavior, we threw out a stern anchor and held our position against the hordes that were moving into the neighborhood.

Coral Serenade was the theme for the parade, so you can see that it was entirely **PAGAN**. Yachts were lighted like Christmas trees and the sound tracks were loud enough to make waves on the ICW. South Florida's newest radio station had musical lighted surfing Santas and speakers blaring rhythm and blues. The Goodyear blimp and Blockbuster Video blimps were overhead, lighted and blinking; land based search lights raced across the tropical sky, fireworks burst from the lead boat carrying the Grand Marshall, Regis Philbin, and helicopters flitted about like dragonflies, their staccato rhythms creating a celebrative invasion atmosphere.

One boat was decorated as Santa's sub pulled by four reindeer.

"Lord, help us."

Another boat had four dancers gyrating and singing "Sock it to me, Sock it to me."

"Lord, have mercy."

They played *We Three Kings Of Orient Are* in reggae.

"Lord, forgive us."

A sailboat with ten wooden soldiers was cute. The next boat had a big neon octopus and a dolphin strumming a base.

"Lord, send snow."

We needed to see cold and bundled choristers and crèches, and stars of David. Instead we were watching a sixty foot cruiser with dancing girls in tight skirts, or no skirts at all. It was awful, I could hardly watch. A sea horse played a saxophone on one lighted boat and a bull frog played a tambourine.

Spectator boats rafted in pods. Gals wore blinking earrings, guys were decked in floral leis. It was an aquatic Sodom, but it was a warm tropical night with the temperature at 78...AND WE WERE HAVING A GREAT TIME.

We packed most of our stuff off the boat in the following days and had UPS pick up fifteen boxes, leaving a survival amount of things for me when I returned. On December 14th we locked up *Genie*, asking a couple of brokers who were cooperating in her sale to look after her. Eva wept.

With a mixture of relief and regret we left the boat. The trip was over. We had completed the whole loop with nothing more serious than a nearly-lost finger, and a deficit financial situation; but we were full of fond memories, photos, and marriage-wrecking as well as marriage-enriching experiences. We had accomplished one of our objectives—to give ourselves great photo opportunities and the material for many stories; but it turned out to be much more than that.

The flight home was long, and homecoming was sweet. Friends, Barbara and Ben, had turned on the house lights, put fresh sheets on the bed and left a basket of muffins and fruit for breakfast.

I fell in love with house and home and marveled at its conveniences and space. What a beautiful place. What grand views of the greening hills. The house didn't move, it was big, and we could take lavish showers and see television with a predictable signal. Eva, not so thrilled, got ready to go back to work. She could live on the boat forever. Not me. I was delighted to be home and would be content to go back to a regular job if she would go back to Florida and sell the boat.

The day after our arrival home, the hospital laboratory staff invited themselves over for a Christmas party so I cut a tree from the yard, trimmed it in record time and Christmas began. On Monday Eva was back to work. I finished some writing chores and got sick. I spent days in bed like a mope waiting for this opportunity to be home.

We spent New Year's Eve in the hot tub and on January 5th said good-bye to each other at the airport at five in the morning. I went back to Florida to sell the boat and write, Eva stayed in California and quickly became engulfed in the tasks at the hospital. Both of us were discontent and wishing for something different. What, we wondered, would be next?

APPENDIX

A POTPOURRI OF INFORMATION

There are people who dream of doing part or all of this trip but lack the necessary knowledge. This section includes essential nitty gritty details and other useful information such as:

THE ROUTE
    Great Loop or Great Circle
    Optional Cruising Routes
    Planning Your Itinerary
    Our Great Loop Cruise Itinerary
    Charts and Guidebooks
    Resources
BOATING EDUCATION
    U. S. Power Squadrons
    U. S. Coast Guard Auxiliary
FINANCING THE CRUISE
    Expenses—Proposed and Actual
    Taxes and Registraton
    Insurance
THE BOAT AND ITS EQUIPMENT
    I'm Not Happy Being That Miserable
    Choosing the boat
    Equipment
        Navigation
        Charts and Publications
        Anchoring

THE ROUTE

Great Loop or Great Circle

We have often heard this cruise called the great circle cruise, but anyone who has taken courses in piloting and navigation knows that the term "great circle" refers to a circle on the surface of a sphere produced by the intersection of a plane that passes through the center of the sphere. On a gnomonic-projection chart, a great circle appears as a straight line. Examples of great circles are the equator and the meridians of longitude.

The 1994 Great Lakes Waterway Guide used the term, the *great loop cruise,* when referring to the route around the eastern United States. We prefer their terminology and have dubbed the route, America's Great Loop Cruise.

Optional Cruising Routes

There is more than one route to take when cruising America's Great Loop. This may be difficult to visualize so get a map of the eastern United States and Canada and follow along.

If you start in Florida as we did, you can choose to take the scenic route up the Atlantic Intracoastal Waterway or if you're in a hurry, go outside and cruise northward in the Atlantic Ocean, coming in when the weather is bad or when you need to provision.

You can cruise the Chesapeake and Delaware Bays, or again go outside and skip them — a big mistake in our view. Chesapeake Bay is one of the most exciting places in the world to explore by boat. Don't miss it.

There is an intracoastal route along much of the New Jersey shore which is passable for very shallow draft boats (under 3 feet). Our trawler had a draft of 4-foot so we went outside from Cape May to New York Harbor — our only open ocean run.

At Waterford, NY, on the Hudson River a major decision must be made — whether to take the Erie Canal westward or continue north to Sorel, Quebec, on the St. Lawrence River via the Champlain Canal, Lake Champlain, and the Richelieu/Chambly Canal System. The determining factor is your boat's height. There are 16 and 17-foot high fixed bridges on the New York Canal System between Troy and Whitehall which you must be able to clear. Sail boats must step/unstep their masts and this can be done at either end of the canal. The Erie Canal, on the other hand, has a 21-foot maximum height limitation.

If you go north through Lake Champlain into the St. Lawrence River and on to Montreal, you again have choices when leaving Montreal. You can continue up the St. Lawrence into Lake Ontario or go up the Ottawa River to the city of Ottawa. From Ottawa you navigate the 40-some locks of the 125-mile long Rideau Canal, entering Lake Ontario at the city of Kingston.

If you elect to cruise the Erie Canal your next decision is made about halfway to Buffalo, near Syracuse. At this point you can take the Oswego Canal to Lake Ontario or continue on to Buffalo and enter the east end of Lake Erie. At the southwest end of Lake Ontario is the St. Lawrence Seaway's Welland Canal with locks that connect Lake Ontario to Lake Erie around Niagara Falls.

For those who choose to enter Lake Ontario, the preferred scenic route is via the Trent-Severn Waterway which meanders through the province of Ontario from Trenton to Port Severn on Lake Huron's Georgian Bay. In Georgian Bay you can cruise northward through the 30,000 islands along the small craft route to Killarney and the North Channel, or you can turn left and cruise along the Bruce Peninsula. From there you can cross Lake Huron or continue to the North Channel. From the North Channel you can lock up to Lake Superior. While that is not part of the Great Loop, it would make a great side trip if you have time.

If you take the route through Lake Erie, you pass Detroit, cross Lake St. Clair and enter Lake Huron near Port Huron via the St. Clair River.

However you enter Lake Huron, all Great Loop boaters will pass under the Mackinac Bridge which separates Lake Huron from Lake Michigan and divides the "hand" of Michigan from the upper peninsula.

Here you have a decision to make — whether to head down the east or the west coast of Lake Michigan. The east coast of the lake is along the state of Michigan while the west coast takes you along Michigan's UP and the State of Wisconsin. Both are scenic and popular. We had relatives in Michigan so that made our choice for us. Next time we will go the other way. The Wisconsin side is the lee side of the lake. Prevailing westerly winds build considerable fetch if you follow the Michigan shore line.

At Chicago you have another decision which is dependent again on the height of your boat. Taking the Chicago River through downtown Chicago was a real thrill but there is a fixed bridge with a 17-foot clearance on the Chicago Sanitary and Ship Canal. If you can't get under that, you must take the Calumet-Sag Channel south of Chicago near the Indiana-Illinois state line. At mile 300.6 there is a fixed bridge with a 19.1-foot clearance.

At Cairo, IL, you must choose whether to stay in the Mississippi River and float on down to New Orleans or take the more popular Tenn-Tom Waterway which most recreational boaters use. To do the latter, go up the Ohio River for a few miles to either the Tennessee River or the Cumberland River. Both are scenic, and well traveled, but the Cumberland has less commercial barge traffic. They nearly meet at Grand Rivers, KY, where a cut makes either accessible at this point. The Cumberland leads to Nashville and on to the Cumberland Plateau. Great Loop travelers follow the Tennessee River to the Tenn-Tom Waterway and Mobile Bay.

At Mobile, AL, you can go out into the Gulf of Mexico or take the Gulf Intracoastal Waterway eastward along the panhandle to Apalachicola or Carrabelle. From there you can head across the Gulf or skirt Florida's Big Bend (Nature Coast) to charming fishing villages—Steinhatchee, Suwanee and Crystal River. You need a shallow draft boat and a good working knowledge of tide tables or you will go aground, but for the well prepared boater this area is a real treat.

At Tarpon Springs/Clearwater you again pick up the Gulf Intracoastal Waterway or go outside in the Gulf to the Cape Coral/Fort Myers area. Here you must make your last major choice of route.

For boats needing less than 49-feet clearance the usual route is the Okeechobee Waterway across south Florida. The other option is around the tip of the peninsula along the Florida Keys.

No matter which way you choose to go along America's Great Loop, you will have a lifetime of experiences and memories to treasure long after the cruise is over. And you will dream about the time in the future when you can make the trip again taking an alternate route to see what you missed the first time.

Planning Your Itinerary

When planning your cruise route and time schedule, keep in mind the prevailing wind direction, current flow, and basic weather patterns. Our route and schedule was determined based on 3 factors:

(1) Major river currents: It is better to go with them (Illinois, Mississippi and Tombigbee) than against them which would increase time and fuel usage.

(2) Traveling with the seasons: We wanted to be the farthest north (Canada) in the middle of summer.

(3) Hurricane season: Expect rougher weather on the east coast in late summer and early fall.

In the interest of economy and comfort, we chose to leave Florida in February, traveling along the Atlantic in the spring, arriving in the north in summer, and making our way southward in the fall. This worked out splendidly.

After formulating your general plan, break the cruise up into smaller legs, allowing plenty of time to accomplish them in comfort without putting a hardship on your vessel or crew. Plan to run no more than 6 hours a day or more than 4 or 5 days in a row. You need time to relax, get groceries, handle correspondence, do laundry and maintain the boat. We usually covered 30 to 50 miles per day, which translated into 150-200 miles per week or 600-700 per month. This left time to sit out storms and travel when we were comfortable and safe.

We had some unavoidable delays which prevented us from rigidly following the original plan, but we had allowed enough time and were able to stay on schedule in spite of the delays. We wanted to explore places, meet people along the way and sip margaritas at sunset. With our schedule we were able to do that.

Our Great Loop Cruise Itinerary

Date	Destination From : To	Statute Miles	Guests
Feb. 1-18 Ft. Lauderdale, Florida (Prepare boat)			
Feb.19-20 Ft. Lauderdale to St. Lucie Inlet		77	
Feb. 21 St. Lucie Inlet to Cocoa		91	
Mar.17-31 Cocoa to Jacksonville Beach		149	
Jacksonville Beach to Thunderbolt, GA		<u>165</u>	
		482	

April 1 Thunderbolt, GA to N. Myrtle Beach, SC		229	
N. Myrtle Beach to Morehead City, NC		150	
Morehead City to Norfolk,VA		<u>205</u>	
(via Dismal Swamp)		**584**	

May 1 Norfolk to Annapolis, MD (via Onancock,			
Tangier Is, Solomons, Oxford, St. Michaels)		335	
Annapolis to Reedy Pt, DE (via Baltimore,			Greg &
Chestertown, Chesapeake City)		182	Tracy
Side trip to Philadelphia, PA and back		87	
Reedy Pt to Cape May, NJ via Cape May Canal		85	Alan
Cape May to New York City at Hudson River entr.		<u>130</u>	
		819	

June 1 NYC (Hudson River) to Burlington,VT (via Cham-			
plain Canal, Vergennes and Lake Champlain)		332	
Burlington to Sorel, Quebec (via Richelieu River			
and Chambley Canal)		120	Ben &
Sorel to Mouth of Ottawa River via Montreal		117	Barbara
Mouth of Ottawa River to Kingston, Ontario via			
the Rideau Waterway		<u>250</u>	
		819	

July 1 Kingston to Trenton, Ontario via Bay of Quinte		113	
Trent-Severn Waterway: Trenton to Bobcaygeon		136	Laura&Tim
Bobcaygeon to Port Severn		99	Cora
Port Severn to Parry Sound via Beausoleil and			& Eric
the Small Craft Channel of Georgian Bay		78	Lelia,
			Mother & Aunt Audrey

Parry Sound to Little Current (Manitoulin Is.)	177	
Little Current to Kagawong (via Benjamin)	<u>38</u>	
Islands)	**641**	

August 1 Kagawong, Ont. to Rogers City via Detour, MI	170	
Rogers City to Mackiinac Is. (Incl. sunset cruise)	62	Teresa & fam.
Mackinac Is. to Harbor Springs via Beaver Is.	91	
Harbor Springs to Grand Haven, MI	225	Joyce, & fam.
Grand Haven to Chicago, IL	<u>140</u>	
	688	

Sept. 1 Chicago to Mississippi River at Grafton, IL		Amy, +
via the Illinois River	327	13 kin
Grafton to Mouth of Ohio River at Cairo, IL	218	
Cairo to Cumberland River (Smithland, KY)	57	
Smithland to Grand Rivers, TN (Green Turtle Bay)	<u>32</u>	
	635	

Oct. 1 Grand Rivers to Pickwick Landing	192	
Pickwick Landing to Demopolis, AL	233	
Demopolis to Bladon Springs, AL	98	
Bladon Springs to Mobile, AL	119	
Mobile to Pensacola, FL (Via Gulf ICW)	<u>75</u>	Phil
	717	

Nov. 1 Pensacola to Carrabelle, FL	207	
Carrabelle to Ft. Myers, FL (Via Steinhatchee,		
Suwanee, Crystal River, Tarpon Springs, and		Karin
the Gulf ICW)	384	
Ft. Myers to Stuart via Okeechobee Waterway	235	
Stuart to Ft. Lauderdale	<u>77</u>	
	913	

Dec. 1 Arrive Ft. Lauderdale	**TOTAL: 6288**

Dec. 2-13 Unpack and ship goods home, clean boat and list for sale
   Visit Key West by car
Dec. 14 Return to California

Charts and Guidebooks We Used

AREA	CHARTS	GUIDEBOOKS
Atlantic Intracoastal Waterway: Florida's East Coast	Maptech (BBA) ChartKit Region 7-Florida East Coast & Keys Maptech, Inc. Andover, MA 01810	Florida Cruising Directory Waterways Etc., Inc. Fort Lauderdale, FL 33335
		Waterway Guide: Southern Primedia Intertec Books Overland, KS 66282
Atlantic Intracoastal Waterway: Georgia, South and North Carolina, & Virginia to Chesapeake Bay	Maptech (BBA) ChartKit Region 6 Norfolk, VA to Jacksonville, FL Maptech, Inc. Andover, MA 01810	Anchorages Along the Intracoastal Waterway Skipper Bob East Rochester, PA 15074
Chesapeake Bay, Delaware Bay, New Jersey to New York Upper Bay	Waterway Guide Chartbook Communications Channels, Inc. Atlanta, GA 30328	Waterway Guide: Mid-Atlantic Primedia Intertec Publishing Overland, KS 66282
Onancock Creek	NOAA Chart # 12228 Chesapeake Bay (Pocomoke & Tangier Sounds)	Guide to Cruising Chesapeake Bay, Chesapeake Bay Communication, Inc., Annapolis, MD 21403
Delaware River to Philadelphia, PA	NOAA Chart # 12311 & Chart # 12312	United States Coast Pilot 3 Atlantic Coast: Sandy Hook to Cape Henry
New York Harbor	NOAA Chart # 12327	Waterway Guide: Northern Primedia Intertec Publishing Overland, KS 66282
Hudson River to Troy, NY	Waterproof Chart #57 (NOAA Charts # 12343, 12347, & 12348)	Waterway Guide: Great Lakes Primedia Intertec Publishing Overland, KS 66282
Champlain Canal & Lake Champlain to Richelieu River (Can.)	Waterproof Charts # 11 & 12 (NOAA Charts # 14786,14782, 14783, 14784, & 14781)	
Richelieu River to Sorel, St. Lawrence River	Small-Craft Charts # 1351 & 1350 Canadian Hydrographic Service	
St. Lawrence River to Montreal, Canada	Chart # 1338-CHS & 1339 (or) Chart # 14208-Defense Mapping Agency, Washington, DC	
Port of Montreal	Chart # 1310-CHS	

Montreal to Ottawa River Entrance	Chart # 1409 & 1410-CHS	
Ottawa River to Ottawa	Small Craft Charts # 1510 & 1511 - CHS	Small Craft Guide, Rideau Waterway and Ottawa River, Canadian hydrographic Services Ottawa, Ontario, Can. K1G 3H6
Rideau Waterway to Kingston on Lake Ontario	Small-Craft Charts # 1512 & 1513 - CHS	Rideau Boating and Road Guide Ontario Travel Guides Toronto, Ontario, Can M6G 2H2
Kingston to Trenton via Bay of Quinta	Charts # 2064 & 2069-CHS	Small-Craft Guide, Lake Ontario Canadian Hydrographic Services Ottawa, Ontario, Can. K1G 3H6
Trent-Severn Waterway, Trenton to Port Severn	Small-Craft Charts # 2021, 2022, 2023, 2024, 2025, 2028 & 2029 - CHS	Trent/Severn Waterway Boating & Road Guide Ontario Travel Guides Toronto, Ontario, Can M6G 2H2
Lake Huron: Georgian Bay, North Channel, to the Straits of Mackinac	Richardson' Chartbook & Cruising Guide, Lake Huron Edition Richardsons' Publishing Inc. Chicago, IL 60608	Ports-The Cruising Guides Georgian Bay/North Channel/ Lake Huron Guide Overleaf Design Ltd. Toronto, Ontario, Can M4L 3V2
Georgian Bay, Killarney to Little Current, Manitoulin Island	Small-Craft Chart # 2205 CHS	Small Craft Guide, Georgian Bay Canadian Hydrographic Services Ottawa, Ontario, Can K1G 3H6
Lake Michigan: Straits of Mackinac to Chicago, IL	Richardsons' Chartbook & Cruising Guide Richardsons' Publishing Co. Chicago, IL 60608	Yachtsman's Guide to the Great Lakes, Seaway Publishing Zeeland, MI 49464
		Michigan Harbors Guide Department of Natural Resources Lansing, MI 30257
Illinois River: Chicago to the Mississippi River	Charts of the Illinois River U. S. Army Corps of Engineers Chicago, IL 60604	Quimby's Cruising Guide The Waterways Journal Inc. St. Louis, MO 63102
Mississippi River: Grafton, IL to Cairo, IL on Ohio River	Upper Mississippi River Navigation Charts U. S. Army Corps of Engineers Rock Island, IL 61204	Waterway Guide: Great Lakes (See above)

Ohio River: Cairo, IL to Smithland, KY on Cumberland River	Ohio River Navigation Charts U. S. Army Corps of Engineers Louisville, KY 40201	
Cumberland River: Smithland, KY to Grand Rivers, KY	Cumberland River Nav. Charts U. S. Army Corps of Engineers Nashville, TN 37202	
Tennessee River: Barkley Canal to the Tennessee-Tombigbee Waterway at Yellow Creek	Tennessee River Nav. Charts U. S. Army Corps of Engineers Nashville, TN 37202	A Cruising Guide to the Tennessee River, The Tenn-Tom Waterway and The Lower Tombigbee River by Marian Rumsey International Marine Publishing Camden, Maine 04843
Tennessee-Tombigbee Waterway: Yellow Creek to Junction of Black Warrior and Tombigbee Rivers	Waterway Charts Tenn-Tom Waterway U. S. Army Corps of Engineers Mobile, AL 36628	The Tenn-Tom Nitty-Gritty Cruise Guide by Fred Myers
Black Warrior and Tombigbee Rivers: Demopolis, AL to Mobile Bay	River Charts Black Warrior-Tombigbee Rivers U. S. Army Corps of Engineers Mobile, AL 36628	CruiseGuide Florence, AL 35630
Mobile Bay	NOAA Chart # 11376	Waterway Guide: Southern (See above)
Gulf Intracoastal Waterway: Mobile Bay to Panama City	Waterway Guide Chartbook Florida's West Coast	Florida Cruising Directory (See above)
Panama City to Carabelle, Gulf of Mexico, West Coast of Florida, and the Okeechobee Waterway	Maptech (BBA) ChartKit-Region 8 Florida West Coast and the Keys Maptech, Inc. Andover, MA 01810	A Gunkholer's Cruising Guide to Florida's West Coast by Tom Lenfestey Great Outdoors Publishing Co. St. Petersburg, FL 33714

Resources

Armchair Sailor
2110 Westlake Ave. N.
Seattle, WA 98109
Website: www. Yachtworld.com/armchair
E-mail: armchair@wolfenet.com
800/875-0852, Fax206/285-1935
Nautical books and charts, cruising guides

Armchair Sailor Books & Charts
546 Hwy. 98E
Destin, FL 32541
800/451-4185, Fax 904/837-1579
Nautical books and charts, cruising guides

Armchair Sailor Newport
543 Thames Street
Newport, RI 02840
Website: www.armchairsailor.com
800/29CHART, Fax 410/847-1219
Marine books, charts, software, vogage planning checklists

Bluewater Books & Charts
Southport Center
1481 SE 17th Street Causeway
Ft. Lauderdale, FL 33316
Website: www.bluewaterweb.com
E-mail: help@bluewaterweb.com
800/942-2583, Fax 305/522-2278
Nautical books and charts, cruising guides, flags

BOAT/U.S.
Catalog Sales Department
880 So. Pickett St.
Alexandria, VA 22304
Website: www.boatus.com
800/937-2628, Fax 800/285-8692
Charts, books, cruising guides, all boating equipment and services

E&B Discount Marine (A West Marine Company)
201 Meadow Road
Edison, NJ 08818
Website: www.ebmarine.com
800-BOATING

Friends of the Trent-Severn Waterway
P.O. Box 572
Peterborough, Ontario K9J 6Z6 Canada

Website: www.ptbo.igs.net/~ftsw/
(or: www.parkscanada.pch.gc.ca/trent
Choose English, National Historic Sites, By province, Ontario)
800/663-2628, Fax 705/750-4816

Friends of the Rideau Waterway
1 Jasper Avenue
Smiths Falls, Ontario K7A 4B5 Canada
Website: www.rideau-info.com/
(or: www.parkscanada.pch.gc.ca/rideau)
E-mail: friends@falls.igs.net
800/230-0016, Fax/Tel: 613/238-5810

The Great Lakes Cruising Club
Suite 1540
20 N. Wacker Dr.
Chicago, IL 60606
Website: wwwglcclub.com
E-mail: info@glcclub.com
312/372-2344, Fax 312/372-2388

Maptech, Inc.
(Formerly The Better Boating Association)
1 Riverside Drive
Andover, MA 01810-1122
Website: www.maptech.com
E-mail: marinesales@maptech.com
888/839-5551, 978/933-3000, Fax 978/933-3040
Charts, electronic or paper

Marine Navigation, Inc.
613 South La Grange Rd.
La Grange, IL 60525
708/352-0606
Navigation charts, publications and nautical books

Mobile Engineer District
P.O. Box 2288
Mobile, AL 36628

Tennessee-Tombigbee Waterway Charts, Black Warrior-Tombigbee River Charts, and Alabama River Charts

Nashville District
Corps of Engineers
P.O. Box 1070
801 Broadway
Nashville, TN 37202
Tennessee River and Cumberland River Charts

Nautical Charts Supply Inc.
90 Hudson Street
New York, NY 1013-2825
212/925-8849

New York Nautical Instruments & Svc
140 W. Broadway
New York, NY 10013-3300
212/962-4522, fax 212/406-8420

National Oceanic and Atmospheric Administration
NOAA Distribution Division, N/ACC3
6501 Lafayette Avenue
Riverdale, MD 20737-1199
800/638-8972, fax 301/436-6829
Nautical charts and related products

Online Marine
P.O. Box 63
Oriental, NC 28571
Website: www.onlinemarine.com
E-mail: info@onlinemarine.com
Sales (Toll-Free): 888/933-BOAT Fax 336/315-9495
Online catalog of discount boating equipment and supplies

Pilothouse
1600 S. Delaware Ave.
Philadelphia, PA 19148-1403
215/336-6414, Fax 215/336-6415

Primedia Intertech Publishing
Waterway Guide
P.O. Box 12901
Overland Park, KS 66282-2901
Web site: www.intertecbooks.com or www.waterwayguide.com
800/233-3359, 800/262-1954, Fax 800/633-6219
The Waterway Guide — intracoastal cruising guides

Richardsons' Publishing Co.
110 W. Cermack Rd., Suite B303
Chicago, IL 60608
312/850-9412, Fax 312/850-9413

Seven Seas Cruising Association
1525 South Andrews Ave, Suite 217
Ft. Lauderdale, FL 33316
Website: www.ssca.org
954/463-243, Fax: 954/463-7183

Tenn-Tom Waterway Development Authority
P.O. Drawer 671
Columbus, MS 39703
E-mail: tenntom@ebicom.net
Website: www.tenntom.org
601/328-3286, Fax 601/328-0363

U. S. Army Engineers
P.O. Box 2004
Clock Tower Building
Rock Island, IL 61204
Upper Mississippi River Charts

U. S. Army Engineers
B-202 Clifford Davis Federal Bldg,
Memphis, TN 38103
Lower Mississippi River Charts
Waterproof Charts, Inc.
320 Cross Street
Punta Gorda, FL 33950-9972

Website: www.waterproofcharts.com
E-mail: iss@waterproofcharts.com
800/423-9026, Fax 941/637-9866

The Waterways Journal Inc.
319 N. Fourth St., Suite 650
St. Louis, MO 63102
Website: www.waterwayj.com
E-mail: Waterwayj@aol.com
314/241-7354, Fax 314/241-4207

West Marine
Catalog Sales Division
P.O. Box 50050
Watsonville, CA 95077-5050
800/538-0775, Fax 408/761-4421
Charts, books, cruising guides, all boating equipment

Women Aboard
P. O. Box 14254
North Palm Beach, FL 33408
561/775 4688, Fax 561/775-4687
Website: www.womenaboard.com

Yacht Registry, Ltd.
3511 Silverside Road, Suite 105
Wilmington, DE 19810
800/321-CORP, 302/477-9800, Fax 302/477-9811
Website: delreg.com/yacht.html
Incorporation service which sets up Delaware corporations

OTHER ONLINE SOURCES: The following online resources serve a variety of functions to help you sell, buy, charter, finance, insure, maintain, equip, and manage your boat. Many provide links to other boating websites. This is not an all inclusive list.

All About Boats	www.allaboutboats.com
Boat Facts	www.boatfacts.com
BoatNet	www.boatnet.com
Boat Owners World	www.boatowners.com

Boat Safe	www.boatsafe.com
Boat Trader Online	www.traderonline.com
Boating America	www.boatingamerica.com
Bob Stephenson's site	www.geocities.com/colosseum/3470
Coastal Cruising Magazine	www.coastalcruising.com
Cruising World Magazine	www.cruisingworld.com/cwdeckpg.htm
DataBoat	www.databoat.com
E-Boating	www.eboating.com
Heartland Boating Magazine	www.heartlandboating.com
Internet Waterway	www.iwol.com
Intracoastal Waterway	www.icw-net.com
Lakeland Boating Magazine	www.lakelandboating.com
Landfall Navigation	www.landfallnav.com
New York State Canal Corp.	www.canals.state.ny.us
NOAA	www.noaa.gov
Passagemaker Magazine	www.passagemaker.com
Power Cruising Page	www.powercruising.com
Shipslog	www.shipslog.com
Trawler World Online	www.trawlerworld.com
U. S. Power Squadrons	www.usps.org
U. S. Coast Guard Auxiliary	www.cgaux.org
U. S. Army Corps of Engineers	www.mvr.usace.army.mil
Yachtworld	www.yachtworld.com
Yachting Net	www.yachtingnet.com

BOATING EDUCATION

We were new boaters with little experience so we knew we needed to educate ourselves on all aspects of boating before attempting our adventure. (See Chapter 1 on our introduction and preparation for the cruise.) We owe a debt of gratitude to the officers, instructors and members of the Costa de Oro (Sail and) Power Squadron (CA) for helping prepare us to complete the cruise on schedule, within budget, and without serious mishap. We highly recommend taking boating courses with either the United States Power Squadrons or the United States Coast Guard Auxiliary.

United States Power Squadrons

The U. S. Power Squadrons is a private, non-profit, non-governmental and non-military organization of adult United States citizens, men and women who are socially compatible and have a common love and appreciation of recreational boating. There are no barriers to membership on the grounds of race, religion or ethnic background. Organized in 1914, USPS is the world's largest private boating organization.

Originally formed as the "power" division of the Boston Yacht Club, USPS now encompasses all boats—whether they be driven by engine, sail or manual power. As a civic service, squadrons of USPS provide a public Boating Course to men, women and youngsters 12 years of age or older for a nominal fee which covers the cost of the instructional materials. Instruction is provided by member volunteers who are knowledgeable and experienced in boating. After successful completion of the course, an interested person may apply for membership in the USPS.

As an alternative to the regular 6-8 week Public Boating Course, a shortened version, Boat Smart, is available to the serious student who desires a concentrated course. Passing Boat Smart also satisfies the educational requirement for membership in USPS.

In addition to the USPS Boating Course and Boat Smart, a PWC (personal watercraft) course, Jet Smart, is available to the public. All three courses have been fully approved by NASBLA (National Association of State Boating Law Administrators) and will satisfy boating education requirements in most, if not all, states.

Members improve their boating knowledge and skills by taking advanced courses on the subjects of Seamanship, Piloting, Advanced Piloting, Junior Navigation and Navigation. In addition to the advanced grades, elective courses in Engine Maintenance, Marine Electronics, Sail, Weather, Cruise Planning and Instructor Qualification are available to members.

Short, self-study courses called USPS Learning Guides are available for a small fee to the public as well as the membership. These include Amateur Radio, Boat Design & Construction, Boat Insurance, Calculators for Navigation, Coast Guard License - Preparation for, Compass Adjusting, Hand Tools, Global Positioning System, Knots Bends & Hitches, Loran-C, Navigational Astronomy - Introduction, Oceanography, Predicted Log Contests, Radar, Sailing - Introduction to, Sight Reduction Methods, Skipper Saver, and Water Sports. These guides are available through West Marine in both their retail stores and catalogs.

Other activities of USPS include Cooperative Charting, which is a program of observing changes or errors in conditions, facilities or aids to navigation as shown on marine and aircraft charts. These are then reported to the National Ocean Survey and aid in the up-dating of the charts and publications of the agency.

Most harbors within the continental United States have a Port Captain, a USPS member who stands ready to advise the membership of local facilities and conditions. This program was developed to help members when cruising or traveling to unfamiliar areas. A directory of Port Captains is available to members who request it.

USPS is constantly at work to develop safe practices of all of its members and is a member of the National Safe Boating Committee.

For information on the United States Power Squadrons' public boating courses closest to you, telephone 1-800-336-BOAT (in Virginia, call 1-800-245-BOAT) or visit their website at www.usps.org.

United States Coast Guard Auxiliary

"The U. S. Coast Guard, charged with the responsibility of maintaining pleasure craft safety standards, recognized the need for positive action. In the 1930's as today, most calls for assistance resulted either from a lack of basic seamanship or, equally serious, ignorance of the law. It was decided that what was needed was a new approach to the problem of water safety.

"The U. S. Coast Guard Auxiliary was established by the Congress of the United States in June 1939 to assist the United States Coast Guard in furthering Boating Safety.

"The Coast Guard Auxiliary has built its foundation on four cornerstones: Vessel Examination, Public Education, Operations and Fellowship. The Auxiliary's Courtesy Marine Examination program offers an annual check of your boat's safety equipment. The Safe Boating Public Education program reaches from the elementary school level with coloring books, to the youth courses, to safe boating courses." (From *Boating Skills & Seamanship Manual*)

The Coast Guard Auxiliary offers a safe boating course called Boating Skills & Seamanship. The course is approved by the U. S. Coast Guard and NASBLA. Other courses available are Sailing And Seamanship and Advanced Coastal Navigation.

To locate the nearest Coast Guard Auxiliary Flotilla in your area check the government listings in your phone book or write to U. S. Coast Guard Auxiliary National Store, 9449 Watson Industrial Park, St. Louis, MO 63126. You can call (toll-free) 800/368-5647 or visit their website at www.cgaux.org.

FINANCING THE CRUISE

Our Expenses — Proposed and Actual

	Proposed	Actual *
Boat Insurance for 1 year:	$2,000.00	$1,885.00
Furnishing, upgrading, etc.:	4,000.00	6,258.58

Fuel:
[Pre-trip estimates:

	Proposed	Actual
Total trip distance = 7,000 miles	8,500.00	3,812.11**

Cruise @ 6 mph (avg.) using 3 gal diesel/hr = 2 mpg
10,000 miles/2 mpg = 5,000 gal/trip @ $1.70/gal]

Repairs & Maintenance:

	Proposed	Actual
$ 500/month x 12 months	6,000.00	7,139.91(r)
[repairs (r), maintenance (m)]		2,030.23(m)

Dockage fees: [Pre-trip estimate: (Jan. 30 - Dec. 31) 336 nights/2=168
(Alternate nights docking & anchoring-average)
40 ft @ $1.15/ft = $ 46.00/night x 168 nights = $7728]

	Proposed	Actual
	7,800.00	5,313.82

Food:

	Proposed	Actual
$300/month/person = $600/mo x 11 months	6,600.00	3,126.12(g)
[Includes groceries (g) and dining out(d)]		1,434.97(d)

Miscellaneous:

	Proposed	Actual
Health insurance	2,575.55	2,575.55
Other (see below)	500.00	3,368.20***
CRUISING EXPENSES	$37,975.55	$36,944.49
Costs recovered when boat sold		(-)5,878.96
NET CRUISING EXPENSES		$31,066.53

*Includes expenses from Feb. 1, 1994 through Dec. 14, 1994 only.
Purchase and sale prices of boat not shown.
**The fuel expense is the total paid beginning with the first large purchase
at the start and including the nearly full tanks when we ended the trip as
well as the fuel used by the generator, so the cost is a little high. It was used

anyway to compute the following:
>   Total Fuel Cost = $3,812.11
>   Total Gallons of Diesel purchased = 2928 Gallons
>   Total Miles Cruised = 6288 statute miles
>   Total Hours Cruised = 900 hours

Using these numbers: Average price = $1.30 / gal.

Average cruising speed at 2000 RPM = 7 MPH using 3.25 gal / hr or 2.15 mi / gal

***Includes expenses for Charts & Guidebooks ($1421.71), Laundry ($174.88), Lockage fees ($184.37), Pumpout ($ 92.96), Clothing ($214.07), Entertainment ($ 247.18), Office expense and postage ($301.81), and other miscellaneous ($1031.22).

While our total expenses may sound high, this was all of our living expenses for the year. Over $13,000 was for upgrading and major repairs. You most likely would not have these expenses if you had your boat already in use. Many of these items would be incurred whether cruising or living at home. We had income from writing, rental property and accrued paid vacation leave to help meet our expenses while cruising. We sold our RV and truck and canceled the insurance on our car. We took bicycles along and used them to get around town rather than rent cars and considered this to be part of the adventure.

This was the trip of a lifetime and as with other traveling we've done, we've never regretted spending money to do it. The memories are worth the expense.

The goal of buying a boat to resell later requires you to buy the boat at a fair price and improve it in ways that make it more marketable, such as replacing worn upholstery, buffing the hull, refinishing teak and refurbishing the bright work. Every negative feature of the boat needs to be corrected. Chipped gel coat, clutter, and dirty lockers turn off buyers. A non-functioning system that may cost $200-$500 to repair or replace may cause a buyer to reduce his offer by $500-$1,000. Selling a used boat is no different than selling a used car. People pay the highest price for vehicles or vessels in top condition. Clean, polish, repair, straighten, replace until you're sick of it. Have an objective person come aboard and evaluate the condition of your boat. Address things that are obviously in need of repair. Borrowing funds for improvement may make sense if you can improve the marketability of the boat and recoup your costs quickly.

If you think a trip like this is beyond your means, here are some questions to ask yourself:

How can we reduce expenses? Might we be able to rent our house? Many cruisers reduce expenses such as house payments, utilities, phone, insurance, etc. by renting their house while they are gone.

Can we work while on the trip? What marketable skills do we have? Can we accumulate paid vacation and holiday leave for several years or take a leave of absence? You may be able to work (consulting, etc.), or leave the boat for a while to return to work and pick up at a later date.

As a last resort, ask your mother, "Hey, Mom, we want to buy a boat and go cruising. How about spotting us a few grand?"

"You want to do what?" she says with her hands on her hips and an incredulous look on her face.

Be creative. It will probably take several years to get the details worked out, but keep dreaming.

Taxes and Registration

When traveling through states you pay sales tax for your purchases according to the tax rate for the area. Other taxes (income, real estate, personal property taxes, etc.) are, generally speaking, paid according to the state considered your primary or permanent residence. That is usually the state that issues your driver's license, where your car is licensed, where you are registered to vote and where you get your mail. When you live or cruise aboard a boat, you may keep your primary residence or change it. If you sold your residence, own only your boat, have no driver's license and use a mail service which forwards your mail, you have a problem. (Or you may have the best of all worlds.) We aren't experts in this area, but think you will probably need to establish a state as your permanent domicile or you may be claimed and taxed by many. If you own any real estate property, that may be the state to consider as your permanent domicile. Consult professional advice on this matter.

When we purchased our boat, we were California residents with a boat we bought in Florida. If we had registered the boat in either state, we would have had to pay the sales (or use) tax on the boat's purchase price, which would have been a hefty fee as both states have high sales tax. Since we weren't taking the boat to California and weren't going to stay in Florida, we chose not to register the boat in either state.

A USCG documented vessel does not have to be registered in a state since it is documented (a national registration, not subject to state registration requirements). Several months prior to the purchase we contacted Yacht Registry, Ltd. in Delaware (See the Resources list to contact them) and formed a Delaware corporation which bought the boat (a documented vessel). Delaware does not have a sales tax so we avoided paying either the California or Florida state sales tax.

To avoid the Florida sales tax we had to sign an affidavit that we would get the boat out of the state in 10 days or be subject to the tax (documented vessel or not). That limitation was extended to 90 days since we made our trip.

Insurance

When getting boat insurance, you are asked in what area you will be cruising. The larger the area, the more your insurance costs. If you don't include an area and need to file a claim, you could be denied coverage if the area was not stated as one of your cruising areas. We thought it better to pay the fee then lie and not include a cruising area. It wasn't very expensive considering all the areas we cruised — east coast, ocean, Canadian waters and inland rivers. Some of the cruise is in foreign waters but not third world situations or high crime areas.

If you are a member of the U.S. Power Squadrons, you can get reasonably priced insurance by calling the United States Power Squadrons Boat Insurance Program (800/763-8777). Also check with Boats U.S. (800/283-2883) and the insurance company that covers your home and cars for comparison quotes.

THE BOAT AND ITS EQUIPMENT

I'm Not Happy Being That Miserable

You hear or read about cruisers who advocate going cheap, forgoing comforts and insurance. We liken that to back packing or tent camping. We've been cold and wet, endured lightning strikes and had water like a mote surrounding our nomadic home. We've bundled kids against the tempest and ate cold beanie weenies under conditions that would qualify for world relief.

Now, in our more mature state, we want to be coddled, both in land travel and in boating. We want creature comforts. Endurance has given way to enjoyment, asceticism to pleasure, penurious spartanism to reasonable indulgence. But we weren't retirees set for life with big pensions and health insurance. We still needed to work and had to maintain our comfort levels within a fairly rigid budget. We travel economically, not first class.

Our investment cost us more than bare boat existence, but mostly in food, fuel and dockage. We recouped most of the cost of the boat. Some other costs, like insurance, were not recovered, but it was worth the peace of mind to have it.

For us it was not prudent to accept the notion of losing the money we had invested in our boat, even though it did not represent our entire life savings. We intended to buy right, improve the boat while we owned it, install necessary safety equipment including up-to-date electronics, and break even when we sold it.

Young people, who haven't worked a lifetime and don't want to wait for retirement to cruise, are probably more interested in saving money and going cheaply. Hardships we endured as 30 and 40 year-olds became intolerable as we moved into the fifties and sixties. Our boat was equipped for people who had worked for years, saved and accumulated, and were ready to enjoy the fruits of their labors. We weren't willing to do it in such a manner that made the trip an endurance test. In classic misstatement, Eva proclaimed, "I'm not happy being that miserable."

We experienced a variety of boating styles along the way. Some folks with retirement incomes of over $100,000/year were traveling in boats we considered substandard. One couple we met along the eastern seaboard were university professors in a trailerable 27-foot sailboat. They had only a six horsepower outboard for power, no heat, air conditioning or hot water. Another small powercruiser was only 20 feet long with extremely cramped quarters which they shared with a dog and two cats. A retired airline pilot and his wife lived aboard a 70's wooden cruiser that needed to have its hull refinished each year. Other retirees were on 50-foot boats with excellent equipment and elaborate decor.

Harry and Margaret from Canada cruised on a single screw trawler that Harry remodeled into a year-long cruiser, avoiding expensive marine features by installing a wood burning stove and patio sliding doors. Pete was a cruiser on an expensive Hatteras who ate out frequently and spent little time on the hook, rented cars and saw all the sights along the way. Our forty-foot cruiser was a giant in Canadian waters but a pittance in harbors like Harbor Springs, Michigan.

There are a range of budgets. You don't have to go cheap and simple and you don't have to live like the rich and famous. Establish your cruising life style according to your budget and needs.

All cruisers have similar experiences, but we were happy we had heat in northern Michigan, air conditioning in Canada, GPS and radar when our visibility was reduced, and good ground tackle when high winds kept us in anchorages for days. An inverter allowed us to use the computer, electric appliances and even a hair dryer when we were at anchor. The only thing we coveted was a fully enclosed flybidge for traveling in all weather.

Choosing the Boat

It took us nearly a year to travel the Great Loop so we wanted a boat that would be a home on the water. Displacement hull trawlers provide ample living accommodations. Staterooms are large, galleys are well furnished, flybridge models have outdoor helms for operating in good weather, decks provide al fresco dining and places for entertaining. Displacement hulls boats are known for their stability and economy. They are stable when cruising open water in the ocean and large lakes and in rough water when at anchor. There were numerous times when the wind blew and the water was choppy but our trawler moved almost imperceptibly. We were amazed how sweet our rest was in the midst of storms.

We heard of people who did this entire Great Loop trip, however, in the amount of time that we spent in a port city getting the boat fixed. They got up at the crack of dawn, were on plane before they had breakfast and didn't shut down until they couldn't see anymore. For these people, the ideal boat is a planing hull screamer that minimizes their time on the water so they can come back and say, "I did the Loop. I didn't see anything but I spent a lot on gas and I set a new record."

We were also concerned about time, but we figured that if we started in Florida in spring, made it to Canada by summer, cruised down the Tenn-Tom Waterway in fall and back in Florida by Christmas, we'd be in pretty good shape. A displacement hull trawler could do that kind of speed and give us the stable home we wanted. Our top speed was 11.5 knots, but we usually cruised around 7-8 knots.

Because we were inexperienced, we chose a twin screw boat because it would give us the greatest opportunity for safety and maneuverability. Learning how to handle the boat was a challenge for Ron, but once he got the hang of it, he was very good. Actually, he wasn't so hot, but the twin screw advantage made piloting the boat in tight quarters a breeze. When we were negotiating near ninety degree turns in Parting Channel off Georgian Bay, we had to literally spin the boat on its axis to stay off the rocks. A single screw boat would have had a dickens of a time doing that. When docking, we could squeeze between boats with considerable ease, thanks to the rotating motion of a boat with twin props; and when we caught a crab pot on the starboard prop, we shut that engine down and continued on the other one. (Darn, we should have done that before attempting to pull the line off the prop and nearly losing Ron's finger in the process.)

There were times, however, when a planing hull boat with higher speeds would have been wonderful. Outrunning storms to the nearest port, making time over large bodies of water, leaving later and arriving at port earlier are real advantages. We remember leaving Beaufort, South Carolina, one day with a sailboat and a planing-hull Bayliner. The sail boat left at 6:30 in the morning; we left around 8:30; the Bayliner left about 10. Around 11 we passed the sail boat who was doing about 4 knots and the Bayliner passed us shortly after noon doing about 20. When we got to Charleston in the afternoon, the Bayliner folks were well into their Margaritas and the be-draggled sailors crawled in hours later.

Fuel consumption was a factor, however. The sailboat probably used a tablespoon, we used gallons and the Bayliner drank like a fish. If economy is a consideration, displacement hull boats are a happy compromise.

Gasoline and diesel engines have their respective benefits and risks. Diesel engines are long-lived and reliable. They often power trawlers. Gasoline engines are lighter weight and achieve higher revolutions, making them ideal for runabouts and planing hull boats. Gasoline is more volatile than diesel fuel and raises the risk for fires and explosions. Most fires are on gasoline-powered boats.

Gas engines are cheaper to buy, however, which may be critical when budgeting for a boat. And single screw boats, both gasoline and diesel, are less expensive than twin engines. Ron argues that our next boat will be a single screw diesel because of reduced initial cost and less maintenance, but he'll sure miss the savoir faire attitude he had with twin screws. He won't be half as cool bringing a boat into the dock in front of the restaurant at Myrtle Beach. With a single screw he may be as clumsy as the sailboat in the lock in the New York Canal System who got sidewise in the lock and tried to impale the lock walls with its stepped mast.

When you choose a boat, both the captain and his mate need to make the decision. Men, honor your wives and choose a boat she'll be happy living in. Women, honor your husbands and understand that he's interested in power, the way the engines sound and the way the ship feels under power. Of course, these can be important to women as well.

If the boat doesn't have updated equipment, budget sufficient funds to include GPS, radar, depth sounders, VHF radios and other gear that will optimize your chances for a safe and happy time at sea. Keep safety first.

Equipment

The following is a list of basic equipment needed for a long term cruise. It is not intended to be an all-inclusive list. Your needs may be different than ours. The size and type of boat will dictate the size and kind of lines and ground tackle needed. Don't skimp. Your safety, and that of the boat and crew, depends on having the proper equipment aboard and knowing how and when to use it.

Navigation Tools and Instruments:
- Compass
- Hand-bearing compass
- Depth sounder
- Speedometer/Knotlog
- Loran or GPS
- Radar
- Plotter and dividers
- Binoculars (7 x 35 or 7 x 50)
- Deck Log

Charts and Publications:
- Charts
- Cruising guidebooks
- Tide and Current tables
- Coast Pilots
- Navigation Rules book (required if boat over 39 feet)

Anchoring:
- 2 or 3 anchors of differing types with adequate rode (We had a 45-lb plow with 200 foot of chain and a 35-lb Danforth with 150 foot of three-quarter-inch nylon line.)
- Electric windlass (This is not only nice to have but a must on a big boat if you want a happy crew.)
- Tripline with float (Can be a plastic one-gallon milk container with lid and a line tied to the handle.)
- Wash down system to rinse mud off anchor and rode when retrieving it (May be a bucket with line attached to handle if your first mate was raised on a farm.)

Docking and locking:
- 4 bow and stern one-inch lines — each more than 1/2 of boat length
- 2 to 4 other three-quarter-inch nylon lines to use as spring lines —one-and one-half times the length of boat
- Minimum of 4 heavy duty fenders with tethers

Fenderboard (optional but very useful in locks)
Boat hooks (at least two)
Heavy-duty electric cables with adapters for 15 or 30 amp (for
        shore power)
Water hose for potable water
Other:
Flashlights and Batteries
VHF Radios — one wired near each helm, one hand-held
        portable model
AM/FM Radio
Dinghy with motor and oars
Life Jackets (also called Personal Flotation Devices or PFD's) –
        Coast Guard approved–one for each person aboard

VHF Radiotelephone

Licenses are not needed to operate a VHF radiotelephone in U.S. waters, but both a ship's station license and an operator's license are required for use in foreign waters such as Canada and Mexico. For information on obtaining these licenses, contact the FCC toll free at (888) 225-5322.

Even though a license is not required, proper radio etiquette is. If you are unfamiliar with proper radio procedures, contact one of the boating education organizations listed on previous pages or the FCC at the number listed above.

Some tips for proper radio operation are:
•Begin by specifying the vessel or land base you wish to raise.
•Always identify yourself by giving the name of your vessel and
        the radio call sign if you have a ship's license.
•Give priority to Distress, Urgency and Safety communications.
•Use the calling frequency to make contact, then switch to an
        unused working channel.
•Instruct everyone on board on radio usage in case of emergency.
•Do not use profane or obscene language.
•Do not request a "radio check". Learn how to test your radio
        before leaving port.
•Keep transmissions brief.

Like the United States, Canada no longer requires a ship's license to use a VHF radio. For more information, contact the FCC at the toll free number listed above.

Tools and Spare Parts (The Man's Point of View)

When we asked our Power Squadron friends what tools to take, they said, "Take a little of everything." That was good advice, but we would go farther. Take every imaginable tool you have. When you're stuck, no matter how much insurance or money you have, or AAA cards in your wallet, there'll be no one near when your boat breaks. You can never have enough tools. Forget the blender, the breadmaker and the crockpot; you want *TOOLS.* This from a guy who isn't particularly handy and was never eager to get in those places where the sun never shines (all problems on boats are in improbable places unsuitable for man or tools...and it's always dark).

Along the way we bought a hand sander, a large crescent wrench, huge channel locks, sand paper, wood screws, glue and Cetol wood finish. We took along a complete set of wrenches and sockets, both English and Metric. What we lacked were large enough sockets for huge nuts on the oil pan and on the propeller shaft, (which Ron never tackled).

Stuffing box nuts require "mothah" channel locks. If you ever have occasion to remove lockers and cabinets in the pursuit of blocked sewage lines (we did), you need hammers, screw drivers, drills, crowbars and a skilled carpenter aboard. (We didn't, but wished we did).

Boats require constant attention. Ron had bruised ribs from hours hanging upside down like a sloth repairing the bilge pump or its switch. The water pump was fickle, stopping mid-shower more than once, and finally had to be replaced. Impellers need to be inspected and replaced. Electrical equipment may require a volt or ohm meter. Wire nuts, wire connectors, electrical tape, silicone seal, and water proofing spray are needed.

Take time to outfit your boat. If possible, take short trips and learn what equipment and tools are still needed.

Don't let your wife take a course in Engine Maintenance. She'll be hanging over you with suggestions and ideas, but her nails will be manicured and she'll be smelling nice (unlike you). She will become catatonic if you suggest she drop down in the engine room with you to change the oil or get her smaller hands into a tight spot to replace the starter. Better yet, insist she take the course by herself, then she'll know everything and you can watch and cheer her on. Ron would much rather do the cooking than tackle the engine maintenance stuff. He'll take his chances on being in the shower when the water pump stops.

Don't forget the snorkel and mask. When you catch a crab pot on the starboard prop, it'll be you guys overboard, even though she's more buoyant. Democracy ends at the water's edge.

CUSTOMS

U.S. and Canadian requirements

When entering Canada you must check with customs. Ship's documents are checked and passengers questioned. Passports are not required, but it may be wise to have them along just in case. We didn't and were okay.

When re-entering the United States, we had to report to U.S. Customs and pay a $25.00 fee.

Weapons Aboard

We have been asked frequently whether we had a gun aboard for protection. We did not. We don't own any guns and have not felt any need to have one. Eva is adamant that guns kill family members more often than criminals, and that producing a gun in the guise of self-defense will provide an intruder with a reason to use his weapon. Ron was sure that under the proper conditions he could become Rambo, so the world was considered a safer place without a gun nearby.

Don't take a gun into Canada. It will be confiscated at the border. If you feel you must have a gun aboard, authorization must be obtained well in advance from the Chief Firearms Officer of the Canadian province you be will visiting. For more information call 800/731-4000 or go to the Canadian Firearms Center website at www.cfc-ccaf.gc.ca. We know of a boater (not in Canada) who lied to the authorities when asked if he had a gun. His boat was searched and a gun found. He was in a heap of trouble, but managed to wiggle out because he was a well-known person.

The community of boaters is wonderfully supporting. While there is risk associated with blind trust in a stranger, no one ever took advantage of us. The brotherhood of boaters implies compassion and consideration; to not accept the good graces of others is to miss the opportunity for friendship. Their model behavior became an inspiration to us and through their example we became more friendly, caring and responsible.

PROVISIONING

Cruising guides have a wealth of information for the cruiser, such as availability of laundry facilities, grocery stores and telephones. Some marinas have courtesy cars for boaters. They may be belching, fuming beasts that give the errand genuine uncertainty, but the only obligation to the user is to put fuel in it. We found locals very accommodating, offering rides or taking us somewhere to get groceries. A pathetic limp or a forlorn look that accompanies a two-mile trek back from a grocery store awakens a sympathetic response from residents who can see that you're a boater. Eva had been picked up on the streets of DeSmet, South Dakota, as a teenager, but she was surprised she got picked up in Elizabeth City, North Carolina with me limping beside her. Side packs on bicycles are necessary for large loads.

Food and Stowage

We had been advised by some to pack it in. "You're going to be a long way from grocery stores," they said, "you better have a week's supply with you...and fill the freezer if you can." This was good advice, but overstated. There were times in the North Channel of Lake Huron when we were out for a number of days, but the Great Loop Cruise is not a wilderness trail. The East Coast is highly populated, New England and Canada have numerous small towns for provisioning, and the midland river towns had grocery stores nearby. Nearby may mean, however, that it's a few miles away. On foot this becomes a problem. With bikes it became a challenge, wobbling around with a gallon of milk, two liters of wine, a twelve-pack of toilet paper, and three boxes of cereal. And we're not including an adequate assortment of Ben and Jerry's ice cream — 3 New York Super Fudge Chunk, 2 Rainforest Chunk and 1 Cherry Garcia.

Clothing

Dress for all seasons. Take a wide range of clothing, but remember that space is limited on most boats. Mornings on the flybridge may be cool but by afternoon the weather is warm. Layering is the best way to assure comfort in all weather. Water is cooler than land, and so is the air. Lined windbreaker jackets and sweaters are a necessity. We wore more wool, rubber and long underwear than we would have guessed. Of course, by the time we were in Canada, we were sweltering and were nearly obscene in our nakedness. But even there in July we had to dress for warmth when it rained. Having full rain gear that covers the entire body can be useful if it is loose fitting and made of breathable material like Goretex.

Plastic zippered bags or garbage bags help keep clothing dry. Laundry facilities can usually be found nearby and it's much quicker than at home because several loads can be done at once.

MISCELLANEOUS INFORMATION

Locks and Locking

Call the lockmaster on your radio. A VHF radiotelephone is a necessity. Communicate with him using the channel in common usage along that section of the waterway. The channels to use are often posted along the way and may vary from area to area. Check your guidebook for information and local customs. In Canada tie up at the blue line only if you wish passage through the lock. Otherwise tie further back.

Await instructions from the lockmaster. It's his lock and thou shalt do as he commands. Proceed into the lock after he gives the signal. Often there is a traffic light signaling when to enter. Enter on a green light. Be alert for instructions and move to an unoccupied wall. Prepare to don life jackets if the dockmaster requires it.

Try to determine in advance where to secure the boat, whether it be bow and stern or center cleat only. Bring the bow into the wall, have your deck hand secure the bow or center cleat. If securing bow and stern, the linesperson then hurries back to secure the stern. It works best to have 2 linespersons, one at the bow and one at the stern. When it was just the two of us, Eva began at either the bow or mid-ships, secured the boat, shut down the engines at the lower helm, then returned to the bow while Capt'n Ron left the upper helm and tended the stern. Our boat had a center cleat and we found that if there was a floating bollard, it worked best to loop the line around the bollard and tie it securely to the center cleat. The boat pivoted around the center cleat and the movement of the boat in the turbulence could be managed by persons with boat hooks at the bow and the stern.

We found a variety of systems were used to secure boats within the lock. In some cases a line was passed up to a lockperson, or they threw one down. The line was wrapped around a cleat and taken in or paid out as the boat rose or fell in the lock. The Canadian canals usually had a series of cables running the depth of the lock chamber and the boat's line was loosely looped around the cables and slid up or down. They had to be tended as the lines could bind on the cables. Others had floating bollards. One had a floating dock inside the lock, and a few had only ladder rungs to secure to. In that case the line was doubled and looped through a rung, then as the boat rose or fell, the linesperson had to quickly remove the line from one rung and loop it around another one.

After the lockmaster gives the signal, leave in the order you entered. Watch out for dead heads in and around the locks.

There were no fees for locking on any of the United States inland waters except the New York State Canal System which has seasonal or two-day passes. The amount due is based on the length of the boat. The Historic Canadian Canals also have a fee based on boat length. Season lockage, single lockages, 12 lockages, or six-day (need not be consecutive) lockage passes are available. For current information and fees call:

New York State Canal Corporation - (518) 436-2983

Rideau Canal, Ontario, Canada - (613) 283-5170

Trent-Severn Waterway, Ontario, Canada - (705) 742-9267

Weather

To say that weather is varied is too simple; but one thing seems certain — it's often windy, and wind to a "stinkpot" boater is not fun. To a sailor, the braver of the two, wind is a blast and the more there is, the sportier it gets. To a 15-foot tall trawler, wind is a problem particularly when docking. And wind on the beam isn't terrific either because wind makes waves and waves broadside to the ship make for a bumpy, if not dangerous ride.

Fetch is the distance that wind travels over water, and large lakes, sounds and river systems offer little resistance to prevailing winds. We were always impressed with how quiet the weather was in protected areas, and how robust and nasty were conditions in open water. Sheltered coves took on real significance for us.

We always had an eye and ear open for the forecast. Every morning we listened to the NOAA weather broadcasts and frequently throughout the day tuned in to the nearest weather channel on our VHF radio. The weather changed quickly and often unexpectedly, sometimes improving but usually deteriorating. We hadn't taken the USPS Weather course before our trip but it would have been beneficial in understanding weather patterns.

On the Great Lakes the marine weather forecast is often given in MAFOR code. It is a forecast of average wind and weather conditions over the open water of the Great Lakes, away from the modifying effects of the shore. The code is given in groups of 5 digits, with each digit referring to the location, time period, wind and weather condition. Write down the numbers as they are given for your cruising area and decode them after the broadcast. Decoding cards are available at many places along the route.

We had a bimini on our fly bridge trawler, but the curtains were primarily at the front, so our sides and back were exposed. This exposure was sufficient to suck the heat out of us and often we were bundled to the nines and still had trouble staying warm. When the weather turned warm, the semi-open bridge was pleasant and at those times the front isinglass came off as well. Twice we sought the shelter of the lower helm, but poor visibility forced us upstairs in the wind and cold.

The eastern side of the United States is wet. Expect about 3 inches of rain each month. Fair weather days are travel days and foul weather days become land-based days. If you're locking through in wet weather the decks will be wet, the lines will be wet, you'll be wet and everything will be cold.

In Canada we anticipated a fair summer, but approaching Sorel, Quebec, on the Saint Lawrence Seaway we experienced the hottest days of our year-long trip with temperatures in the upper 90s and no winds. Weeks later, but still in summer, we experienced some of the coldest days of our trip in DeTour Village, Michigan, on Lake Huron. Strong winds with a great fetch kept us tied to the dock on Harbor Springs for several days, and all the way down the Michigan coastline we had uncomfortable winds, interspersed with days when the winds were less than 10-15 knots. We learned after a while that winds 20 knots and higher were reason to stay in town because waves could quickly build making passage uncomfortable or dangerous. Winds on the bow were preferred to beam winds or tail winds because the boat could better handle waves breaking on the bow better than waves striking midships or coming from the stern. Following seas were some of our most difficult travel days on the ocean and large lakes.

When cold fronts approach and walls of darkness are in your future, button down the hatches and seek shelter. If you're at a slip or dock, stay put until the weather improves. If you're caught in heavy weather with decreased visibility, slow or stop, sound your position as required, and keep an eye on the radar for nearby boats. Seek the shelter of nearby land masses that will break the force of high winds.

Medical and Other Professional Services

Obtaining good medical care along the route is always a concern. We needed the services of an emergency room physician and a dentist on our trip as well as barbers and beauticians. If you travel with pets, you may need veterinary services. We found good caregivers along the way. The best source is personal recommendation. Ask at the marina where you are docked. People went out of their way to be helpful to us; the boater community is exceptional in this way.

Eva's regular beautician wrote on an index card the brand name, color, and other necessary information about the care of her hair, and she took that to shops along the way when she needed to have her hair done.

Mail Forwarding and Bill Paying

This is a problem for most cruisers whether they are traveling by boat or a land yacht (RV, motorhome, etc.). There are a lot of retirees who elect to spend a great deal of time on the go. This dilemma has been solved by a number of methods.

The method we used was to have the people living in our house collect, screen and forward the mail to us wherever we were. They got a big priority mail envelope and collected the mail in it and about every two weeks we would call and give them an address to send it to. With the post office priority mail we usually got it 2-3 days after they sent it, unless it was a weekend or holiday. We found that if we called them on the weekend and the mail was sent on Monday or Tuesday, we usually received it on Thursday; so we had to know where we were going to be. They addressed the package with the name of our boat as well as our name and marked it in large black letters: HOLD FOR ARRIVAL. Usually it was sent to a marina, but sometimes we had it sent "General Delivery" to the local post office if the facility was close enough for us to walk or ride our bicycles. One post office refused to give the mail to us without proper identification so be sure to take your wallet when you go for the mail. Guidebooks have information about mail pickup, addresses and phone numbers of marinas.

We handled our own finances so when we got a new batch of mail, we sat down and immediately paid bills, as many were due by the time we got them. Our income checks were automatically deposited in our checking accounts at home so the money was in the accounts when bills needed to be paid. Transfers between accounts were handled by phone. With computers and on-line banking, much of this can be accomplished via computer and modem. We got cash from ATMs but found that there frequently was a service charge (sometimes at both ends), so we withdrew enough to last a couple of weeks each time and charged nearly everything on the credit card. Before we left we got a credit card that was tied to an airline frequent flyer program and we used that card for all purchases. By the end of the year, we had accumulated enough points for a free airline ticket.

Many people have grown children living nearby to handle these tasks, but all of our children had moved out of the area, so we relied on our friends to help us out. We reimbursed them for expenses and tried to compensate them in other ways.

Some used their bank for bill paying, or paid a mail forwarding service. We also know of one couple with a "what will be" attitude who just left, letting health insurance lapse and other problems to be resolved however they may.

We had the most trouble getting our mail in Canada. It took much longer than in the United States. We missed the mail on more than one occasion and it was a real problem trying to recover it. We learned that several more days were needed and that priority mail doesn't mean anything there. We finally gave up and just asked to have it sent to our first U.S. port. There is now a global priority mail service with the U.S. Post Office which may be worth using.

Our Visa charge card was accepted in most places in Canada, but getting cash was a problem. We found that the Bank of Montreal which had a branch in most towns was our best bet. Their ATM was a Cirrus affiliate and the exchange rate was the best. We didn't know exactly how much money to subtract from our checking account until we got the bank statement, but we got pretty good at guessing.

Anchorages and Dockage

Dockage at marinas ran from $.50/ft of boat length to $1.50/ft. at the time we took our cruise. Sometimes this fee included electrical hookup and sometimes there was an additional charge for each 30 amp hookup.

Following is a list of places that we anchored or docked free of charge. Some of these places may no longer be available, so be sure to check your guidebook for current information before arrival. Information on type of bottom and holding conditions may be obtained from charts and guidebooks of the area.

All are anchorages, unless noted as a dockage. (*) indicates a superb anchorage or a "must" stop.

    USA:

Atlantic Intracoastal Waterway (ICW)
    Florida: Alligator Creek - South Amelia River
    Georgia: St. Simons Island - near Golden Isles Marina
        Buck Creek (Bear River)
        Dock at Daufuskie Island (Had special permission)
    South Carolina:
        Beaufort - near Downtown Marina
        Charleston - near City Marina
        Georgetown - in harbor
        Dock at N. Myrtle Beach - Barefoot Landing
    North Carolina:
        Oriental - in harbor

Belhaven - in harbor
Dock at Elizabeth City (*)
North Carolina/Virginia Border:
Dock in Dismal Swamp - welcome station at state boundary
Chesapeake Bay:
Virginia:
Deltaville - Fishing Bay in Piankatank River
Onancock - Onancock Creek
Maryland:
Crisfield - Somer's Cove
Solomons - Back Creek
Hudson's Creek - Little Choptank River
Fairlee Creek
New Jersey:
Delaware Bay: Greenwich - Cohansey River
Manasquan Inlet - Dock at Shrimp Box Restaurant
Jersey City - Tide water basin (Morris Basin) near Ellis Island
(This is a marina now.)
New York:
Hudson River - Bear Mountain State Park (near Bear Mountain
Bridge)
Hudson River - Dock at Ft. Edward Yacht Basin
Lake Champlain - Port Henry harbor
Vermont:
Otter Creek - Dock at Vergennes town dock (*)
CANADA:
Quebec:
Ste. Jean-sur-Richelieu - dock at wall near first lock (free when
lock closed)
Ontario:
Bay of Quinte - Big Bay between Massasauga Pt. and Horse Pt.
(*)
Georgian Bay
Bayfield Inlet near Gibraltor and Elm Tree Islands
Eastern Outlet French River north of Obstacle Island, Dores
Run(*)
Covered Portage Cove near Killarney(* may be crowded)
North Channel
The Pool at the end of Baie Fine off Frazer Bay(*)

Croker Island
South Benjamin Island between S. & N. Benjamin Islands(*)
USA:
Michigan:
    Charlevoix - Round Lake
    Frankfort - harbor
    Manistee Lake
    Pentwater Lake
    Whitehall/Montague - White Lake
Illinois:
    Illinois River - Dock at Joliet city wall
    Illinois River - Hennepin - behind Hennepin Island
    Illinois River Mile #38 - Twin Islands
    Dock off Mississippi River - Kaskaskia River at lock wall
    Dock Ohio River Lock # 53 - Lock wall
Kentucky:
    Tennessee River - Ft. Heiman in cove at mile # 62.6
Tennessee:
    Tennessee River - Birdsong Creek at mile # 103.5
    Tennessee River - Marsh Creek at mile # 138.4 (*)
    Tennessee River - Indian Creek at mile # 168.4
    Tennessee River - Pickwick Lake, N. Lower Anderson Branch,
        Shadow/Corner Cove
Mississippi:
    Tenn-Tom Waterway - Bay Springs Lake, Coot Cove (near Little
        Coot Cove) behind Mackey Spit
    Tenn-Tom Waterway - Blue Bluff Lagoon near Campground area
        at Aberdeen (*)
Alabama:
    Tenn-Tom Waterway - Sumter Recreation Area near
        Gainesville(*)
    Tombigbee River - Bashi Creek mile # 145 (*)
    Tombigbee River - Three Rivers Lake mile # 63.8
    Tombigbee River - Big Bayou Canot, South mile # 9.7
Gulf Intracoastal Waterway:
    Alabama - Ingram Bayou mile # 164
    Florida:
        Choctawatchee Bay - east end near bridge at mile # 250
        Pearl Bayou near Panama City mile # 295

Apalachicola - harbor
Dog Island - Tyson's Harbor
Tarpon Springs - Anclote River at Powerplant Cove
Tarpon Springs - Pappas Restaurant
Stump Pass near Thornton Key at mile # 41
Okeechobee Waterway: Lake Okeechobee Rim Route mile # 63 in
"Y" shaped basin
Atlantic Intracoastal Waterway (ICW) - all in Florida:
Peck Lake mile # 992
Lantana - south of bridge mile # 1031
Maule Lake near N. Miami Beach

Low Cost Dockage

We found inexpensive (often a low flat fee) docking at the following places:

Carolina Beach State Park Marina
Tangier Island
Poughkeepsie Yacht Club - Hyde Park, NY
Kingston (NY) City Docks
St. Anne de Bellvue, Quebec - lock wall
Rideau and Trent-Severn Waterways - lock walls. Bathroom
facilities but no other services. Dockage fee is based on boat
length.
Beausoleil Island (Georgian Bay Islands National Park)
Fryingpan Island, Sans Souci (Georgian Bay) - Henry's Fish
Restaurant
Beardstown, IL - tied to barge at Logsdon Tug Services
LaBelle, FL - River Edge Motel and Dock
St. Lucie, FL - St. Lucie Recreation Area

A Pre-boarding Letter To Our Guests:

What To Bring:

You won't need much more than the essentials on your stay with us — swim suit, sunglasses and suntan lotion for starters.

Clothing should be lightweight and casual for a boater's "laid-back" lifestyle. T-shirts and shorts are about as dressed up as you're gonna get. One dressier but still casual outfit may be used on a rare occasion if we want to "do the town". A warm sweater, light jacket, wind breaker or foul weather gear is handy to have along for the cool evening or sudden shower. A pair of comfortable jeans or sweat suit is recommended in case of cool weather.

Bring plenty of sunscreen, (no oils, please, which make the decks slippery!). A hat or visor and deck shoes are recommended. You may want to bring motion sickness medication (or wrist straps), chapstick, and insect repellent.

Storage space on board is limited, so DO NOT bring large or boxy suitcases. (There's nowhere to put them!) Duffel bags are best as they fold and collapse for easy storage. If you arrive in a car, you could unpack and store suitcases in your car. The best advice is to pack light!

Other items you may want to bring are: binoculars, cassette tapes or CD's, camera, video camera if compact, and reading material.

Passenger VS. Guest:

The federal government (U.S. Coast Guard) has redefined it's definition of a "passenger" as opposed to a "guest". According to the current definition, recreational boaters who take out their friends and receive voluntary offerings are not being "paid" and therefore do not have to be licensed. Voluntary sharing of expenses for food, fuel, and other supplies for the outing is no longer considered payment and therefore is acceptable. We would love to be able to pick up the tab for all expenses while you are aboard with us; but due to our own financial situation, we simply cannot afford to do that, so we ask that you, please, be prepared to help us out in the area.

Expectations:

If you have ever been in an RV unit or a boat, you know that space is limited and living in close quarters can be trying at times. There is almost no space to call your own. Our boat has 2 staterooms (bedrooms), one for us and one for our guests. We would expect that you confine your personal items to your stateroom and keep the common areas uncluttered and clean for the use of everyone on board.

We would also expect that you be willing and able to assist in cooking and cleanup. This is an equal opportunity boat where the men help in the galley and the ladies may take a turn at the helm. We may rotate couples for each meal, with one couple responsible for cooking and the other couple doing the cleanup, then switching for the next meal. Other suggestions are welcome.

Welcome aboard and let's have fun cruising together.

INDEX

About the Authors

Ron Stob was a travel writer and photographer for the San Luis Obispo County (California) *Telegram-Tribune* from 1984 through 1998, taking readers on hikes, river-rafting excursions and motor trips along the back roads in search of the obscure and unusual. He has written books on travel from Santa Barbara to Big Sur — *Back Roads of the Central Coast, More Back Roads of the Central Coast* and *Exploring San Luis Obispo and Nearby Coastal Areas.*

He and his wife, Eva, write and photograph for a variety of publications, including *Heartland Boating, Highways, Power and Motoryacht, Trailer Boats Magazine, Wildlife Conservation* and *Bluegrass Unlimited.* Their photographs often appear on magazine covers.

The Stob's have traveled throughout all 50 of the United States and abroad. Together, they learned about boats and cruised for nearly a year aboard their forty-foot trawler, *Dream O'Genie.* This book is the story of a 6300-mile cruise encompassing 145 locks around Eastern North America, known as the Great Loop or Great Circle Cruise.

In August 1999, they formed America's Great Loop Cruisers' Association, a network of boaters who cruise or dream of cruising the coastal and inland waterways of the Great Loop. (Go to www.greatloop.com for information.) The membership has rapidly grown to include cruisers from nearly every state as well as foreign countries.

Ron and Eva reside with Canoe, their cat, along the shores of the Little Tennessee River on Tellico Lake in the hills of East Tennessee. They travel and discover America's scenic areas in their 5th-wheel travel trailer, and explore the inland waterways in their trailerable cruiser, *Li'l Looper.*

To order more copies,
use Order Form on reverse side.

Order Form

For postal orders, send completed form with check, money order or credit card information to:

    Raven Cove Publishing
    P. O. Box 168
    Greenback, TN 37742-0168, USA

Telephone orders: 865/856-7888
Fax orders: 865/856-7889
For inquiries by E-mail: REStob@aol.com or
    REStob@greatloop.com
Visit Website at www.greatloop.com for special offer and information about America's Great Loop Cruisers' Association.

- -

Please send __ copies of "Honey, Let's Get a Boat..." @ $18.95 ea.
              (US$) $_____ x # __ = $ _____
Sales tax: (Please add 8.00% for books shipped to Tennessee addresses.)   Tax, if applicable = $ _____
Shipping: (Add $2.00 /book for book rate, $3.50 /book for priority mail.)   Shipping = $ _____
              Payment Total = $ _____

Ship to:
Name:_____
Address: _____
City: _____State:_____Zip:_____
Telephone: _____/_____
E-mail: _____
Payment by: (Circle one)   Check   Money Order   Credit card
Charge my credit card: Visa MasterCard AmExp Discover
Card #_____
Expiration Date:_____
Cardholder Name:_____
Signature: _____